PROGRESSIVE Skills in English

in English

Level 2   Course Book

Terry Phillips and Anna Phillips

with Nicholas Regan

Garnet

EDUCATION

Published by
Garnet Publishing Ltd.
8 Southern Court
South Street
Reading RG1 4QS, UK

First edition 2011

ISBN: 978-1-85964-678-6

British Library Cataloguing-in-Publication Data
A catalogue record for this book is available from
the British Library.

Production

Project managers:	Richard Peacock, Nicky Platt
Editorial team:	Emily Clarke, Sarah Mellowes, Richard Peacock, Nicky Platt, Rod Webb
Research:	Lucy Phillips
Design:	Ed Du Bois, Mike Hinks
Illustration:	Doug Nash
Photography:	Clipart, Corbis, Digital Vision, Getty Images, Image Source, Photodisc, Istockphoto, Shutterstock
Audio and DVD:	EFS Television Production Ltd.

Every effort has been made to trace the copyright holders
and we apologize in advance for any unintentional
omissions. We will be happy to insert the appropriate
acknowledgements in any subsequent editions.

The authors and publisher would like to thank the following
for permission to reproduce from copyright material:

Fred Rompelberg for photograph on page 50

Wikipedia for photograph on page 54 (This Wikipedia and
Wikimedia Commons image is from the user Chris 73 and
is freely available at http://commons.wikimedia.org/wiki/
File:Benz_Patent_Motorwagen_1886_(Replica).jpg under
the creative commons cc-by-sa 2.5 license.)

Printed and bound
in Lebanon by International Press: interpress@int-press.com

Contents

Topics

Listening	Speaking	Reading	Writing	Knowledge area
1 Coming of age	Festivals	Fireworks, horses and bulls	Celebrations	Culture and civilization
2 Who? What? When?	Transport inventions	A brief history of space travel	The historic moment	Technology
3 Arts and media	Advertising	The values of magazines	Media studies research reports	Arts and media
4 Classifying sports	Sports in education	Board games	For and against	Sports and leisure
5 A balanced diet	Portions	How to eat healthily	Obesity	Nutrition and health

Skills

Listening	Speaking	Reading	Writing
1 • understanding signpost language: following a sequence of events including *before / after doing*	• showing understanding: echo + comment • showing understanding: echo + question • showing lack of understanding: echo	• finding information quickly: using capital letters for proper nouns • predicting content: using prepositions	• spelling: with a single vowel • spelling: with a pair of vowels • comparing events and ideas
2 • understanding signpost language: recognizing the organization of a lecture	• talking about research	• finding information quickly: using numbers • predicting content	• connecting ideas with *and / but*
3 • predicting content from linking words	• taking part in a tutorial	• distinguishing between fact and possibility	• designing a questionnaire • recording and displaying results
4 • note-taking: classification	• giving a talk with slides	• referring back *then / there*	• spelling schwa • paragraph structure: point, explanation, example
5 • revision	• revision	• revision	• revision

Grammar

Listening	Speaking	Reading	Writing
1 • present simple: *he / she / it / they* • *after / before doing*	• present simple open questions • present simple negatives	• extra information about the complement • extra information about the object	• time prepositions
2 • grammar of dates • *in … vs … ago*	• checking questions	• extra information about the subject • nominalization	• subject and object pronouns • possessive adjectives
3 • grammar of lexical cohesion: verbs into nouns	• introductory phrases • asking for an opinion	• subject and object pronouns • possessive adjectives	• pre-modifying nouns: percentages and quantifiers
4 • verb valency: prepositions after the verb	• modals: *must / should*	• zero conditional	• articles: *the* vs zero article
5 • revision	• revision	• revision	• revision

Phonology, Everyday English and Portfolio work

Listening	Speaking	Everyday English	Portfolio
1 • vowels – long: /uː/	• vowels – short vs long: /ʌ/ vs /uː/ • consonants: /t/ vs /d/ • intonation: interest; surprise	• the right things to say	Festivals around the world
2 • consonants: /tʃ/, /ʃ/ (*tion*)	• consonants: /tʃ/, /ʃ/ (*tion / tu*)	• using technology	Great transport inventions
3 • diphthongs: /eɪ/, /aɪ/	• diphthongs: /eɪ/, /aɪ/	• talking about the media	Mass-media usage
4 • diphthongs: /əʊ/, /aʊ/	• diphthongs: /əʊ/, /aʊ/	• talking about games	Team games
5 • revision	• revision	• revision	Fast food

Introduction

This is Level 2 of *Progressive Skills in English*. This course is in four levels, from Intermediate to Advanced. In addition, there is a remedial / false beginner course, *Starting Skills in English*, for students who are not ready to begin Level 1.

Progressive Skills in English is designed to help students who are at university or about to enter a university where some or all of their course is taught in English. The course helps students in all four skills:
Listening – to lectures
Speaking – in tutorials and seminars
Reading – for research
Writing – assignments

Progressive Skills in English is arranged in five themes. Each theme is divided into four sections, one for each skill. Each skill section has five core lessons as follows:

Lesson 1: *Vocabulary for the skill*
pre-teaches key vocabulary for the section

Lesson 2: *Real-time practice*
practises previously learnt skills and exposes students to new skills; in most cases, this lesson provides a model for the activity in Lesson 5

Lesson 3: *Learning skills*
presents and practises new skills

Lesson 4: *Grammar for the skill*
presents and practises key grammar points for the skill

Lesson 5: *Applying skills*
provides practice in the skills and grammar from the section; in most cases, students work on a parallel task to the one presented in Lesson 2

In addition, there are three extra elements in each theme:

Everyday English	presents and practises survival English for everyday life
Knowledge quiz	tests students on their learning of key vocabulary and knowledge
Portfolio	offers extended practice and integration of the skills in the theme

Theme 1

Culture and civilization

- Coming of age
- Festivals
- Fireworks, horses and bulls
- Celebrations

1.1 Vocabulary for listening   Coming of age

A   Activating knowledge

Discuss these questions.

In your culture, when do you …

1. give presents?
2. send cards?
3. have parties?
4. say *Congratulations*?

B   Understanding vocabulary in context

1. Study the list of words on the right. Find a synonym for each of the words and phrases below. 🔊 **1.1** Listen to a talk about births, marriages and deaths, and check your ideas.

   a. at the present time   *nowadays*
   b. old
   c. actions
   d. beginning
   e. party
   f. method
   g. disappear
   h. age group
   i. give
   j. group
   k. time

2. Complete these sentences with information from the talk.

   a. Anthropologists study …
   b. We have celebrations for …
   c. We have rituals, for example, when …
   d. Rituals often include …
   e. A special day of celebration is called …
   f. Nowadays, some traditions …

C   Developing critical thinking

Discuss in groups.

1. What festivals do you have in your country?
2. What does each festival celebrate or remember?
3. What rituals are involved in each festival?
4. Which festivals or rituals (if any) are dying out?

---

adult (*n*)
ancestor (*n*)
anthropologist (*n*)
attend (*v*)
birth (*n*)
celebrate (*v*)
celebration (*n*)
ceremony (*n*)
childhood (*n*)
congratulations (*n*)
death (*n*)
die out (*v*)
event (*n*)
festival (*n*)
generation (*n*)
God (*n*)
(the) gods (*n*)
guest (*n*)
influence (*n*)
light (*v*)
marriage (*n*)
nowadays (*adv*)
occasion (*n*)
official (*adj* and *n*)
origin (*n*)
party (*n*)
pass down (*v*)
present (*n*)
primitive (*adj*)
procedure (*n*)
religious (*adj*)
ritual (*n*)
set (*n*)
special (*adj*)
take place (*v*)
tourist (*n*)
traditional (*adj*)
vote (*n* and *v*)

1.2 Real-time listening *Seijin no hi*

A **Reviewing vocabulary**

Study the photographs on the opposite page.

1. Where is each ceremony taking place?
2. What rituals are involved?

B **Activating ideas**

Juri Taku is an anthropology student. She is going to talk to her study group about a festival in Japan. Make a list of questions you expect to hear the answers to.

What is the festival called?

C **Predicting the next word**

1. ◉ **1.2** Listen to the talk once. Juri pauses a few times during her talk. Guess the next word on each occasion.
2. ◉ **1.3** Listen again and check your ideas.
3. Which questions in Exercise B does Juri answer?

D **Making notes**

Make notes about Juri's talk in the table on the right.

E **Understanding spoken definitions**

How does Juri define these words?

1. *Seijin no hi*
2. *seijin shiki*
3. town hall
4. kimono

F **Identifying words from the stressed syllable**

1. Mark the stressed syllable on these words from the talk.

   a. gov ern ment   ....
   b. cel e brat ed   ....
   c. cer e mo ny   ....
   d. 'fes ti val   ___1___
   e. of fi cial   ....
   f. at tend   ....
   g. ad ult   ....
   h. tra di tion al   ....
   i. pre sent (*n*)   ....
   j. spe cial   ....

2. ◉ **1.4** Listen to some sentences. Number the words above in order.

> 1. I'm going to talk to you today about a **festival.**

Where is the festival?	Japan
What is it called?	
Who is it for?	
When is it?	
Why is the occasion important?	
What happens on the day?	
Do the people wear special clothes?	
What happens after the ceremony?	

A Reviewing key words

1. Study the pairs of words on the right.
2. 🎧 1.5 Listen. Tick the word you hear in each case.

B Identifying a new skill

1. Write one word in each space.

   a. I'm ____going____ to talk _____ you today _____ a festival in Japan.

   b. _____, a government official makes a speech.

   c. _____, he gives small presents to the new adults.

   d. _____ going to the ceremony, the girls put on traditional dresses.

   e. _____ attending the ceremony, the new adults go to special parties.

   f. _____, the young people go home.

2. Read the Skills Check. Check your answers.

C Recognizing a sequence of events

You are going to hear about two more coming-of-age ceremonies. 🎧 1.6 Listen and number the events in order.

Sweet Sixteen in the USA

	changes shoes
	dances with father
	lights candles
	sits in a chair
	watches a video

Goyuje in Korea

	bows to the guest
	changes clothes three times
	drinks from a special cup
	is given a new name
	listens to advice
	receives good wishes
	visits the grave of an ancestor

D Identifying vowel sounds

Work in pairs.

1. What do all the words below have in common?

   new few true blue suit you do who too shoe used move

2. Read the Pronunciation Check. Check your answers.

3. How do you pronounce all the other words in the Pronunciation Check?

1.	☐	festival	✓	first of all
2.	☐	sell	☐	celebrate
3.	☐	ceremony	☐	money
4.	☐	sent	☐	present
5.	☐	ritual	☐	written
6.	☐	part	☐	party
7.	☐	traditional	☐	dish
8.	☐	event	☐	evening
9.	☐	pass	☐	past
10.	☐	official	☐	officer

Skills Check

Follow the signposts!

Speakers often help listeners with signpost words. The words help listeners to understand the organization of their talk.

Introducing the topic	*I'm going to talk to you today about …*
Talking about a sequence of events	*First(ly) / Second(ly) / Third(ly) …* *Then / Next / Later …* *After (that / the speech), …* *Finally …*

Pronunciation Check

Hearing vowels: /uː/

The vowel sound in *new* is written in many ways. But each way can make other sounds.

ew	*new, few*	*sew*
ue	*true, blue*	*colleague*
u	*used*	*cut, put*
ui	*suit*	*build*
ou	*you*	*about*
o	*do, who*	*go*
oo	*too*	*book*
oe	*shoe*	*does*
o-e	*move*	*love*

Always check the pronunciation of a new word with these letters.

The verb *be*   Other verbs   ①

subject	verb	complement
The event	is	traditional.
The ceremony	is	very old.
The events	are	traditional.
The festivals	are	very old.

subject	verb	object
The girl	lights	16 candles.
The girl	wears	a special dress.
The adults	go	home.
The girls	put on	traditional dresses.

When you listen, it is quite difficult to decide if a **noun subject** is singular or plural.

Listen for other clues in the sentence or paragraph.

However, it is quite easy to decide if a **pronoun subject** is singular or plural.

Listen for the pronouns.

subject	verb
He / She / It	goes
They	go

A   Identifying singular and plural

🎧 **1.7** Listen. Is each subject singular or plural?

The house is very interesting.   Singular.

We can join two sentences in a sequence with *after* and *before*.   ②
Sometimes the next word is a **gerund** = infinitive + *ing*.

first event	second event
The girl lights 16 candles.	Then she sits on a chair.
After ligh**ting** 16 candles, [pause] **the girl** sits on a chair.	
The girls put on special dresses.	Then they go to the town hall.
Before go**ing** to the town hall, [pause] **the girls** put on special dresses.	

Note:
• There is **no subject** in front of the first verb, e.g., *lighting*, *going*.
• The **subject** of both verbs comes after a small pause.

B   Identifying the subject

🎧 **1.8** Listen. Number the subjects in order. There are extra subjects you do not need.

1. After getting money from the bank, **the man** goes to the supermarket.

	the boy		the children		the official		
	the boys		the interviewer	1	the man		the official
	the candidate		the light		the manager		the officials
	the candidates		the lights		the men		the student
					the woman		the students

1.5 Applying new listening skills Quinceañera

A Reviewing vocabulary

Match each verb with words from the right column to make phrases about special events.

1. give ☐ a party
2. make 1 presents
3. wear ☐ special events
4. go to ☐ special food
5. eat ☐ speeches
6. spend ☐ special music
7. have ☐ traditional clothes
8. listen to ☐ time with the family

B Following a talk

Adriana Hernandez is going to talk about a special event in her country.

🔊 1.9 Listen to her talk. Make notes of the important points.

• where?

• when?

• who?

• why?

• what?

C Checking understanding

Ask and answer questions about the Quinceañera in pairs.

> Where does it take place?

> In Mexico.

D Transferring a new skill

Is there a special birthday for people in your country?
Who is it for? What happens on that day?

1.6 Vocabulary for speaking   Birthdays

A   Reviewing vocabulary

1. Look at each word in the box on the right. Is it a verb, an adjective or a noun? Mark the correct part of speech.
2. 🌐 **1.10** Listen and repeat each word.
3. Make a sentence with each word.

> ritual   traditional   symbol
> modern   event   origin   adult
> official   celebrate   death
> marriage   light   wear

B   Understanding new vocabulary in context

1. Look at the photograph and discuss the questions.
   a. What are the people in the photograph celebrating?
   b. What traditional items can you see?
   c. What's going to happen next?
2. Find at least five words from the list on the right in the photograph. Practise saying each word.

C   Practising new vocabulary

1. 🌐 **1.11** Listen to four short talks about birthday traditions: *presents*, *parties*, *candles* and *cards*. Make one or two notes about each topic.
2. 🌐 **1.12** Listen to some words from the talk. How many syllables are there in each?
   culture – 2
3. Work in groups of four. Choose one of the topics. Give the information to the rest of the group.

D   Developing critical thinking

Discuss these questions in groups.

1. How important are birthdays in your culture?
2. What special songs do you sing at festivals or celebrations?
3. What special food do people cook for important events?
4. When do people send cards?

actually (*adv*)
birth (*n*)
birthday (*n*)
bonfire (*n*)
candle (*n*)
card (*n*)
colourful (*adj*)
conditions (*n*)
congratulations (*n*)
culture (*n*)
dancing (*n*)
dress (*n* and *v*)
during (*adv*)
each (*adv* and *pron*)
evil (*adj*)
fire (*n*)
guide (*n*)
huge (*adj*)
last (*v*)
local (*adj*)
luck (*n*)
lucky (*adj*)
meal (*n*)
nearly (*adv*)
original (*adj*)
originally (*adv*)
powder (*n*)
procession (*n*)
race (*n* and *v*)
reflect (*v*)
relative (*n*)
represent (*v*)
ring (*n*)
song (*n*)
spirit (*n*)
statue (*n*)
sunrise (*n*)
surprise (*n*)
symbol (*n*)
through (*prep*)
wreath (*n*)

1.7 Real-time speaking   Local festivals

A   Activating ideas

Tell your partner about five special days in the year in your country.

> Mother's Day is special. July 9th is special because it's National Day.

B   Studying a model

You are going to hear two students talking about a local festival.

1. Read the conversation. What are Speaker A's questions?

2. 🔊 1.13 Listen to the conversation. Complete A's questions.

A: Are there any traditional festivals in your country ?

B: Yes, we have one in the summer. It's called *Noc Swietojanska* in Polish. I like it a lot.

A: ?

B: Yes. It means 'night'. Saint John's Night. We celebrate the longest day of the year, and the shortest night. It's on 23rd June.

A: ?

B: Well, people dress in colourful traditional clothes. There is music, dancing and fireworks. The young women make wreaths of flowers with candles on them.

A: ?

B: If a woman is single, she makes a wreath – a ring of flowers. Then she puts the flowers on a lake or river. When a young man finds it, he falls in love with the girl – that's the tradition.

A: ?

B: No, they don't. In some places, they make a fire and jump over it.

A: ?

B: Because it shows that they are strong and brave.

A: ?

B: We make the food during the day, too. The men prepare the music and the lights outside.

A: ?

B: It starts at about eight o'clock. We dance and talk and eat. The party continues through the night – it doesn't stop until sunrise.

A: ?

B: Yes, they do. But they're very tired!

C   Practising a model

1. 🔊 1.14 Listen to the conversation again. What do you notice about the intonation of the questions?
2. Role-play the conversation in pairs.
3. Talk with your partner about a festival in your region or country.

D   Developing critical thinking

Why are traditional festivals important for people?

A Activating ideas

Look at the photographs.

1. How does each person look?
2. Why does each person look this way?

B Studying models

1. 🌐 1.15 Listen and match each phrase with one of the conversations.
2. Practise each conversation.

Are you tired?	Has something happened?	Hi, there! Happy birthday!
I passed my test!	What's wrong?	You look a bit stressed.

1
A: ....
B: Oh, I didn't get the job.
A: Bad luck. I'm sorry.
B: Thanks.

4
A: ....
B: Yes, I am. We've just had a new baby.
A: Congratulations! Is it a girl or boy?
B: A boy.

2
A: ....
B: Oh, thanks!
A: And here's a card.
B: That's really nice of you. Thank you!

5
A: ....
B: Yes. I've got an important exam tomorrow.
A: Well, good luck. I'm sure you'll be fine.
B: Thanks. I hope so.

3
A: What's the matter? ....
B: Yes. My grandmother has died.
A: Oh, I'm so sorry.
B: Thanks. We were really close.

6
A: ....
B: Sorry? Which test?
A: My driving test.
B: Well done! That's great!

C Practising a model

Work in pairs. Role-play conversations for these situations.
One of you:

- got 78 per cent for the last assignment.
- is 21 today.
- has decided to get married.
- has an interview tomorrow.
- was not chosen for the sports team.
- has had a death in the family.
- stayed up late last night to revise.

Echoing and commenting

A Saying consonants

1. Read Pronunciation Check 1. Which sound is voiced and which is unvoiced?

2. Circle one word in each pair below. Say the word that you circled. Tick the words you hear.

   a. try   dry   e. site   side
   b. three   tree   f. both   boat
   c. write   ride   g. den   then
   d. tie   die   h. cart   card

B Saying vowels

1. Read Pronunciation Check 2. Which spellings have the sound /uː/?

2. Mark these words /ʌ/ or /uː/ according to the (underlined) sound.

   a. club   /ʌ/   f. useful   _____
   b. cool   _____ g. rude   _____
   c. come   _____ h. run   _____
   d. two   _____ i. colour   _____
   e. few   _____ j. cut   _____

3. 🔊 1.16 Listen and check. Say the words.

C Identifying a new skill

1. Read the Skills Check. How can you show interest?

2. 🔊 1.17 Listen. Tick the reply you hear.

   a. My cousin got married last week.
      ☐ Your cousin? Did you go?
      ☐ Married? But he's very young!
   b. I got a present today.
      ☐ That is not interesting for me.
      ☐ A present? That's nice.
   c. I'm taking my exam tomorrow.
      ☐ Tomorrow? Are you going to pass?
      ☐ Tomorrow? Yesterday was better.

3. Which replies above are good?

D Practising a new skill

1. 🔊 1.18 Listen to some sentences about traditional events.

2. Work in pairs. Say some of the sentences. Give a reply to show you understand.

   > We eat delicious cakes at New Year.

   > Cakes? What kind?

   > At New Year? That's interesting.

Pronunciation Check 1

Saying consonants: /t/ and /d/

The sound /d/ is always voiced. It is always spelt d or dd.

Examples: *do, tradition, find, address*

The sound /t/ is always unvoiced. It is always spelt t or tt.

Examples: *town, meeting, separate, better*

Both sounds are made by touching the top of the tongue against the roof of the mouth.

Do not confuse /t/ and /d/ **with** /θ/ and /ð/.

Examples: *tin* for *thin; dis* for *this*

Pronunciation Check 2

Saying vowels: /ʌ/ and /uː/

The sound /ʌ/ is short. When the letter u is stressed, it often makes the sound /ʌ/.

Examples: *luck, sun, just, but*

The sound /uː/ is long. The letters ew, oo and ue often make the sound /uː/.

Examples: *new, flew, blue, true, food, too*

Other common words with the sound /uː/ are: *you, who, do.*

Skills Check

Showing understanding

When a person gives us some new information, we must show that we understand. We can do this by echoing important words. We often add a question or a comment.

Examples:

A: *Originally it was in September, not July.*

         echo   question

B: *In September? Did they change it recently?*

OR

B: *In September? Why did they change it?*

A: *The children sing a special song.*

         echo   comment

B: *The children? That's nice.*

Use your voice and your face to show the speaker you are interested or surprised.

To make a question with the verb *be*, we use the verb followed by the subject.   ③
For other verbs, we make a question with an **auxiliary** in front of the subject.

question	verb	subject	extra information	
What	is	the best part	of the day	?
Who	are	they		?

question	auxiliary	subject	verb	extra information	
Where	do	they	learn	the dance	?
When	does	it	start		?

A   Asking questions

1. Complete the questions about your partner's country with the correct word from the box below.

> Who   ~~What~~   Why   Where   When   Which   How many

a. *What*_____ is the origin of the name of your country?

b. _____ do most people live – in the countryside or in the city?

c. _____ do you eat the biggest meal – at midday or in the evening?

d. _____ is the leader of your country?

e. _____ days in the year are holidays?

f. _____ days a week do children go to school?

g. _____ do people enjoy festivals?

2. Ask and answer the questions above in pairs.

To make a negative with the verb *be*, we add *not* after the verb.   ④
For other verbs, we put an **auxiliary after the subject** and add *not*.

S	*be*		C	S	aux		V	extra information
You	are		happy.	You	do		need	money to get in.
She	is		here.	She	does		make	special foods.
It		not	difficult.	It		not	happen	every year.
We	are		ready.	We	do		celebrate	birthdays very much.
They			in the room.	They			send	cards.

B   Producing negatives

Make negative sentences in the present simple. Use some of the words below.

sports	understand	easy
children	like	difficult
cars	drive	tall
vegetables	play	married
assignment	have	here
friend	be	ready
sister	eat	strong

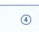

My friend doesn't play sports.

My sister isn't married.

A **Reviewing sounds**

1. Which (underlined) vowel sound is different in each line?

   a. d<u>o</u>ne   s<u>o</u>me   (h<u>u</u>ge)
   b. b<u>u</u>t   g<u>oo</u>d   b<u>u</u>ll
   c. f<u>oo</u>d   c<u>u</u>lture   sh<u>oe</u>
   d. l<u>u</u>ck   c<u>o</u>ver   l<u>oo</u>k
   e. h<u>u</u>t   stat<u>ue</u>   m<u>u</u>sic
   f. n<u>ew</u>   c<u>o</u>lour   c<u>oo</u>l
   g. j<u>u</u>st   j<u>ui</u>ce   y<u>ou</u>ng
   h. m<u>o</u>ve   w<u>ou</u>ld   w<u>oo</u>d

2. Use some of the words above to talk about the pictures.

   > The people are covering the girl's face with colours.

B **Activating ideas**

Your partner is going to talk about a festival. Make eight questions to ask him/her, using these words.

- name?
  > What's it called?
- place?
- origin?
- clothes?
- who for?
- important?
- events on the day?

C **Researching information**

Work in two groups. Group A: Read the text on page 172, Group B: Read the text on page 171. Make notes to answer the questions in Exercise B.

D **Using a key skill**

1. In your group, prepare to talk about your festival. Check that you can answer all of the questions.

2. Make pairs – a student from Group A with a student from Group B. Talk about the festivals.

   > There's a bonfire.

   > A bonfire? Why do they have that?

   > The people carry a huge statue.

   > Sorry? I don't understand.

E **Developing critical thinking**

Make Groups A and B again. Compare what you heard. Are there any differences in the versions? Which is probably the correct version?

Reading: Fireworks, horses and bulls

1.11 Vocabulary for reading Guy Fawkes Night

A Reviewing vocabulary

All the words below are connected with festivals. What is the full word in each case?

1. fes _tival_
2. att
3. cel
4. cer
5. rit
6. ori
7. tra
8. rel
9. cul

B Understanding vocabulary in context

1   2   3   4

1. Read the website text. Find these words and phrases in the photographs.

> firework display parade Houses of Parliament
> Guy Fawkes cart figure costume

2. Find words with these meanings.

a. try to be better than others
b. before
c. when you are unsuccessful
d. happens
e. make something more beautiful
f. join or do an activity
g. wear special clothes
h. the past participle of the verb *light*
i. brings people
j. an advertisement on a large piece of paper

File   Edit   View   Favorites   Tools   Help

http://www.fireworks.com

What to see and do in November

If you visit England in November, you will see posters for firework and bonfire celebrations. Go to one of the events. They are great fun!

Guy Fawkes Night is a traditional event in England. It started in 1607. Two years earlier, a man called Guy Fawkes tried to destroy the Houses of Parliament in London. He was unsuccessful. Now every year, on 5th November, people celebrate his failure.

One of the best celebrations takes place in Lewes, in the south of England. The event attracts about 70,000 visitors. There are five bonfire societies in the town. They compete to put on the best display. Each society has its own traditional costumes. For weeks before the event, each society makes a figure of Guy Fawkes or another unpopular person. They decorate carts with the figures and other items.

On the day of the event, many of the people from the town take part. They dress up like Guy Fawkes and other historical figures. In the evening, there is a big parade through the town. People carry flags in all the colours of the rainbow. Then the five separate bonfires are lit. After the bonfires, there are firework displays. Finally, people have something to eat – usually sausages and burgers these days!

anniversary (n)
attract (v)
centre (n)
compete (v)
competition (n)
connect (v)
costume (n)
decorate (v)
display (n)
dress up (v)
earlier (adv)
event (n)
exhibition (n)
failure (n)
figure (n) [= model]
firework (n)
flag (n)
historical (adj)
jockey (n)
last (v)
lit (v) [= past participle]
look like (v)
parade (n and v)
peculiar (adj)
popular (adj)
population (n)
poster (n)
race (n and v)
recover (v)
ribbon (n)
situated (adj)
society (n) [= club]
spectator (n)
take part (v) [in]
take place (v)
ticket (n)
tourism (n)
tourist (n)
unsuccessful (adj)
visitor (n)

A Activating ideas

Prepare to read the text opposite. Answer these questions.

1. Where is the text from?
2. Who is the text for?
3. What is the text about?
4. What information do you expect to find in the text?

B Predicting content

Cover the text opposite. Read the topic sentences on the left below. Read the sentences on the right below. Which paragraph do you think each sentence comes from?

1. Siena was once an important centre for banking and for art.

2. Siena is best known today for a horse race.

3. For three days before the event, flags fly from houses and shops.

4. On the day of the event, the young men and women of the city dress up in colourful costumes from the Middle Ages.

5. Finally, at exactly 7.30 p.m., the race begins.

	It only lasts 90 seconds.
	The Black Death of 1348, however, killed thousands of people.
	Then, in the late afternoon, there is a parade in the Piazza del Campo.
	The flags belong to the 17 *contradas*, or areas of the city.
	Thousands of visitors come to the city every year just to see it.

C Understanding a text

Read the text. Find out the meaning of any new words. Make notes to answer these questions.

1. Where is Siena?
2. What is the Palio?
3. When was the first ever race?
4. When does it take place?
5. What sort of clothes do the people wear?
6. When does the race start?
7. Where does it take place?
8. How many horses take part?
9. How long is the race?
10. When does it finish?

C. Italy

D Transferring information

Make a table of the important information about the Palio for visitors to Italy.

Great traditional events around the world

1: The Palio in Siena

Siena is a city of around 56,000 people. It is situated in central Italy, 120 kilometres south of Florence and 200 kilometres northeast of Rome. It is built on a high hilltop.

Siena was once an important centre for banking and for art. The Black Death of 1348, however, killed thousands of people. In some ways, the city never recovered.

Siena is best known today for a horse race. It is as old as Siena, in other words, nearly 3,000 years old. It takes place on 2nd July and 16th August each year. The race is called the Palio. It is famous throughout the world. Thousands of visitors come to the city every year just to see it.

For three days before the event, flags fly from houses and shops. The flags belong to the 17 *contradas*, or areas of the city. Young men from ten of the *contradas* take part in each race.

On the day of the event, the young men and women of the city dress up in colourful costumes from the Middle Ages. First, in the morning, they walk around the streets, looking like actors from a Shakespeare play. Then, in the late afternoon, there is a parade in the Piazza del Campo. This is the main square in the centre of the city. After that, there is an exhibition of flag throwing, with lots of drumming.

Finally, at exactly 7.30 p.m., the race begins. It only lasts 90 seconds. In that time, the horses and jockeys race three times around the piazza. After the race, the men and women from the winning *contrada* carry their flags through the city. Then there are special dinners in each *contrada*. The most special, of course, is in the restaurants of the winning *contrada*.

A Reviewing vocabulary

What do the underlined words mean in the sentences below from the text in Lesson 1.12?

1. The Black Death of 1348, however, killed thousands of people.

   It's a disease.

2. In some ways, the city never recovered.

3. Young men from ten of the contradas take part in each race.

4. ... the young men and women of the city dress up in colourful costumes from the Middle Ages.

5. After that, there is an exhibition of flag throwing, ...

6. ... and jockeys race three times around the piazza.

B Using capital letters

1. Read Skills Check 1. Which type of word in English always has capital letters?

2. Find and underline all the proper nouns in the text in Lesson 1.12.

C Predicting content

1. Read Skills Check 2. What part of speech can come in front of a preposition? What part of speech can come after a preposition?

2. Study the phrases below. What type of information do you expect to read next?

   a. The girls put on ... *some kind of clothes.*
   b. The people dress up in ...
   c. The town has a population of ...
   d. The people take part in ...
   e. The doll looks like ...
   f. The young people of ...
   g. I went to an exhibition of ...
   h. The car reached speeds of ...
   i. The people give thanks to ...

3. Find words in the box to complete each sentence above.

   > 160 kph   50,000   an opera   the President
   > Krishna   medieval costumes   modern sculpture
   > silver tiaras   the neighbourhood

Skills Check 1

Finding information quickly: using capital letters

All proper nouns in English – names, nationalities, places, months, etc., start with a capital letter.

Examples: *Siena, July, Shakespeare*

Proper nouns often give you the answers to research questions.

Skills Check 2

Predicting content: using prepositions

Prepositions often prepare the reader for the type of information that will come next.

Examples:

The city ...	type of information
is built on ...	a hill a river the coast
was built in ...	a date a period of history
is situated in ...	a part of a country
is known for ...	a person a product an event
is south of ...	a city a feature (e.g., lake)
is a centre for ...	an industry the arts

Extra information about a complement or an object is often in a prepositional phrase. ⑤

subject	verb	complement / object	extra information
Siena	is	a city	of around 56,000 people.
Siena	was (once)	an important centre	for banking and for art.
It	is	famous	throughout the world.
... each society	makes	a figure	of Guy Fawkes or another unpopular person.
They	decorate	carts	with the figures.

A **Finding subject, verb, complement and extra information**
Divide each sentence in this text with /. Mark *S*, *V*, *C*, *E* (extra information).

     S   V   C   E

1. Venice /   is   / a city / of around 300,000 people.

2. Venice was once an important centre for trade.

3. Every year in September, there are boat races in the city.

4. For many days before the event, people fly flags from their houses.

5. On the day, there is a parade along the Grand Canal.

6. The first race is for children from different areas of the city.

7. Then there are races for men and women from the areas.

8. After the races, there are big dinners in each of the areas.

B **Finding extra information about the complement or the object**
Find each piece of *extra information* below in the text on page 23.
What does it refer to in each case?

1. _posters_   for firework and bonfire celebrations

2. _____ in England

3. _____ in London

4. _____ in the south of England

5. _____ in the town

6. _____ of Guy Fawkes or another unpopular person

7. _____ with the figures and with other items

8. _____ and other historical figures

9. _____ through the town

10. _____ in all the colours of the rainbow

A   Reviewing vocabulary

All the words below might appear in a tourist guide.
Complete each word.

1.   is _lan_ d
2.   co_____t
3.   pop_____n
4.   agr_____al
5.   cap_____l
6.   att_____t
7.   vi_____r
8.   ev_____t
9.   har_____t
10.   dec_____e

Figure 1: *Location of Bali*

B   Understanding a text

1.   Prepare to read the text opposite.
2.   Read the text. Make notes of the key information. Use,
     for example, *where*, *when*, *what*. Remember to look for:
   - capital letters for proper nouns.
   - information after prepositions.
   - extra information about the object or complement.

C   Understanding new words in context

Find each word below in the text. Work out the part of
speech. What does the word mean?

1.   coconut   _n_   _kind of fruit_
2.   buffalo   _____   _____
3.   chariot   _____   _____
4.   ribbon   _____   _____
5.   connect   _____   _____
6.   mount   _____   _____
7.   tail   _____   _____
8.   steer   _____   _____
9.   peculiar   _____   _____
10.   spectator   _____   _____

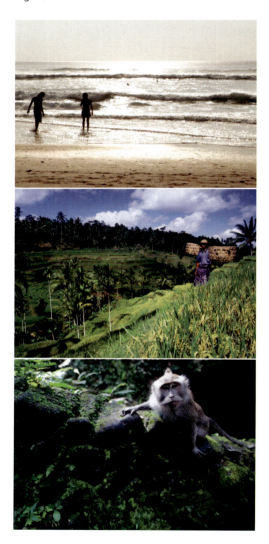

D   Developing critical thinking

Which of the following types of tourist would enjoy the Bali
event? Explain your answers.
   - families with young children
   - teenagers
   - retired people

Great traditional events around the world

2: Bull racing in Bali

Bali is a small island in Indonesia. On the western coast of the island there is a town called Negara. It has a population of around 34,000. The area around Negara is agricultural. They grow coconuts and bananas there. It is about 50 kilometres west of the capital, Denpasar.

Bali is a popular tourist island, but for most of the year very few people go to Negara. However, in late summer, the area attracts many visitors. Why? Because every two weeks in September and October there is a very unusual event. The young men of Negara race bulls.

The event began about 100 years ago. Nobody is really sure about the origins of the event. Perhaps it was part of a festival giving thanks to God for a successful harvest.

The bulls are not ordinary farm animals. They are special water buffalo. People choose them for their speed and their colour. Their only job is racing. Each jockey has two bulls and a chariot or small cart.

On the day, the jockeys prepare for the race. First they decorate their carts with flags and ribbons. Then they connect the two bulls together. After that, they tie the pairs to the chariots. Finally, they mount the chariots and take hold of the tails of the bulls.

The race starts! The jockeys use the tails to steer the animals during the race. They run for two kilometres, downhill. Sometimes, over 40 chariots take part. The bulls reach speeds of 50 kilometres per hour.

It is a peculiar race. The bulls do not all run at the same time, so it is very difficult for spectators to know the winner. But it is certainly very exciting.

1. Who studies societies in the past and primitive societies?	
2. Who tried to destroy the British parliament in 1605?	
3. Who is the Holi festival for?	
4. What is a harvest?	
5. What are rituals?	
6. What is a wreath?	
7. What are buffalo?	
8. What was the Black Death?	
9. What is a statue?	
10. What are *Seijin no hi* and *Quinceañera* examples of?	
11. What do the candles on a birthday cake represent?	
12. When do girls come of age in:	
a. Japan and Korea?	
b. the USA?	
c. Mexico?	
13. When were the Middle Ages?	
14. Where is Bali?	
15. Where do people celebrate Saint John's Night?	
16. Where do people celebrate San Fermin?	
17. Where does the Palio take place?	
18. How old is the Holi festival?	
19. How long does the Palio race last?	
20. How do people decorate the Negara chariots?	

1.16 Vocabulary for writing   Fasting

A Reviewing vocabulary

There is one spelling mistake in each of these words from Theme 1.
Rewrite each word correctly.

1. ceremoney *Ceremony*
2. costum
3. decarate
4. exibition
5. influense
6. occassion
7. proceedure
8. rituel
9. traditonal
10. visiter

B Building vocabulary and knowledge

Complete the text below. Use a word from the list on the right in each case.
Make any necessary changes.

The origins of fasting

Fasting is going without food ⌃⁶. Every major religion has asked its followers to

___*fast*___ . But the _____ goes back to primitive societies.

Fasting rituals have appeared in all societies. Fasting has two main purposes. Firstly,

it _____ before an important event. For example, in some cultures, a

child must fast before the coming of age ritual. In other cultures, fasting

_____ before a hunt or a _____ in a war. Secondly, it is often

connected with _____ cleaning of the body. A person is closer to God

after fasting. There are two well-known periods of fasting. The Islamic tradition of

fasting is still practised _____ the Muslim world. The Christian tradition

of fasting during a period called Lent has _____ died out.

C Using fixed and semi-fixed phrases

The text above is very simple. We can add extra information at the beginning
or the end of many sentences. Where can you add each of the following
pieces of information? See the example (6) in the text above.

1. According to anthropologists,
2. According to many religions,
3. ancient and modern
4. at certain times of the year
5. during the holy month of Ramadan
6. for a period of time
7. On the other hand,

---

according to
anthropologist (n)
anthropology (n)
around (prep)
  [= approximately]
balloon (n)
battle (n)
cultural (adj)
die out (v)
during (prep)
earlier (adj)
fast (n and v)
  [= not eat]
happen (v)
hold (v) [= happen]
holy (adj)
largely (adv)
Lent (n)
luck (n)
mosque (n)
on the one hand
on the other hand
pray (v)
prayer (n)
relative (n)
religion (n)
ritual (n)
social science (n)
sunrise (n)
sunset (n)
Thanksgiving (n)
throughout (prep)
tradition (n)
victorious (adj)
war (n)

A Reviewing vocabulary

Complete each verb to make a phrase about festivals.

1. c elebrate   an event
2. m   preparations
3. d   hands
4. s   relatives
5. v   the graves of ancestors
6. p   through the streets
7. s   prayers
8. g   thanks to God
9. p   special clothes
10. c   special food

B Activating ideas

The spidergram on the opposite page contains notes for a text about a festival.

1. How many sections will the text contain?
2. Why are there two **events** under **Origins**?
3. Can you supply any of the missing information?
   where? = Muslim countries throughout the world

C Gathering information

1. Work in four groups. Each group reads a text about Eid al-Fitr.

   Group A: Read the text on page 172.
   Group B: Read the text on page 169.
   Group C: Read the text on page 171.
   Group D: Read the text on page 174.

2. Each group completes one section of the spidergram.
3. Work in groups of four, with one student from each of the four groups. Complete the rest of the spidergram.

D Describing a festival

1. Read the assignment on the right.
2. Complete the essay. Use your spidergram notes to help you.

The start of Eid

Eid prayers

Henna decoration   Fireworks for Eid

Eid foods   Prayers at the graves

Faculty of Social Science and Cultural Studies

Anthropology and the modern world
Assignment 3

Describe an annual festival in one or more countries. Give details of the origins of the festival and the way it is celebrated today.

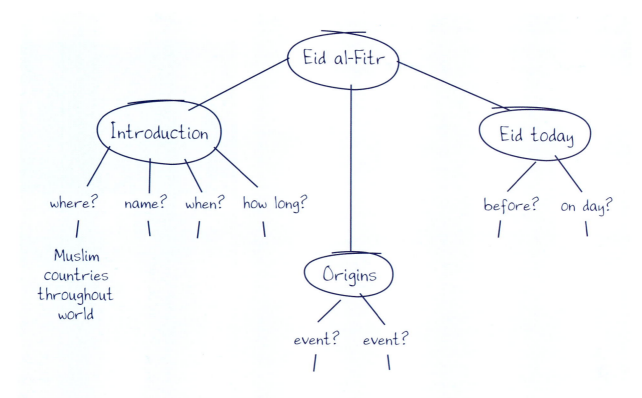

Eid al-Fitr
Introduction

Eid al-Fitr is celebrated ....

The name ....

The festival takes place ....

During the holy month of Ramadan, ...

Eid al-Fitr lasts ....

Origins

The first Eid ....

Some people believe ....

Other people say ....

....

Eid al-Fitr today

Before the festival, ...

....

On the day of the event, ...

....

Spelling vowel sounds; using fixed phrases

A Developing vocabulary

1. Which **single vowel** is missing from each set of words?
   What is the sound in each word?

   a. h___ppen   l___st   s___ys   w___nt

   b. pr___pare   sp___cial   n___w   th___y

   c. g___ve   fest___val l___ke   th___rd

   d. m___ney   cl___thes   h___liday w___men

   e. b___y   p___t   ___p   ___se

2. Which **pair of vowels** is missing from each set of words?
   What is the sound in each word?

   a. c_____ntry   y_____   h_____se

   b. m_____n   _____rly   br_____kfast

   c. ball_____n   c_____k   g_____d

   d. th_____r   rec_____ve   n_____ghbour

   e. f_____lds   fr_____nds   countr_____s

3. Read Skills Check 1 and check your answers.

B Identifying a new skill

Read Skills Check 2. Then find and correct seven mistakes in the text below.

New Year's Day

At a time, New Year's Day was celebrated on 15th March in Europe. Nowadays, it has been celebrated on 1st January. Other people believe that it is lucky to clean the house on New Year's Day.

Other people are saying that you should eat a particular kind of food to get good luck for the year. At some countries, people spend the day with their relatives. Before day, in the UK people send cards. On the day, there are going to be football matches and a big parade through the centre of London.

C Practising a new skill

Study the pairs of phrases in Skills Check 2 again. Complete each pair of sentences with true information from your own knowledge.

In some countries, people celebrate Christmas.
In other countries, people celebrate the birth of the Prophet Muhammad (PBUH).

Skills Check 1

Spelling vowel sounds

1. With one letter
Here are some examples of **different sounds** from a **single vowel**.

a	happen	last	says	want
e	prepare	special	new	they
i	give	festival	like	third
o	money	clothes	holiday	women
u	buy	put	up	use

2. With two letters
Here are some examples of **different sounds** from a **pair of vowels**.

ou	country	you	house
ea	mean	early	breakfast
oo	balloon	cook	good
ei	their	receive	neighbour
ie	fields	friends	countries

Always learn the spelling of the vowel sound(s) in a new word.

Skills Check 2

Comparing events and ideas

We often want to compare actions or ideas. We can use a pair of fixed phrases to introduce the actions or ideas.

In some countries, …
In other countries, …

Some people believe that …
Other people say that …

At one time, … + past simple
Nowadays, … + present simple

Before the day, … + past simple
On the day, … + present simple

The most common time prepositions are *in, on, at*. ⑥
- in = more than a day   e.g., in the Middle Ages, in 1607, in July
- on = a day   e.g., on 5ᵗʰ November, on Monday, on the day of the event
- at = parts of a day   e.g., at 6.30 p.m., at sunrise, at night

There are common **exceptions**.
- in e.g., in the morning, in the afternoon, in the evening
- at e.g., at the weekend (BrE), at Christmas
- on e.g., on the weekend (AmE)

There are several other time prepositions, including:
- for = general time periods   e.g., for years, for centuries
- during = specific time periods   e.g., the Middle Ages, the 1600s, July
- around = approximate date, time   e.g., around 10ᵗʰ March, around 7 p.m.
- from / to = start and finish times   e.g., from January to March, from 6.00 to 8.00 p.m.

There are **no prepositions** with these words and expressions:
yesterday, today, tomorrow, last week / month / year, etc., next week / month / year, etc.

A Using time prepositions

Write the correct preposition in each space. You do not need a preposition in some cases.

1. _____ 1890
2. _____ 4.00 p.m.
3. _____ April
4. _____ April _____ June
5. _____ Eid
6. _____ five days
7. _____ many years
8. _____ 10ᵗʰ March

9. _____ National Day
10. _____ night
11. _____ morning _____ night
12. _____ sunset
13. _____ the day of the event
14. _____ the evening
15. _____ the moment
16. 10.00 a.m. _____ 12 noon

17. _____ the second week
18. _____ yesterday
19. _____ the weekend
20. _____ three months
21. _____ Tuesday
22. _____ midnight
23. _____ last week
24. _____ the 17ᵗʰ century

B Using fixed phrases of time

Complete the sentences with a possible time word or period in each space. Invent the details.

1. The festival was first celebrated in _the Middle Ages / the 11ᵗʰ century / ancient times_ .

2. At one time, it lasted for _____.

3. The festival changed during _____.

4. Nowadays, it lasts for _____.

5. Every year, it starts on _____ and ends on _____.

6. For _____ before the festival, people prepare.

7. Then, on _____ there are many events.

8. In _____, there is a parade through the streets of the town.

9. Then, in _____.

10. Finally, at _____ people light fires and let off fireworks.

A **Reviewing vocabulary and grammar**

There is one wrong word in each sentence. Find it and correct it.

1. The festival ~~is~~ *was* first celebrated hundreds of years ago.

2. The festival takes part on the first Monday of June.

3. The festival takes one day.

4. According of tradition, the event was originally a harvest festival.

5. Some people speak that the festival started in the seventeenth century.

6. Other people say that it began in the sixteen century.

7. Special sports events are holding on the day.

8. On the evening, there is a big dinner for all the family.

9. Before start the meal, the family say prayers.

10. Everyone give thanks for something, for example good health.

B **Thinking and organizing**

You are going to describe another festival. Read the research notes on the right.

1. How many sections are there in the essay?
2. What is the main tense in each section? Why?

C **Writing**

Write about Thanksgiving.
Remember to use:
- present simple and past simple passive, where possible.
- time prepositions correctly.
- fixed phrases to compare, e.g., *At one time*, …

D **Editing**

Write about the interview process.
Exchange essays with a partner. Read his/her essay. Mark the essay with *?*, *S*, *G* and *P*.

E **Rewriting**

Read your essay again. Look at the *?*, *S*, *G* and *P* marks on your first draft. Write the essay again.

<u>Thanksgiving</u>

<u>Introduction</u>

North America = 'the act of giving thanks'
4th Thu in Nov (USA) / 2nd Mon in Oct (Can.)
1 day.
C17th group of religious people in N.A.

<u>Origins</u>

1:
- 1st = 1621
- gave thanks for harvest
- Sept, Oct or Nov – 3 days

2:
- not connected with harvest
- day of fasting / prayer originally
- changed to thanksgiving festival 1623 = started to rain during prayers

<u>Thanksgiving today</u>

Before:
- children make special things at school
- people make special clothes for parade
- lorries decorated with figures
- large balloons attached to lorries = figures of animals / cartoon characters

On day:
- lorries driven through streets
- special sports events, e.g., US football
- evening = family dinner
- before meal – prayers
- everyone gives thanks, e.g., food, good health, friends, neighbours
- eat turkey, pot roasts, pumpkin pie

Portfolio Festivals around the world

A Activating schemata

1. Look at the photographs above. What are some of the key features of festivals around the world?
2. Why do festivals share these features?

B Gathering information (1)

1. Divide into three groups. Group A: 🎧 **1.19**, Group B: 🎧 **1.20**, Group C: 🎧 **1.21**. Listen to information about three festivals. Make notes to answer the questions.

   - What is it called?
   - What does the name mean?
   - Where is it?
   - When is it?
   - How did it start?
   - How do people prepare for the event?
   - What happens on the day?
   - Do people wear special clothes?
   - Do people eat special food?

2. Work in groups of three, one student from each group, A, B and C. Exchange information about your festival.
3. Which festival would you like to attend? Explain your answer.

C Gathering information (2)

1. Work in pairs. Read one of the texts about great traditional events: *The Venice Regatta* or *The Holi Festival* on pages 38 and 39. Make notes.
2. Explain the information you read about to your partner. Your partner should make notes.

D Giving a talk

Choose one of the festivals from your portfolio notes. Write a short talk. Give your talk in a small group.

E Writing

Choose the festival you are most interested in. Write a short essay about the festival.

Great traditional events around the world

3: The Venice Regatta

Venice is a city of around 300,000 people. It is situated in northeast Italy, nearly 400 kilometres north of Rome. It is built on a system of canals. Many journeys through the city are on gondolas or long boats rather than in cars or on foot.

Venice was once an important centre for trade. In the Middle Ages, ships sailed from there for all parts of the known world. However, in the 16th century, the city declined, although by 1800 it was already a popular tourist resort.

Many people visit Venice today for the annual boat races, or regatta. It takes place on the first Sunday in September. Perhaps it started to celebrate a parade through the city in 1489. Queen Caterina of Cyprus, a Venetian herself, came to give her island to Venice.

For many days before the event, the people of the different areas fly flags from their houses. They prepare their costumes — brightly coloured clothes from the Middle Ages.

On the day, they dress up and parade along the Grand Canal. Then, at 3.30 p.m., the boats line up behind a rope stretched across the canal. They travel along the canal to a pole, go round the pole and come back.

There are four races. The first race is for children, the second for women, the third for men and the fourth for champions. In each race, the different areas compete against each other. After the races, local people and tourists travel up and down the canals in boats of all sizes. There are clowns and artists in the city's squares. There are big dinners in each of the areas.

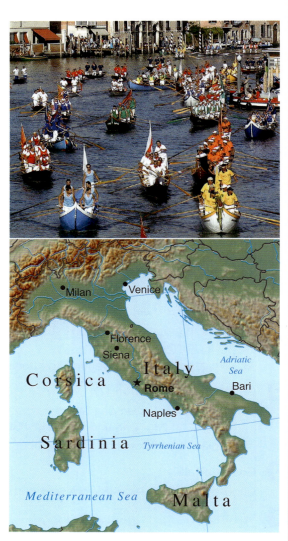

Great traditional events around the world

4: The Holi Festival

Jaipur is a city of around 2.5 million people. It is situated in the state of Rajasthan in northeast India, 260 kilometres southwest of New Delhi. It is called the Pink City because many of the houses in the old city are painted pink.

Jaipur was founded in 1727 by the ruler of the area. It is built on a grid pattern, like New York. It is one of the three cities of India's Golden Triangle. The other two are New Delhi, the capital, and Agra, the site of the Taj Mahal. The city is now a popular tourist destination.

Many people visit Jaipur each year for the Holi Festival. It takes place around 25th March. *Holi* means 'burning' in Sanskrit, the ancient language of the country. The festival celebrates an old legend. People have probably celebrated the festival for thousands of years.

Holi is celebrated all over India, but in Jaipur they celebrate with elephants. For many days before the event, people paint their elephants – trunks, heads and feet. They also cover the elephants in gold cloths and jewels.

On the day, there is a parade of elephants and horses. There are also traditional dances in the streets. Then there is a game of elephant polo. People normally play this game on horses, but in Jaipur they use elephants. Finally, there is a tug of war between elephants and people. In each game, there is one elephant against 19 men and women. The elephant often wins!

People do not wear their best clothes for the Holi Festival because, after the events, the young people start throwing bags of brightly coloured powder. Many people go home with hair the same colour as the buildings!

Theme 2

Technology

- Who? What? When?

- Transport inventions

- A brief history of space travel

- The historic moment

2.1 Vocabulary for listening Power sources for travel

A Revising vocabulary

How can you travel from one place to another? Complete this list of ways.

1. You can ride a *bicycle*.
2. You can sail a …
3. You can drive a …
4. You can fly a …
5. You can go by …
6. You can get on a … or get in a …

B Understanding vocabulary in context

1. Complete the table.
2. 🔊 2.1 Listen and check your ideas.

Table 1: *Power sources for travel*

power source	walking	boat/ship	bicycle	horse	car	train	plane	spacecraft
human	✓							
animal								
wind								
steam								
electricity								
petrol								
rocket								
jet								

C Developing critical thinking

Discuss these questions.

1. Why are there very few jet cars?
2. Why are very few cars powered by electricity?
3. Why are there no planes which use human power?
4. What will be the next power source for travel?

ago (*adv*)
aircraft (*n*)
astronaut (*n*)
electricity (*n*)
engine (*n*)
field (*n*) [= area]
helicopter (*n*)
human (*n* and *adj*)
in my opinion
in the air
invent (*v*)
invention (*n*)
inventor (*n*)
jet (*n*)
jumbo jet (*n*)
later (*adv*)
main (*adj*)
method (*n*)
motorcycle (*n*)
on land
on sea
other (*adj* and *pron*)
petrol (*n*)
power (*n* and *v*)
power source
propeller (*n*)
ride (*v*)
rocket (*n*)
sail (*n* and *v*)
shuttle (*n*)
source (*n*)
space (*n*) [= universe]
spacecraft (*n*)
steam (*n*)
track (*n*)
transport (*n*)
transportation (*n*)
travel (*n* and *v*)
wheel (*n*)

A Activating ideas

Look at the forms of transport on the opposite page.

1. Number the inventions in order – the earliest = *1*.
2. Discuss in groups. Which of these inventions is the greatest in the history of transport?

B Understanding the organization of a lecture

You are going to watch a lecture on the history of transport. ⊙ **2.2** DVD **7.A** Watch the first part of the lecture. What is the lecturer going to talk about?

C Making notes

1. ⊙ **2.3** DVD **7.B** Watch the second part of the lecture. Copy names and dates from the box on the right under the correct picture.
2. Which methods of transport are not mentioned in the lecture?

D Understanding an opinion

⊙ **2.4** DVD **7.C** Watch the final part of the lecture. Which invention does the lecturer think is the most important invention? Why does she have this opinion?

E Hearing short vowel sounds

Look at the words on the right. They are all from the lecture. They all have short vowel sounds.

1. Write each word in the correct column, according to the (underlined) vowel.
2. ⊙ **2.5** Listen and check your answers.

F Hearing long vowel sounds

Look at the words below. They are all from the lecture. They all have long vowel sounds.

1. Write each word in the correct column, according to the (underlined) vowel.
2. ⊙ **2.6** Listen and check your answers.

after	called	conc**e**rned	c**ou**rse	~~each~~	far
flew	last	more	move	p**eo**ple	s**ou**rce
steam	transp**or**t	use	world		

sea	car	first	horse	new
/iː/	/ɑː/	/ɜː/	/ɔː/	/uː/
each				

1903		Macmillan
	Benz	1888
1839		Pener
	Stephenson	1775
1830		Indonesian natives
Wright brothers		40,000 years ago

bec**au**se	engine	~~history~~	jet	p**e**trol	r**o**cket
that	track	tr**a**nsport	was	went	what
	when	which	wind		

ship	land	tell	on
/ɪ/	/æ/	/e/	/ɒ/
history			

A

B

C

D

E

F

G

H

A   Reviewing vocabulary

🎧 **2.7** Listen to some sentences. Tick the best way to complete each sentence.

1.	☑	inventions	☐	inventing
2.	☐	travelling	☐	transport
3.	☐	land	☐	ground
4.	☐	invented	☐	invent
5.	☐	air	☐	wind
6.	☐	track	☐	road
7.	☐	sky	☐	air
8.	☐	opinion	☐	mind
9.	☐	world	☐	place
10.	☐	civilizations	☐	cultures

B   Identifying a new skill (1)

1. 🎧 **2.8** Listen to the first part of the lecture in Lesson 2.2. What is the lecturer doing in this part?

2. Read Skills Check 1 and check.

3. 🎧 **2.9** Listen to the introductions to some more lectures. Organize your notes.

Festivals

1. origins
2. most important
3. best tourist attractions

C   Identifying a new skill (2)

1. 🎧 **2.10** Read Skills Check 2 and listen to the extracts. What is the lecturer doing in each extract?

2. 🎧 **2.11** Listen to some extracts from the lectures in Exercise B. How does the lecturer signal the change of topic in each case? Number the phrases.

   a. OK, now let's look at …   ....
   b. Right, that's …   ....
   c. So we have heard about …   ....
   d. So we have seen …   ....
   e. So, first …   ....

3. Read Skills Check 3. What are the missing letters – *sh* or *ch*? 🎧 **2.12** Listen and check your ideas.

   a. fre........   f. mu........
   b. ea........   g. resear........
   c. relation........ip h. ....ange
   d. mat........   i. whi........
   e. ....uttle   j. ....eck

Skills Check 1

Recognizing the organization of a lecture

The introduction to a lecture often gives you the order of sub-topics.

Use the introduction to pre-organize your notes.

First, I'm going to talk about … = 1
After that, I'll tell you …   = 2
Finally, I'm going to say …   = 3

Skills Check 2

Recognizing change of sub-topic

Lecturers often indicate change of sub-topic very clearly.

So, first, what are the main methods of transport …

So, there are several methods of transport. But when …?

So, we have heard about the main inventions in the field of transport. But which invention …?

In my opinion, …

Skills Check 3

Hearing blends: *ch, sh*

The letters *ch* make the sound /tʃ/.
The letter *sh* make the sound /ʃ/.
change, match, which, each
ship, fresh, short, English
The final letters *~tion* often have the sound *shun*. The stress is always on the vowel before *~tion*.
in-'ven-tion, ce-le-'bra-tion, con-gra-tu-'la-tions
The final letters *~ture* often have the sound /tʃ ə/.
lecture, picture

2.4 Grammar for listening Years and dates

Dates
⑦

in writing	in speech		
1 January	on the 'first of 'January	on 'January the 'first	on 'January 'first
April 10	on the 'tenth of 'April	on 'April the 'tenth	on 'April 'tenth
March 3	on the 'third of 'March	on 'March the 'third	on 'March 'third
11/9 or 9/11	on the e'leventh of Sep'tember	on Sep'tember the e'leventh	on 'nine e'leven

Years

in writing	in speech		
2000	in two 'thousand		
1815	in 'eighteen fif'teen		
1850	in 'eighteen 'fifty		
1901	in 'nineteen 'hundred and 'one	in 'nineteen oh 'one	in 'nineteen 'hundred 'one
1910	in 'nineteen 'ten		
1926	in 'nineteen twenty-'six		
2001	in two 'thousand and 'one	in 'twenty oh 'one	in two 'thousand 'one
2010	in two 'thousand and 'ten	in 'twenty 'ten	in two 'thousand 'ten
2020	in two 'thousand and 'twenty	in 'twenty 'twenty	in two 'thousand 'twenty

Time periods

In 1964, she arrived in the USA. Nine years **later** … = in 1973

In 1964, he got married. Nine years **earlier** … = in 1955

It's 2011 now. Ten years **ago** … = in 2001

A Understanding years and dates

1. 🔊 **2.13** Listen and write the year.

   1. 1762
   2.
   3.
   4.
   5.
   6.
   7.
   8.
   9.
   10.

2. 🔊 **2.14** Listen and write the date.

   1. 1/2
   2.
   3.
   4.
   5.
   6.
   7.
   8.
   9.
   10.

3. 🔊 **2.15** Listen and complete Table 1 below.

> The first carts with wheels appeared around 3500 BCE.

Table 1: *A transportation timeline*

	The first wheeled carts
	The first horses for transportation
	The first horse-drawn bus
	The first steam-powered car
	The first hot-air balloon
	The first petrol-engine car
	The first motorcycle
	The first powered flight
	The first flight faster than sound
	The first man on the Moon

A Activating ideas

  1. Can you name any of the flying inventions on the right?

  2. In what order were they invented?

B Preparing to listen

  1. How do you say these dates?
- 1900
- 1905
- 1910
- 1914
- 1936

  2. How do you say these names?
- Whittle
- Boeing
- Wright
- Sikorsky
- Goddard

C Listening and note-taking

You are going to watch another lecture about transport inventions.

🔊 **2.16** [DVD] **7.D** While you watch the lecture, remember to:
- write the main topic at the top of your notes.
- make a note of the sub-topics.
- make a note of the key information as follows:
  - when?
  - what?
  - who?
- make a note of any opinions the lecturer gives.

| 1.
2.
3.		
when?	what?	who?

Speaking: Transport inventions

2.6 Vocabulary for speaking Automobile inventions

A Reviewing vocabulary

The words and phrases below are from the Listening section. Find pairs. Explain the connection.

| aircraft astronaut electricity engine in space in the air jet
jumbo jet on land power propeller rocket sail sea shuttle
space spacecraft steam track |
|---|

aircraft – propeller: Some aircraft have propellers.

Mary Anderson	Giuliana Tesoro
Grace Hopper	Stephanie Kwolek

B Understanding new vocabulary in context

1. 🔊 2.17 Listen to a text about female inventors. Match each invention from the box to the photograph of the inventor above.

windscreen wipers Kevlar fire-resistant materials computer programs

2. Discuss this question.

    How does each invention make vehicles safer or faster?

3. Study the words on the right. Which words did you hear in the talk? What is the pronunciation in each case? Listen to the talk again and check your ideas.

C Developing critical thinking

Read this statement: *There are more male inventors than women.*

1. Was this true in the past? Why (not)?

2. Is it true today? Why (not)?

3. Will it be true in the future? Why (not)?

according to (*prep*)
apparently (*adv*)
brake (*n*)
break (*v*)
button (*n*)
click on (*v*)
coin (*n*)
control (*n* and *v*)
cover (*n*)
female (*adj*)
hard (*adj*) [= not soft]
industrial (*adj*)
insert (*v*)
(the) Internet (*n*)
machine (*n*)
male (*adj*)
material (*n*)
motorcar (*n*)
pardon?
practical (*adj*)
press (*v*)
product (*n*)
push (*v*)
record (*n*)
replace (*v*)
rider (*n*)
run out of (*v*)
safe (*adj*)
safety (*n*)
screen (*n*)
set (*v*) [= fix]
speed (*n*)
substance (*n*)
switch on (*v*)
technology (*n*)
vehicle (*n*)
work (*v*) [= operate]

A Previewing vocabulary

Put the words below into five groups, according to the (underlined) vowel sound.

> bel<u>ie</u>ve   ~~dr<u>e</u>w~~   s<u>u</u>re   m<u>o</u>re   p<u>ar</u>don   w<u>or</u>ld   <u>ear</u>lier   sp<u>ee</u>d   tw<u>o</u>   wh<u>o</u>   h<u>al</u>f   rec<u>or</u>d (v)   r<u>ea</u>d

/uː/	/iː/	/ɑː/	/ɜː/	/ɔː/
drew				

B Activating ideas

1. Look at the website on the right.
   - What is it about?
   - How many pieces of information does it give?
2. Cover the conversation below. 🔊 **2.18** Listen and complete the missing numbers and dates in the website.

C Studying a model

1. Uncover the conversation. Complete the gaps.
2. 🔊 **2.19** Listen again and check.

> A: Did you know there are over a billion <u>bicycles in the world</u>?
>
> B: Only a million?
>
> A: No, one billion, apparently. It says here that it was invented in the 19th century by Kirkpatrick Macmillan and now _____.
>
> B: When was it _____?
>
> A: In 1893 … Wow!
>
> B: What?
>
> A: According to this, the speed record for a bicycle is two hundred _____. It was set in 1995. Apparently he was riding _____.
>
> B: Amazing.
>
> A: But it seems that Leonardo da Vinci actually drew a picture of a bicycle more than three _____.
>
> B: Pardon? Who _____?
>
> A: Da Vinci. D-A and V-I-N-C-I. The famous Italian painter and inventor drew a bicycle.
>
> B: No he _____! I read about that. Apparently, someone else drew the bicycle in Leonardo's notebook in 1970.
>
> A: Are you _____? But it says here that _____.
>
> B: Maybe – but you shouldn't believe everything _____.

3. Role-play the conversation in pairs.

D Developing critical thinking

Why is information on the Internet sometimes wrong?

Four things you didn't know … about the bicycle

There are over _____ bicycles in the world. Nearly _____ of them are in China.

The bicycle was invented by Kirkpatrick Macmillan in _____.

The speed record for a bicycle is _____ kilometres an hour. The rider was Fred Rompelberg in _____.

Leonardo da Vinci, the famous Italian painter and inventor, drew a picture of a bicycle in _____.

Everyday English **Using technology**

A Activating ideas

1. Look at the pictures above. What are the people doing?
2. Have you ever had a problem with these pieces of technology?

B Studying models

1. Which sentence below goes in each conversation?

a. The photocopier is broken.
b. Have you ever used the SPSS program?
c. How do you set the time?
d. How does this thing work?
e. Do you know how to use the book checkout?
f. I can't get the washing machine to work.

1
A: _____
B: Put in the powder.
A: I've done that.
B: OK. Pull this thing out. Put the coins in here. Push it in. Switch it on.

2
A: _____
B: Press the 'Menu' button and go to 'Settings'.
A: OK, and then I choose 'Date and time'?
B: That's right. We're an hour behind Berlin.

3
A: _____
B: Follow the instructions on the screen.
A: 'Insert coins.' OK. 'Press Button A.'
B: When the light flashes, it takes a picture.

4
A: _____
B: No, it isn't. It's run out of paper.
A: How do you put more paper in?
B: It says here: 'Open cover. Insert paper. Replace cover.'

5
A: _____
B: Yes, I have. But I'm not very good at it.
A: Do you know how to input new data?
B: Click on 'Data view'.

6
A: _____
B: Just put the book on the scanner.
A: But it won't read my library card.
B: Let's ask for help.

2. 🔊 **2.20** Listen and check.

C Real-time speaking

1. Practise the conversations.
2. Role-play conversations about these pieces of technology.

- camera
- computer printer
- media projector
- ID swipe card
- MP3 player
- library catalogue
- TV remote control
- parking meter

2.8 Learning new speaking skills Talking about research

A Saying blends

1. Put these words into two groups, according to the <u>underlined</u> sounds.

> pic<u>t</u>ure <u>sh</u>ould informa<u>ti</u>on pu<u>sh</u> <u>ch</u>oose
> resear<u>ch</u> inven<u>ti</u>ons <u>s</u>ure lec<u>t</u>ure swi<u>tch</u>

2. Read the Pronunciation Check. Check your answers.

3. ⓑ 2.21 Listen. Say the words you hear.

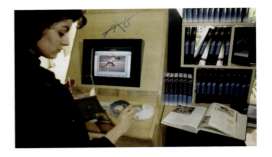

B Identifying a key skill

1. ⓑ 2.22 Listen and complete the sentences.

   a. It _seems that_ humans can never travel to other stars.

   b. _____, people from Asia sailed across the Pacific 600 years ago.

   c. _____ here that the motorcycle was invented in 1885.

   d. _____ to this, the first cars were always black.

   e. _____ you _____ the scientific name for a horse is *equus caballus*?

   f. _____ bamboo sometimes grows a metre a day.

2. Read the Skills Check and check your answers.

3. Find more examples in the conversation in Lesson 2.7.

C Practising a new skill

Read each piece of information below. Tell your partner about it. Your partner replies.

> *Apparently, in most cities, a bicycle is faster than any other vehicle.*

> *Really? Where did you read that?*

Pronunciation Check

Saying blends: /tʃ/ and /ʃ/

/tʃ/ and /ʃ/ are pronounced with the lips forward and round. They are unvoiced sounds.

The sound /ʃ/ is the sound in English to ask for silence: *Shhh!* It is usually spelt *sh, -ti-* or *su*.

Examples: *ship, dictionary, location, sure*

The sound /tʃ/ is made by putting /t/ before /ʃ/. It is usually spelt *ch, tch* or *-tu-*.

Examples: *check, each, watch, picture*

Skills Check

Talking about research

We often want to tell another person about our research.

Learn these ways.

1. To introduce information:
   Did you know that ...?
   It says (here) that ...
   Apparently, ... It seems that ...
   According to (this) ...

2. To comment or show interest:
   Amazing. That's interesting.
   How did they do that? Really?

> Steam trains are still used all over Africa, Asia and South America.

> The Wright brothers were not the first people to fly.

> It is not possible to travel faster than the speed of light.

> Most people walk about three kilometres in half an hour.

> If a person cycles every day, he/she feels ten years younger.

> People who fly in balloons don't know where they are going to land.

> In the UK, they drive about 500 billion kilometres a year.

> The average Formula 1 car has 80,000 parts.

> **Flying is still the safest way to travel.**

> Every year in Wales, a race is held between the local train and 1,000 people on foot.

We can check statements if we don't hear them correctly, or if we don't believe them.   ⑧

1. With *be*

	subject	verb	complement
checking ...	Kevlar	is	a very hard material.
the **subject**	*What is a very hard material?*		
the **complement**	*What is Kevlar?*		

2. With **other verbs**

	subject	verb	object	extra information
checking ...	Fred Rompelberg	rode	a bicycle	at 268 kilometres an hour.
the **subject**	*Who rode a bicycle at 268 kilometres an hour?*			
the **object**	*What did he ride at 268 kilometres an hour?*			
the **extra information**	*How fast did he ride a bicycle?*			

We stress the **question word**. We use a **rising intonation**.

A   Completing checking questions

1. Complete the checking question in each case.

   a. The French Revolution was in 1789.
     When _____?

   b. The Incas built a city on a 2,000-metre mountain.
     _____ *a city on a mountain?*

   c. Apparently, penicillin comes from a fungus.
     Pardon? _____?

   d. It seems Henry the Eighth had six wives.
     Pardon? _____ *many wives did he have?*

   e. It says here that too much water makes you ill.
     Sorry? _____ *you ill?*

   f. Some animals sleep in winter to save energy.
     Sorry? Why _____ *in winter?*

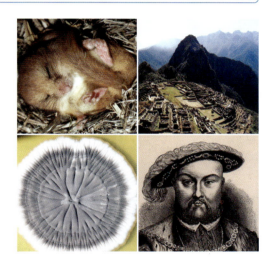

2. 🔊 **2.23** Listen and check.

3. Role-play the conversations. Remember to use the correct stress and intonation.

B   Asking questions

Ask checking questions for each of these statements.

Student A

a. Steam trains are still used all over Africa, Asia and South America.

b. They found an important shipwreck under the sea.

c. The force of gravity makes things fall.

Student B

d. Animals use different colours to hide from each other.

e. The Polynesians discovered America first.

f. Chinese New Year starts between 21ˢᵗ January and 20ᵗʰ February.

A   **Reviewing sounds**

1. Say each pair of words below. Make sure your partner can hear the difference.

	A	B
1.	she's	cheese
2.	ship	chip
3.	shoes	choose
4.	shop	chop
5.	shore	chore
6.	wash	watch
7.	wish	which
8.	dish	ditch

2. 🔊 **2.24** Listen. Then practise saying these sentences.

   a. Which cheese did she choose?
   b. You wash the dishes. I'll watch TV.
   c. Is that a chip shop?
   d. Was the ship near the shore?

B   **Researching information**

Work in groups.

> **Group A:** Read about the invention of the helicopter on page 174.
> **Group B:** Read about the invention of the motorcar on page 172.

Learn the information about your invention. Do not take notes!

C   **Using a key skill**

Work in pairs, with one from Group A and one from Group B. Tell your partner about your research. Use the language you have learnt in this section.

> It said that he began work on helicopters in 1910.

> When did he begin work on helicopters?

> Apparently, he called his car a 'motor carriage'.

> Sorry? What did he call it?

shop | chop
shore | chore
dish | ditch

2.11 Vocabulary for reading   The solar system

A   Reviewing vocabulary

Choose the correct word in italics to complete each sentence. Circle the word.

1. The rider got *on* / *in* the motorbike.
2. The age of flying began just over a hundred years *behind* / *ago*.
3. The steam engine was a very important *invent* / *invention*.
4. The *pilot* / *driver* of the plane has a lot of experience of flying.
5. There are many different methods of *travel* / *transport*.
6. The shuttle takes *sailors* / *astronauts* up into space and brings them back to Earth.
7. The *head* / *captain* ordered the men to start the ship's engines.
8. *According* / *Apparently* to some websites, the Wright brothers were not the first people to fly in a powered plane.

B   Understanding vocabulary in context

Complete the text below with words or phrases from the list on the right. Make any necessary changes.

C   Developing critical thinking

At one time, people thought that the Sun went round the Earth. Why did they think that?

Hundreds of years ago, people in Europe believed that the Earth was the centre of the ....universe........ They thought that the Sun and all the .... went round the Earth. However, at the start of the 16th century, a Dutchman called Copernicus said: 'The Earth and all the planets .... the Sun.'

We know now that the Sun is a .... at the centre of our Solar System. Some .... say that there are nine .... in our system. Others believe that there are only eight. Pluto is usually the .... planet from the Sun, but it is so small that some people say it is not a planet

.... The Earth is the third planet from the Sun. It is the planet that we .... It has a natural .... which orbits the Earth. It is called .... Our .... is in space. No human being went into space until the second half of the 20th century. In 1969, men .... on the Moon and returned safely to Earth. Now, spacecraft .... almost every month. Many scientists think that the next object for space .... is the planet Mars.

astronomer (n)
at all
attack (v)
carbon (C) (n)
castle (n)
discover (v)
enemy (n)
explode (v)
exploration (n)
far (adv)
fire (v)
further (adv)
(the) furthest (adv)
gunpowder (n)
inhabit (v)
journey (n)
kill (v)
land (v)
launch (v)
mainly (adv)
mark (v)
  [= show a change]
mix (v)
(the) Moon (n)
natural (adj)
orbit (n and v)
oxygen (O) (n)
parachute (n)
planet (n)
satellite (n)
(the) Solar System (n)
star (n)
sulphur (S) (n)
(the) Sun (n)
universe (n)
weapon (n)
wound (v) [= injure]

A Activating ideas

What is the connection between fireworks and space travel?

B Predicting content

1. Look at the opposite page for 30 seconds. What is the text about?

2. Read the topic sentences on the left below. Then read the statement beside each one. Is it true or false? If it is false, correct it.

1. The new invention of gunpowder was mainly used by the Chinese in fireworks.	*Paragraph 1 will probably be about Chinese fireworks.*	True? But 'mainly' = used for something else too?
2. Between the tenth and 13th centuries, Arab traders in China learnt about gunpowder.	*Paragraph 2 will probably be about Arab traders.*	
3. Cannons could blow huge holes in castle walls.	*Paragraph 3 will probably be about castles.*	
4. Werner von Braun, a German scientist, studied the rockets of the ancient Chinese and the cannons of medieval Europe.	*Paragraph 4 will probably be about cannons in medieval Europe.*	
5. On 8th September 1944, the first rocket hit London.	*Paragraph 5 will probably be about the future.*	

C Understanding a text

Read the text opposite. Deal with any new words. Match each question below with an answer.

1. What happened around 800 BCE? ☐ Fireworks and as the power source for cannons.
2. What is gunpowder? ☐ Space travel.
3. What did the Chinese use gunpowder for? [1] Someone invented gunpowder.
4. When did gunpowder arrive in Europe? ☐ A mixture of S, KNO_3 and C.
5. What did Europeans use gunpowder for? ☐ Fireworks and rockets.
6. Why did gunpowder lead to the end of castles? ☐ Some time around the 13th century.
7. What was the power source of von Braun's rockets? ☐ Liquid oxygen.
8. What did von Braun want to use his rockets for? ☐ Because cannons with gunpowder could blow holes in the castle walls.

D Transferring information

Make a timeline of the key information in the text.

A brief history of space travel

Part 1: Gunpowder, cannons and rockets

In about 800 BCE, a person in Ancient China mixed sulphur (S), potassium nitrate (KNO_3) and carbon (C). He set fire to the mixture. It exploded. The mixture was gunpowder.

The new invention of gunpowder was mainly used by the Chinese in fireworks. One of these fireworks was the rocket. Someone discovered that rockets could be very big. These big fireworks could be weapons. The Chinese sometimes fired rockets at their enemies. They didn't know it, but their invention led, over 1,000 years later, to space travel.

Between the tenth and 13th centuries, Arab traders in China learnt about gunpowder. They took it to Europe. People there also used it for fireworks. However, the Europeans mainly put gunpowder in new guns called cannons. Cannons were weapons for blowing holes in castle walls. There are reports that cannons were used at the battle for Seville in 1248.

Cannons could blow huge holes in castle walls. The arrival of gunpowder in Europe, therefore, led eventually to the end of castles because there was no safety inside a castle any more. But what has all this got to do with space travel?

Werner von Braun, a German scientist, studied the rockets of the ancient Chinese and the cannons of medieval Europe. In December 1934, von Braun invented a rocket which travelled a long way. The fuel of the rocket was not gunpowder, but liquid oxygen. Nazi Germany attacked London with the rocket at the end of the Second World War. But what about space travel?

A Chinese rocket

A cannon of the Middle Ages

A medieval castle

On 8th September 1944, the first rocket hit London. It killed three people and wounded 17. Before the end of the war, over 500 rockets were launched. They killed nearly 9,000 people and injured more than 25,000. Von Braun once remarked to one of his colleagues: 'The rocket worked perfectly, but it landed on the wrong planet.'

A   Reviewing vocabulary

What does the underlined word mean in each sentence from the text in Lesson 2.12?

1. In about 800 BCE, a person in Ancient China mixed sulphur, potassium nitrate and carbon. He set fire to the mixture.

2. The new invention of gunpowder was mainly used by the Chinese in fireworks.

3. The Chinese sometimes fired rockets at their enemies.

4. Between the tenth and 13th centuries, Arab traders in China learnt about gunpowder.

5. There are reports that cannons were used at the battle for Seville in 1248.

6. The arrival of gunpowder in Europe, therefore, led eventually to the end of castles …

7. The fuel of the rocket was not gunpowder, but liquid oxygen.

8. Nazi Germany attacked London with the rocket …

9. It killed three people and wounded 17.

10. Von Braun once remarked to one of his colleagues: 'The rocket worked perfectly, but it landed on the wrong planet.'

B   Identifying a key skill (1)

1. Read Skills Check 1. What numbers are often written as words?

2. Find and underline all the numbers in the text in Lesson 2.12.

C   Identifying a key skill (2)

1. Read Skills Check 2. What part of speech is *mainly*?

2. What do you expect to read after each of these sentences?

   a. The people of the area mainly lived in villages.
      Some people lived in towns and cities.

   b. Early cars mainly used petrol as a power source.

   c. Von Braun was mainly interested in space travel.

   d. Liquid oxygen is mainly used to power space rockets.

   e. This article is mainly about the Ancient Chinese.

   f. The festival of Eid al-Fitr is mainly for Muslims.

Skills Check 1

Finding information quickly: using numbers

Numbers can be in **figures** or words.

Examples:

Figures: *800, 17, 1248*

Words: *three, thirteenth*

Writers often put in **words**:

- numbers 1 to 10
- centuries

Always look for numbers in a text. They often give you the answer to research questions.

Always make a **timeline** of events in a chronological text.

Skills Check 2

Predicting content: using the adverb *mainly*

Adverbs often help you to predict information in the text.

Example:

The new invention of gunpowder was ***mainly*** *used … in fireworks …*

=

The text will probably give another use for gunpowder.

=

These big fireworks could be weapons.

Extra information about the subject ⑨

subject	extra information	verb	object / complement
A person	in Ancient China	mixed	S, KNO_3 and C.
Arab traders	in China	learnt about	gunpowder.
The fuel	of the rocket	was not	gunpowder.

The extra information about a **subject** is sometimes in a prepositional phrase.

A Finding the subject and the verb

1. Find and circle the verb in each sentence below.

   a. The earliest picture of a parachute was drawn in around 1485 CE.
   b. An inventor in Italy made the drawing.
   c. The drawing by an Italian, Leonardo da Vinci, shows a man hanging from four ropes.
   d. The four ropes of the parachute are attached to a frame.
   e. The sides of the frame are just over seven metres.
   f. The frame of the device is the base of a pyramid.
   g. The pyramid on top of the frame has the same height as the base.
   h. According to da Vinci, the size and the shape of the device are extremely important.

2. Underline the subject in each sentence. What is the extra information about the subject?

We can make a complete sentence into the subject of a new sentence. ⑩

subject	verb	adverbial
Gunpowder	arrived	in Europe.

subject	verb	object
It	led to	the end of castles.

subject	extra information	extra information	verb	object
The arrival	of gunpowder	in Europe	led to	the end of castles.

It is good to find the original sentences in these cases. They help you understand the long sentence.

B Finding the original sentences

Make a verb from the red word in each case. What were the original sentences?

1.	The invention of the steam engine by James Watt led to faster travel on land and at sea.	James Watt invented the steam engine. It led to faster travel on land and at sea.
2.	The flight of Orville Wright in *The Flyer* in 1903 was the start of the air age.	
3.	The design of a helicopter by Sikorsky in 1910 did not result in the production of working machines.	
4.	The launch of von Braun's rockets during the Second World War was the start of the space age.	
5.	The death of Hitler in 1945 marked the end of the Second World War in Europe.	
6.	The failure of Guy Fawkes to blow up Parliament in 1605 is celebrated every year in Britain.	

A Match the questions and answers.

1. What can you race?
2. What can you inhabit?
3. What orbits the Earth?
4. When do you need a parachute?
5. Who can you pray to?
6. What does a primitive society not have?
7. What does a glider not have?
8. What does an astronomer study?
9. Where are the Tropics?
10. Where does a submarine go?
11. What do scientists do with a hypothesis?
12. What do you do with a firework?
13. Why are some animals becoming extinct?
14. What can you use a rocket for?
15. What do nearly all insects have?

- [ ] They try to prove it.
- [ ] Space.
- [ ] North and south of the Equator.
- [ ] Under the water.
- [ ] An engine.
- [1] Horses, cars, other people, etc.
- [ ] As a weapon or to get into space.
- [ ] A house, a town, an area, a country, etc.
- [ ] Wings.
- [ ] The Moon.
- [ ] God or the gods.
- [ ] Climate or human activity.
- [ ] Set light to it.
- [ ] A lot of technology.
- [ ] To escape from a damaged plane.

B Match the opposites.

1. friend
2. be born
3. inland
4. insert
5. horizontal
6. positive
7. take off
8. put
9. agricultural
10. accept

- [ ] land
- [ ] negative
- [ ] reject
- [ ] industrial
- [ ] on the coast
- [ ] remove
- [1] enemy
- [ ] vertical
- [ ] die
- [ ] take

C Match the words with similar meanings.

1. almost
2. attend
3. around
4. conclude
5. everyone
6. field
7. bay
8. hobby
9. maybe
10. rude
11. reach
12. participate
13. continue
14. happen
15. power

- [ ] end
- [ ] impolite
- [ ] take place
- [ ] interest
- [ ] perhaps
- [ ] get to
- [1] nearly
- [ ] take part
- [ ] all the people
- [ ] energy
- [ ] about
- [ ] harbour
- [ ] area
- [ ] go on
- [ ] go to

2.16 Vocabulary for writing   Transport

A   Reviewing vocabulary

Complete the table with one or two words in each space.

transport	person	place	verb: infinitive	verb: past simple	verb: past participle
car	driver / passenger				
bicycle					
plane					
boat					

B   Building vocabulary

Write a word or phrase from the list on the right for each dictionary definition. Check your answers in a dictionary.

___land___   come back to the ground in a plane or helicopter; *The plane ran out of fuel, but the pilot managed to ~ safely.*

_____   a kind of boat that can go under the water; *The ~ went down six metres.*

_____   a toy which flies; it is often in the shape of a diamond; *The children flew the ~ for a long time, then the boy let go of the string.*

_____   move a boat through the water with long pieces of wood; *There was no wind, so they ~ed the boat back to the harbour.*

_____   a group of ships with guns; *The US ~ has more than 280 fighting ships.*

_____   make a car, boat, plane, etc., go at the correct speed and in the correct direction; *He couldn't ~ the car and it went off the road.*

_____   leave the ground in a plane or helicopter; *Pilots must check everything before they ~.*

_____   a plane without an engine; *You can fly for a long time in a ~ if the weather conditions are right.*

_____   have an accident in a car, plane or helicopter; *He lost control of the car and it ~ed into a wall.*

_____   something which transports people on land, such as a car, a bus, a motorbike; *This road is closed to motor ~.*

C   Using new vocabulary

Cover the definitions in Exercise B. Write a sentence for each of the words.

Submarines are very important in sea battles nowadays.

accept (v)
aircraft (n)
attach (v)
brief (adj)
control (n and v)
crash (n and v)
demonstrate (v)
design (n and v)
drive (v)
engineer (n)
engineering (n)
flight (n)
fly (v)
glider (n)
historic (adj)
hot-air balloon (n)
jet (adj and n)
kite (n)
land (v)
lose (v) [= not have]
lose control (v)
navy (n)
pilot (n)
powered (adj)
printing (adj)
propellor (n)
realize (v)
reject (v)
repair (v)
row (v)
safety (n)
submarine (n)
take off (v)
test (v) [= try out]
underwater (adj)
vehicle (n)
win [a contract] (v)
wing (n)

2.17 Real-time writing The first powered flight

A Reviewing vocabulary

Complete each sentence about flying.

1. On 15th January, 2009, the _pilot_ of flight 1549 got into his plane.

2. He started the _____ .

3. The plane _____ off from La Guardia Airport, New York.

4. It _____ for a few minutes without any problems.

5. Then suddenly the engine lost _____ .

6. The _____ was too far away. They could not return.

7. The pilot _____ on the Hudson River.

8. The _____ went under the water.

9. But the pilot managed to _____ the plane.

10. It _____ , but no one was injured.

B Activating ideas

1. What are the similarities between the three things in the photos?

2. What are the main differences?

C Using the present simple

Study the table at the top of the opposite page.
Answer the questions below.

1. How is the information organized?

2. What is the connection between all the events?

3. What tense is used?

4. What grammatical items are missing?

5. What is the main event?

D Using the past simple

1. Study the first sentence of the biography of the Wright brothers on the opposite page. What tense is used?

2. Complete *The early years* with the correct verbs in the correct form.

3. Complete the other three sections with information from the timeline.

E Developing critical thinking

Why did the Wright brothers succeed when many other people had failed?

A box kite

The Wright glider

The Wright Flyer

Department of Aeronautics and Astronautics

The history of flight
Assignment 6

- Make a **timeline** of events in the lives of Wilbur and Orville Wright.
- Write a short **biography** of the two brothers. Focus on their first powered flight.

	The early years
1867	Wilbur Wright b. Indiana, USA
1870?	family moves Dayton, Ohio
1871	Orville Wright b. Ohio, USA
1889	Wilbur and Orville start printing company, Dayton
1892	start bicycle shop, Dayton, sell / repair bicycles, design bicycles, build them
1896	famous pilot dies in glider crash; Wilbur and Orville interested in flying
	Development of the invention
1899	put wings on bicycle; fly it like kite
1900	build glider – keeps crashing, build wind tunnel, test glider
1901–1903	learn to control glider; build plane – 2 wings; engine for plane – 2 propellers, The Flyer
	The historic moment
1903	17/12 – O. flies 35 m. in 12 secs = changes world forever!
	Later life
1904–1908	build bigger, better planes
1909	win contract to build planes for US Army
1912	Wilbur d.
1915	Orville sells company; works as aircraft engineer
1930	jet engine is invented
1939	helicopter is invented
1948	Orville d.

The Wright brothers

The early years

Wilbur Wright was born in 1867 in Indiana in the USA and lived for several years in Indiana, but his family moved to Dayton, Ohio, in about 1870. His brother, Orville, ... in 1871. In 1889, the brothers .... a printing company in Dayton. Three years later, they .... a bicycle shop. At first, the brothers .... and .... bicycles. Later, they .... bicycles and .... them. In 1896, a famous pilot .... in a glider crash. The brothers .... about the crash and .... interested in flying.

Development of the invention

In 1899, ... A year later, ...
.... At first,
.... After that, ... Finally,
....
....

The historic moment

....
....

Later life

....
....

2.18 Learning new writing skills Connecting ideas with *and* and *but*

A Spelling key words

Write the past tense of each verb.

1. is   *was*
2. are   ....
3. build   ....
4. go   ....
5. learn   ....
6. make   ....
7. put   ....
8. keep   ....
9. buy   ....
10. become   ....

B Identifying a new skill

Which word do you use to join each piece of information –
and or *but*? Make other necessary changes.

1. He was born in 1867 in Indiana.
   a. *and he*   lived there for several years.
   b. *but he*   moved to Dayton, Ohio, in about 1870.

2. The Wright brothers went to high school.
   a. .... They did quite well.
   b. .... They didn't graduate.

3. They heard about the crash.
   a. .... They became interested in flying.
   b. .... It did not change their plans.

4. The glider flew well.
   a. .... It kept crashing.
   b. .... They learnt how to control it.

5. They bought an engine for the glider.
   a. .... They put the engine in the plane.
   b. .... It was too heavy.

6. In 1909, the brothers won a contract to build army planes.
   a. .... Wilbur died just three years later.
   b. .... They built many planes in the next three years.

Read the Skills Check to check your answers.

C Using logical connectors

Read the start of each sentence about a fictional inventor.
Write something logical after each connector.

1. She was born in 1954 in Paris, France, and …
2. She went to university in 1972, but …
3. She joined an engineering company after university, but …
4. She finally got a job in aeronautics in the USA and …
5. She worked on the NASA Space Program and …
6. She designed many parts of the first Space Shuttle, but …

Orville Wright in the bicycle factory

Skills Check

Connecting ideas

A lot of short sentences with the same
subject are quite hard to read.

Examples:

Wilbur was born in 1867.
He lived in Indiana for three years.
He moved to Ohio in 1870.

It is good English to join short sentences.

The most common joining words are
and and *but*.

We use **and** to add expected information.

We use **but** to add unexpected
information.

Examples:

*He was born in 1867 in Indiana **and** he*
lived there for several years.

*He was born in 1867 in Indiana, **but***
his family moved to Dayton, Ohio, in
about 1870.

If two sentences have **the same
subject**, you can join them with *and*
or *but* and delete the subject of the
second verb.

Example:

The brothers built a glider and ~~they~~
flew it like a kite.

⑪

person	subject pronouns	object pronouns	possessive adjectives
1st singular	I	me	my
2nd singular	you	you	your
3rd singular	he / she / it	him / her / it	his / her / its
1st plural	we	us	our
2nd plural	you	you	your
3rd plural	they	them	their

Do not repeat nouns in a text. Replace them with pronouns or possessive adjectives.

Wilbur Wright was born in 1867 in Indiana.
Wilbur Wright lived for several years in Indiana.
Wilbur Wright's family moved to Ohio in about 1870.

Wilbur Wright was born in 1867 in Indiana.
He lived for several years in Indiana.
His family moved to Ohio in about 1870.

The brothers built a glider.
The brothers flew the glider like a kite.

The brothers built a glider.
They flew it like a kite.

But be careful. Sometimes, you **must** repeat the noun. If you don't, the reader will be confused.

The brothers built an engine for the plane.
The brothers put the engine in the plane.

The brothers built an engine for the plane.
~~They put it in it.~~ They put it in the plane.

A Joining sentences

1. Replace the nouns in the text below with pronouns and possessive adjectives where possible.
2. Join sentences and delete the subject of the second sentence where possible.

Alberto Santos Dumont was born in 1873.
Alberto was born in Brazil in South America.
Alberto's father owned a large farm.
Alberto's father knew about machines.
Alberto worked on Alberto's father's farm.
Alberto learnt engineering from Alberto's father.
In 1891, Alberto's father sold the farm.
Alberto's father moved Alberto's father's family to France.
In Paris in the 1890s, Alberto took flights in hot-air balloons.
Alberto became interested in hot-air balloons.
Alberto started designing hot-air balloons.
Alberto built a hot-air balloon.
Alberto made controls for the hot-air balloon.
Alberto called the hot-air balloon *The Brasil*.
Alberto attached a petrol engine to the hot-air balloon.
The hot-air balloon was the first hot-air balloon with a petrol engine.
Hot-air balloons with engines and controls are called 'airships'.
On 18th September 1898, Alberto flew Alberto's airship for the first time.
In 1901, Alberto flew Alberto's airship around the Eiffel Tower.
Alberto became the most famous person in the world.

Alberto Santos Dumont was born in 1873 in Brazil in South America.
His father owned a large farm and knew about machines.

A Reviewing vocabulary and grammar

One word is missing from each sentence. Add the word in the correct place.

1. Robert Fulton ⟋ born in Pennsylvania, USA, in 1765. *was*
2. He went to school, but not go to university.
3. He moved Philadelphia in 1782.
4. In 1786, he went to London study art.
5. From 1793 to 1797, he worked an engineer in England.
6. In about 1800, realized that New York needed a good system of water transport.
7. In 1807, he built a steamship from an earlier design by a man John Fitch.
8. On 18th August 1807, he demonstrated steamship on the Hudson River.
9. He went to build other boats, including a steamship for the US Navy.
10. Robert Fulton died 14th February 1815.

Fulton's steamship

Drebbel's submarine in the River Thames

B Thinking and organizing

You are going to write a short biography of an inventor. There are four sections to the biography:

- The early years
- The development of the invention
- The historic moment
- Later life

Study the timeline of Drebbel's life on the right. Divide the timeline into four sections.

C Writing

Write about the life and main invention of Cornelius Drebbel. Remember to:

- use the past simple, active and passive.
- add extra ideas after *and / but*.
- join sentences with the same subject.
- use pronouns and possessive adjectives.

D Editing

Exchange essays with a partner. Read his/her essay. Mark the essay with *?*, *S*, *G* and *P*.

E Rewriting

Read your essay again. Look at the *?*, *S*, *G* and *P* marks on your first draft. Rewrite the essay.

<u>Cornelius Drebbel</u>

1572	b. Alkmaar, Netherlands
1579–1585	goes to school (not university)
1586–1590	becomes apprentice to printer; learns chemistry; starts inventing
1595	designs water supply system for Alkmaar
1604	moves to England demonstrates inv. to K. James I
1604–1610	works for K. James; makes fireworks, special clock, etc.
1618–1619?	builds first submarine – uses earlier design (Will. Bourne) rowing boat (wood + leather) but sailors need O underwater so makes O from potassium nitrate (KNO₃)
1620	23 / 8 demonstrates submarine; goes up and down R. Thames; 4m. under water; British Navy rejects!
1620–1628	better sub = Drebbel II; 6m. under water; but not accepted; D. gets no money
1629–1633	very poor in London
1633	d. London

A Activating schemata

Look at the photographs of transport inventions above.

1. What is each invention?
2. How did it change transport?

B Gathering information (1)

Divide into three groups. Group A: 🔊 **2.25**, Group B: 🔊 **2.26**, Group C: 🔊 **2.27**.

1. Listen to the information about another invention. Make notes to answer these questions.

   - What is it called?
   - What does it do?
   - Who invented it?
   - What nationality was he/she / were they?
   - When was he/she / were they born?

   - Where did he/she/they work?
   - How did he/she/they invent it?
   - When did he/she/they invent it?
   - How did the invention develop?

2. Work in threes, one student from each group, A, B and C. Exchange information about your invention. Make notes.

3. Which of the three inventions is the most important, in your opinion? Explain your answer.

C Gathering information (2)

1. Work in pairs. Read one of the texts, *A brief history of transport safety 1* or *2* on pages 70 and 71. Make notes.

2. Explain the information you read about to your partner. Your partner should make notes.

D Giving a talk

Choose one of the inventions from your portfolio notes – *Kevlar, car windscreens, train ventilator, parachutes, radar*. Write a short talk. Give your talk in a small group.

E Writing

Think about transport today. Think of an invention to improve safety. Write a short essay explaining the invention, how it works and why it is useful.

A brief history of transport safety

Part 1: What goes up … must come down

A parachute is a device for bringing a person safely down to earth from a great height. It took hundreds of years before someone invented a parachute that actually worked.

In 852 CE, a man called Armen Firman jumped from a minaret in Cordoba in Spain. He only had a big coat to save himself. He was hurt when he landed, but he did not die. Three hundred years later, in 1178, a man jumped from a minaret in Constantinople, also wearing a large coat. He died from his injuries.

Although some people believe that the Chinese had working parachutes by the 12th century, the earliest picture of a parachute is by Leonardo da Vinci. The famous Italian artist and inventor was born in 1452. At school, he apparently upset his teachers by asking too many questions. He was interested in everything. He left school at the age of 15 to become an artist. He made hundreds of drawings in his notebooks, including one of a parachute, between 1483 and 1486.

Da Vinci's drawing shows a man hanging from four ropes. Each rope is connected to the corner of a square frame. The frame is the base of a pyramid, covered in cloth. The sides of the frame are just over seven metres, and the pyramid has the same height. The size and shape were important, according to da Vinci. He believed that this size and shape could support the weight of a man. He wrote: 'Anyone can jump from any height with no risk at all.' However, nobody believes that he actually made his device, or tried it out.

A Croatian man called Faust Vrancic went to school in Italy and saw da Vinci's drawing in about 1595. He made his own parachute and tested it in 1617. He jumped off a tower attached to the device … and survived.

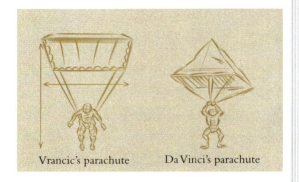

Vrancic's parachute   Da Vinci's parachute

The design of the parachute was lost for over a hundred years, but it was reinvented in 1783 by a Frenchman called Sebastien Lenormand. Some people say he also gave it its name, from two French words – *para* meaning 'against' and *chute* meaning 'fall'. Two years later, another Frenchman, Jean-Pierre Blanchard, threw a dog out of a hot-air balloon, attached to a parachute. It landed safely. He followed the dog in 1793, when his hot-air balloon caught fire. He also survived.

Parachutes have many uses nowadays. They bring spacecraft safely to land, they slow down sports cars, and they are even used in sport. They are part of the equipment of all air-force pilots around the world. Passenger airliner pilots do not have them, however. Nor do their passengers.

A brief history of transport safety

Part 2: **Ra**dio **D**etection **A**nd **R**anging

When we are sailing or flying in the daytime, we can normally see other planes or ships around us. But what happens at night, or in fog? At one time, ships and planes were in danger. It took 30 years after the first manned flight for someone to find the answer.

In 1887, a German scientist called Hertz discovered an interesting fact about radio waves. He found that they passed through some materials, like wood, but bounced back from others, like metal.

Seven years later, a Dutchman, Christian Huelsmeyer, invented a device to improve safety at sea. His device enabled one ship to detect or find other ships, even in fog or at night. However, the device could not give the actual location or the distance of these other ships. Navies around the world were not interested in the invention. Scientists in many countries, including France, Germany and the United States, worked on the problem through the 1920s, but it was finally solved by a British scientist, Robert Watson-Watt.

Watson-Watt was born in 1892 in Scotland. He studied engineering at University College, Dundee. In 1915, he started work as a meteorologist – a person who studies weather. He became involved in tracking thunderstorms. The lightning in storms produces radio signals and, in 1923, he had the idea of using an oscilloscope to show the radio waves.

He used the information about the location of storms to warn pilots. They could then take a route around the storm.

Then, in 1935, he invented a device to send out radio waves and draw a picture of the reflections on an oscilloscope. The picture showed the location of an object, such as a plane, and its distance. It also showed the size of the object and its speed. He called the device Radio Detection and Ranging, because *range* is another word for 'distance'. The name of the invention soon became *radar*, from the first letters of these words.

It is possible that radar helped Britain to win the Second World War, because the British system was better than the German system, and it was difficult for German planes to attack without being 'seen'.

Radar is still used today to track weather systems, but it is also used at all airports and on all planes. It is also used on all ships. It has improved safety in the air and at sea enormously.

Theme 3

Arts and media

- **Arts and media**

- **Advertising**

- **The values of magazines**

- **Media studies research reports**

Listening: Arts and media

3.1 Vocabulary for listening   The mass media

A   Revising vocabulary

What do all the items in the box below have in common?

> television   radio   newspapers   magazines   mobile phones   the Internet

B   Understanding vocabulary in context

1. Use a word or words from the list on the right to complete the text below. Make any necessary changes.

Nowadays there are many information organizations. For example, we have television, radio, newspapers and, of course, the Internet. They all provide .... and information to the general public. The word for all of these organizations is .... It is an unusual word because it is a plural. The singular word is *medium*. This word has different meanings in everyday English. But here it means *a way of communicating*. For example, we can say 'The Internet is the most important .... today.'

We often talk about the *mass media*. The word .... means *a large amount*. So we use the phrase for media that .... a large number of people.

The mass media have a lot of influence on the .... This is because modern technology can give the news very fast to millions of people. So the media have a very big .... In television and radio, we say information is .... to viewers and listeners. This means it is .... over a very wide area, perhaps over the whole world at the same time. People in many different countries often watch the same .... events .... on television, for example.

2. 🌐 **3.1** Listen and check.

C   Using new vocabulary

1. 🌐 **3.2** Listen. Make notes about each event.
2. What point is the speaker making with these two examples?

D   Developing critical thinking

What *kind* of events are in the news every day? Name three main kinds.

---

advertisement (*n*)
advertising (*n*)
appear (*v*)
as a matter of fact
audience (*n*)
bias (*n*)
breaking news (*n*)
broadcast (*n* and *v*)
channel (*n*)
character (*n*) [= letter]
crowd (*n*)
distribute (*v*)
distribution (*n*)
explanation (*n*)
(the) general public (*n*)
in fact
in many cases
incidentally
influence (*n*)
literacy (*n*)
live (*adj*)
(the) mass media (*n*)
medium (*n*)
   [= way of communicating]
message (*n*)
   [= what you want to say]
(the) news (*n pl*)
printing (*adj* and *n*)
privacy (*n*)
product (*n*)
reach (*v*)
   [= get to a target]
reporter (*n*)
scene (*n*)
service (*n*)
terrorist (*n*)
therefore (*adv*)
transmission (*n*)
transmit (*v*)

....

....

....

....

....

A Activating ideas

Look at the illustrations on the opposite page.

1. What does each illustration show?
2. 🔊 **3.3** Listen and check your ideas.

> E. This is one of the first newspapers.

B Understanding the organization of a lecture

You are going to watch a lecture on the early history of the mass media.

Study the student notes on the right. 🔊 **3.4** [DVD] **8.A** Watch the introduction to the lecture. What is the lecturer going to talk about in the lecture? Correct the student notes.

> <u>Mass media for news and</u>
> <u>entertainment: history</u>
>
> 1. Spoken news
> 2. Written news – Rome, China
> 3. Printing, early newspapers

C Understanding the key information

1. 🔊 **3.5** [DVD] **8.B** Watch the rest of the lecture. Is each sentence true (*T*) or false (*F*)?

a.	People did not get news of events in early history.	F	They got news in speech.
b.	The first written news appeared in Ancient Greece.		
c.	The first printed text appeared in Ancient China.		
d.	Gutenberg invented the printing machine in 1464.		
e.	Gutenberg's machine made printing easy but expensive.		
f.	Printed books were not popular at first.		
g.	The first advertisements appeared in 1477.		
h.	There was a link between printing and literacy.		
i.	The lecturer thinks the mass media is linked with advertising.		
j.	We can only advertise products and services in the mass media.		

2. Correct the false statements above.
3. What is the assignment?

D Identifying words from the stressed syllable

1. 🔊 **3.6** Listen to some sentences. Number the words below in order.

> 1. When did the mass media for news begin?

a. 'his to ry ....
b. lit e ra cy ....
c. me di a ___1___
d. pro cess ....
e. pub lic ....
f. ap peared ....
g. com mu ni cate ....
h. com mu ni ca tion ....
i. dis trib u ted ....
j. trans mit ting ....

2. Mark the stressed syllable in each word.

E Developing critical thinking

Study the graph on the right. How do you feel about the information?

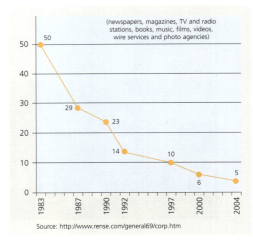

(newspapers, magazines, TV and radio stations, books, music, films, videos, wire services and photo agencies)

Source: http://www.rense.com/general69/corp.htm

Figure 1: *Number of corporations that control a majority of US media*

A Reviewing key words and phrases

🔊 **3.7** Listen to some sentences. Tick the word you hear.

1.	☐	fine	✓	define
2.	☐	news	☐	new
3.	☐	two	☐	to
4.	☐	two	☐	too
5.	☐	each	☐	reaches
6.	☐	even	☐	event
7.	☐	round	☐	around
8.	☐	boards	☐	bored
9.	☐	how	☐	however
10.	☐	four	☐	therefore

B Identifying a new skill

1. Read these extracts from the lecture in Lesson 3.2. What sort of information is the lecturer going to give next, in each case?

   a. *Mass* means 'big', so …

   b. Mass media reaches a large number of people. In fact, …

2. Read the Skills Check and check.

C Practising a new skill

🔊 **3.8** Listen to some extracts from a lecture. Predict the next part from the linking word.

1. *There are advertisements during most mass-media news programmes because …*

	mass-media news companies are very big.
	one minute of TV news could cost the company $20,000.
1	the mass-media companies do not make money from the news itself.
	they add the sound.
	they employ people to link the news items.

D Identifying vowel sounds

1. Put the words below into two groups, according to the (underlined) vowel sound.

> case def<u>i</u>ne expl<u>ai</u>n k<u>i</u>nd m<u>a</u>ke r<u>a</u>dio
> t<u>i</u>me w<u>ay</u> wh<u>y</u> ass<u>i</u>gnment

2. Read the Pronunciation Check. Check your answers.

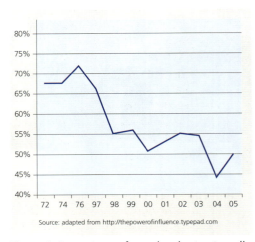

Figure 1: *Percentage of people who trust media news 'a lot' or 'quite a lot'*

Source: adapted from http://thepowerofinfluence.typepad.com

Skills Check

Predicting content from linking words

Speakers often introduce the next piece of information in a talk.

Examples:

*Mass means 'big', **so** …*

*Mass media reaches a large number of people. **In fact,** …*

Listen for words and phrases to help you predict the function of the next information.

word / phrase	next information
but / however	contrary, opposite point
and / in addition	more information
so	result
because	reason
in fact, / actually	extra information same subject

Pronunciation Check

Hearing vowels: /eɪ/ and /aɪ/

These are two diphthongs (or double vowels). They end in the /iː/ sound.

/eɪ/ – *way, same, expl<u>ai</u>n, <u>a</u>ncient*

/aɪ/ – *time, kind, Ch<u>i</u>na*

We can often make verbs into nouns by adding letters. Speakers often use related verbs and nouns in the same section of a talk.

- Sometimes, it is easy to **hear** that these words are related. They have the same stress and almost the same sound.
- Sometimes, it it harder to hear the relationship, because the stress moves, or because the stressed syllable sounds different.

Examples:

1. *About 60 BCE, the first newspaper* **appeared** *in Ancient Rome. However, its* **appearance** *was not the start of mass-media news.*

2. *They* **communicated** *a message to a large number of people. Let's look at the early development of this kind of* **communication**.

3. *There was no method of* **transmitting** *speech to a large number of people.* **Transmission** *of speech … started with the invention of the radio in the late 19th century.*

1. Same stress

a'ppear	a'ppearance
a'ppoint	a'ppointment
be'have	be'haviour
se'lect	se'lection

2. Different stress

co'mmunicate	communi'cation
ex'plain	expla'nation
dis'tribute	distri'bution
'advertise	ad'vertisement
pre'fer	'preference

3. Different syllable sound

trans'mit	= /m ɪ t/	trans'mission	= /m ɪ ʃ/
pro'duce	= /d ʒ uː s/	pro'duction	= /d ʌ k/
o'ccur	= /k ɜː/	o'ccurrence	= /k ʌ/
de'scribe	= /s k r aɪ b/	de'scription	= /s k r ɪ p/

A **Identifying words from the stressed syllable**

🔊 **3.9** Listen to some sentences. Each sentence contains one of each pair of words on the right. Do you hear the noun or the verb in each case?

> 1. The festival **is celebrated** in August.

B **Predicting related word forms**

🔊 **3.10** Listen to a sentence. Try to hear the important verb. Which noun do you expect the speaker to use later in the text? Say the noun.

> 1. In this talk, I'm going to tell you how to **apply** to university.

> application

	verb		noun
1.	✓ celebrate	☐	celebration
2.	☐ combine	☐	combination
3.	☐ produce	☐	production
4.	☐ compete	☐	competition
5.	☐ explore	☐	exploration
6.	☐ motivate	☐	motivation
7.	☐ qualified	☐	qualification
8.	☐ describe	☐	description
9.	☐ participate	☐	participation
10.	☐ prepare	☐	preparation

	advertisement		measurement
1	application		organization
	attendance		situation
	decision		transmission
	explanation		behaviour

A   Reviewing vocabulary

1. 🔊 **3.11** Listen to each sound. It is the stressed syllable of a word connected with the mass media. Can you identify the word?

2. 🔊 **3.12** Listen and check your ideas.

a. me   media / medium

b. tel   ....

c. chan   ....

d. me   ....

e. miss   ....

f. mun   ....

g. vert   ....

h. port   ....

i. ven   ....

j. news   ....

1

2

3

B   Preparing to listen

The news is everywhere nowadays. Is mass-media news a good thing or a bad thing? Use the table below to list advantages and disadvantages.

C   Listening and note-taking

You are going to watch another lecture about mass-media news. 🔊 **3.13** DVD **8.C** While you watch, remember to:

- write the main topic at the top of your notes.
- make a note of the sub-topics.
- make a note of key information under each sub-topic.
- predict the next communicative purpose.

Mass-media news: advantages and disadvantages	
+	—
1. fast – many reporters / good comms	1. needs stories all the time = not really news?

Speaking: Advertising

3

3.6 Vocabulary for speaking — Stereotypes

1   2   3   4   5

A   Reviewing vocabulary

1. Ask your partner for another form of these words from the Listening section.

> appearance   distribute   explanation   privacy   behave

> *appearance – appear*

2. Make a sentence with each word.

B   Understanding new vocabulary in context (1)

1. 🔊 **3.14** Listen. Complete each conversation with a word from the list on the right. Make any necessary changes.

   1   A: What's a _____?
          B: It's the main article in a magazine.

   2   A: What's the difference between _____ and *advert*?
          B: There's no difference. They're both short for *advertisement*.

   3   A: Does _____ mean people at a concert?
          B: Yes. And it means the people who see an _____.

   4   A: Do you spell _____ with *~ise* or *~ize* at the end?
          B: You can use either. The pronunciation is the same.

2. Practise the dialogues in pairs.

3. Discuss the following questions.
   - What is a stereotype? What is wrong with stereotypes?
   - What's the difference between a *stereotype*, a *generalization* and an *impression*?

C   Understanding new vocabulary in context (2)

1. 🔊 **3.15** **DVD** **8.D** Watch a tutorial about groups of people. Number the words below in the order you hear them.

   _____ impression   _____ stereotype   _____ issue

   _____ reality   _____ generalization   _____ community

2. Mark the stress on the words above.

D   Developing critical thinking

Which photos above show / go against stereotypes?

---

ad (*n*)
advert (*n*)
advertisement (*n*)
audience (*n*)
avoid (*v*)
biased (*adj*)
community (*n*)
cosmetics (*n*)
critic (*n*)
definitely (*adv*)
design (*n* and *v*)
disabled (*adj*)
documentary (*n*)
ethnic (*adj*)
exhibition (*n*)
feature (*n*)
generalize (*v*)
image (*n*)
impression (*n*)
issue (*n*)
magazine (*n*)
minority (*n*)
mostly (*adv*)
otherwise (*adv*)
persuade (*v*)
portray (*v*)
purpose (*n*)
reaction (*n*)
reality (*n*)
report (*v*)
review (*n*)
sexist (*adj*)
shocking (*adj*)
show (*v*)
sort (*n*)
stereotype (*n*)
stereotypical (*adj*)
stuff (*n*)
target (*adj* and *n*)

A Activating ideas

Look at the magazine advertisements on the right.
Discuss these questions.

1. What is each advertisement selling?
2. What stereotypes does each advert show?

B Studying a model

Look at this conversation from a tutorial about advertising in magazines.

1. Discuss the meanings of the words in bold in the conversation.
2. Complete each gap with a suitable adjective.
   🔊 **3.16** Listen and check your ideas.

A: Where do you think the first advert is from?

B: I think it comes from a women's magazine.

A: And who is the **target audience**?

B: _Young_____ women.

C: I agree. Maybe _____ women, too.

A: What is the **purpose** of the ad?

C: To sell cosmetics.

A: Why is the target audience interested in adverts like this?

C: Because most women want to look _____.
   They feel it's _____.

B: That's a stereotype!

C: Maybe. But it's _____.

A: And how does the ad **persuade** them to buy the product?

C: The woman is very _____. The message is: if you
   use this make-up, you will look _____, too.

A: Do you think it's a _____ advert?

B: I don't like it. In my opinion, the **image** doesn't represent reality.

A: And how about you?

C: I don't believe it's a _____ advert. It's not reality, but I think it's very _____.

A: Who **created** the ad? Who **designed** it?

C: I think an advertising agency designed the image.

B: I agree. And the cosmetics company paid for it. I think it was very _____.

3. Role-play the conversation in threes.

C Practising a model

Talk about the other advertisements on this page. Use A's questions from the conversation above.

Talking about the media

A. .... B. .... C. .... D. .... E. .... F. _1_

A Activating ideas

1. Look at the pictures above. Which areas of the media are they examples of?
2. How often do you use each area?

B Studying models

1. Which question below goes with each conversation?

    a. Have you seen the new *Vogue*?
    b. Did you see that documentary last night?
    c. What sort of media do you work with?
    d. Have you read the review of the book?
    e. Do you read the papers?
    f. Are you going to see the Rembrandt exhibition?

2. 🔊 **3.17** Listen and check.

1
A: ....
B: No. The shop has run out.
A: There's an article on the Milan Fashion Week.
B: I'll get one tomorrow.

2
A: ....
B: Yes, I saw it in the literature magazine.
A: What do you think?
B: I think it was a bit biased.

3
A: ....
B: That awful thing on Channel 7 about cinema?
A: Yes. Didn't you like it?
B: No. I didn't think much of it.

4
A: ....
B: TV and film mostly. How about you?
A: Photography.
B: That's interesting.

5
A: ....
B: Yes, every day.
A: Do you have a favourite?
B: No, I like to read all the different styles.

6
A: ....
B: Yes. When is it on?
A: It starts tomorrow for three months.
B: Good. I really like his stuff.

C Practising a model

1. Practise the conversations.
2. Role-play conversations beginning with these questions.
    • Have you seen the *Computer* magazine?
    • What did you think of the photo exhibition?
    • Do you listen to the radio much?
    • Do you think advertising to children is wrong?
    • Are you going to see the new film at the Showcase?
    • What news websites do you read?
    • What do you think of advertising by e-mail?

A Saying diphthongs

1. Put these words into two groups according to the (underlined) vowel sound.

> while my case way change otherwise buy
> maybe always find fight paper like they wife

2. Read the Pronunciation Check.
3. 🔊 3.18 Listen. Say the words.

B Identifying a key skill

1. Read the Skills Check. Answer these questions.
   a. What should you do before a tutorial?
   b. What should you do during a tutorial?
2. Why are these things important?

C Practising a key skill (1)

1. Study the statements at the bottom of the page and complete the table. Compare your ideas in pairs.
2. Form your opinion about each statement. Add more examples and ideas.

D Practising a key skill (2)

1. 🔊 3.19 Listen to an extract from a tutorial. Practise the conversation.
2. Turn the other statements in Exercise C into questions. Then discuss them in groups.

> What is the most important subject at school?

> In my opinion, Maths is the most important subject because you need it for every job. For example, in a shop or a bank.

> I agree. But I think English is also very important. It's an international language.

Pronunciation Check

Saying diphthongs: /eɪ/ and /ɑɪ/

A **diphthong** consists of **two sounds**. The first sound is stronger than the second.

Examples:

/eɪ/: *like, my, fight, buy, find*

/ɑɪ/: *say, they, paper, weigh, great*

Note that there are many different spellings for these two sounds.

Skills Check

Taking part in a tutorial

You must take part in discussions with tutors and other students.

Before a tutorial, you must:

- research the topic, e.g., *The influence of television on children.*
- form an opinion about it, e.g., *It is bad.*

During the tutorial, you must:

- give your opinion, e.g., *I think television is a bad influence on children …*
- give reasons for your opinion, e.g., *… because children often copy bad behaviour.*
- give an example, e.g., *For example, if they watch a violent programme, they might copy it.*

---

statement	for	against
Maths is the most important subject at school.	You need maths in every job.	English is an international language so it is more important.
TV is a bad influence on children.	Children copy bad behaviour.	Some TV is educational.
Boys and girls should go to mixed schools.	Boys behave better with girls in the class.	
It is better to be an extrovert than an introvert.		Extroverts can sometimes bully other people.
Sociology is more useful than psychology.		
Some people can't find a job because they are lazy.		At the moment, there are not many jobs.

3.9 Grammar for speaking   Introductory phrases

We often give an opinion with an introductory phrase. We put any negative in the introductory phrase. ⑬
We can follow *think*, *feel* and *believe* by *that*, but in spoken English we usually leave *that* out.

introductory phrase				statement
I		think		an advertising agency designed it.
We	(don't)	feel	(that)	there are too many advertisements on television.
They		believe		the news is very interesting at the moment.

A   Using introductory phrases

Give your opinion about these things. Use words from each box.

> *I think TV adverts are entertaining.*   *I agree.*   *I'm sorry, I disagree.*

I (don't) think	smoking	is	a good / bad idea.
	mobile phones		a great / frightening experience.
	TV adverts		really expensive.
I (don't) feel	hard work	are	entertaining.
	qualifications		boring / interesting.
	television		important.
	living in a different country		useful.
I (don't) believe	having a lot of money	can be	very good / bad for you.

We can ask for an opinion with *think*. ⑭

with be

Q word	question	statement
—	Do you *think*	the advert is good?
Why	do you *think*	the ending is bad?

with other verbs

Q word	question	statement
—	Do you *think*	the advert works?
Why	do you *think*	people buy it?

B   Making questions

1. Tick the correct questions below.
   a. Where is this advert from? ☐
   b. Where this advert is from? ☐
   c. Where you think this advert is from? ☐
   d. Where do you think this advert is from? ☐
   e. Where do you think is this advert from? ☐
   f. Where do you think it comes from? ✓
   g. Where do you think does it come from? ☐

2. What happens when we put *Do you think* in front of a question?

3. Read the tables above and check your ideas.

LIFE IS AN EXTRAORDINARY JOURNEY

C   Using *think*, *feel*, *believe*

1. 🔊 **3.20** Listen and answer some questions about the advert on the right.

2. Ask and answer about the advert in pairs.

3.10 Applying new speaking skills Analyzing TV ads

A Reviewing sounds

Say the words below. Make sure your partner can hear the difference.

1.	wait	white	6.	way	why
2.	late	light	7.	trade	tried
3.	main	mine	8.	replayed	replied
4.	race	rice	9.	A	I
5.	lake	like	10.	may	my

B Activating ideas

You are going to take part in a tutorial on the topic of TV advertisements.

1. Complete the questions below.

Source

Where is the advert from?

_____ created it?

Audience

_____ is the target audience?

_____ is the target audience interested in adverts like this?

Purpose

_____ is the purpose of the advert?

_____ does the advert persuade people to buy the product?

Reaction

_____ you like the advert?

_____ the advert is effective?

2. Think of a TV ad you love or hate. Answer the questions above.

C Researching information

Work in groups. Find three filmed adverts on the Internet.

1. Watch the adverts without the sound. What do you think the people are saying?
2. Watch the adverts with the sound.
3. Think about the questions in Exercise B. Make notes.

D Using a key skill

Discuss the adverts in your group.

Remember to:

- take turns.
- support your opinions with examples.
- mention any use of stereotypes.
- mention any avoidance of stereotypes.
- use *I think / I don't think* ...
- ask for opinions with *do you think?*

> Who do you think the target audience is?

> Why do you think it is for that audience?

> I think it's mothers with small children.

> I don't think older children like those things.

3.11 Vocabulary for reading   Values

A Reviewing vocabulary

All the words below are connected with media. What is the full word in each case?

1. att..............
2. aud..............
3. bro..............
4. dis..............
5. imp..............

6. me..............
7. por..............
8. pri..............
9. ste..............
10. tra..............

B Understanding vocabulary in context

Complete the text with words or phrases from the list on the right. Make any necessary changes.

What is the value of your mobile phone? The word .... normally means the cost or price of something. But the plural – .... – has a different meaning. Your values are the important things in your life. For some people, family life is the most important thing. For other people, the most important thing is a set of religious .... Finally, your values are your opinions or ...., e.g., *How should young people behave towards older people?* At one time, values came from religion and parents. But perhaps nowadays some people get their values from the mass media. There .... be a problem with this.

The mass media shows .... all the time. The message is: 'Money is the most important thing.' Money buys the .... of celebrities. However, there is some interesting research into modern values. According to .... in Western Europe, young people do not think money is very important (see Figure 1). Will they feel the same in a few years' time? What .... will the mass media have on their values?

Figure 1: 'Money is very important to me.'
(Survey in Western Europe 1994)

C Developing critical thinking

How much does the mass media influence *you* in your choice of the following?

- clothes
- appearance, e.g., hairstyle, make-up
- likes and dislikes, e.g., music, books
- attitudes
- behaviour

---

affect (*v*)
appeal (*n* and *v*)
attitudes (*n pl*)
  [= how you see things]
attract (*v*)
belief (*n*)
celebrity (*n*)
collection (*n*) [= group]
cope (*v*)
cover (*n*)
decline (*n*)
demographic (*adj*)
effect (*n*)
elderly (*adj* and *n*)
e-zine (*n*)
feature (*n* and *v*)
image (*n*) [= picture]
lifestyle (*n*)
market sector (*n*)
(the) mass media (*n*)
may (*v*)
persuasion (*n*)
powerful (*adj*)
principle (*n*)
promote (*v*) [= support]
publisher (*n*)
reader (*n*)
sector (*n*)
self-image (*n*)
specialist (*n*)
survey (*n*)
target (*n* and *v*)
teen (*adj* and *n*)
title (*n*) [= name]
value (*n*)
values (*n pl*)

A   Activating ideas

Study the magazine covers on the right. What sort of person reads each magazine? Think about:

- demographic group.
- interests.
- occupation.

B   Predicting content

1. Prepare to read the article on the opposite page.
   Then think of an answer to the question in the subheading:
   How do publishers make money from magazines?

2. Cover the text. Read the topic sentences on the left below.
   Match each topic sentence to the next sentence in the paragraph.

3. Uncover the text opposite. Check your answers.

a. In 1881, the first real magazine in the world appeared.	☐ They attract readers in a number of ways.
b. Magazines today are not for everybody.	☐ Because they do not make their money from the sales of the magazine.
c. Magazines target particular groups.	ⓐ It was published by a man called George Newnes.
d. Publishers want to attract the right kind of reader to each title.	☐ Each title appeals to a particular market sector.
e. Why do magazine publishers want to attract a particular market sector?	☐ Nowadays, there are different magazines for each kind of person.
f. Nowadays, magazines do not contain titbits of information for everybody.	☐ Do they also *influence* their readers?
g. So magazines reflect their readers' interests in a very clear way.	☐ Firstly, there are demographic groups.

C   Understanding the text

Read the statements below. Decide if each statement is true (*T*) or false (*F*). Then read the text opposite and check your ideas. Correct the false statements.

1.	At one time, magazines appealed to one kind of person.	F	all kinds of people
2.	The elderly are a demographic group.		
3.	Readers are attracted to a particular magazine by the name and nothing else.		
4.	Advertisers want to reach everybody with their adverts.		
5.	Magazines definitely influence their readers.		
6.	Magazines affect people's values.		

In the next two weeks, we look at

magazines

This week:

How do publishers make money from magazines?

In 1881, the first real magazine in the world appeared. It was published by a man called George Newnes. He called it *Titbits* because the word means 'interesting little pieces of information'. It was for all kinds of people. Newnes made money from selling his magazine to a large number of people.

Magazines today are not for everybody. Nowadays, there are different magazines for each kind of person. In 2008, there were about 2,800 magazine titles in the UK alone.

Magazines target particular groups. Firstly, there are demographic groups. We have magazines for teens, for the elderly, etc. Secondly, we have interest groups. There are sports magazines, hobby magazines, and so on. Finally, some magazines nowadays appeal to people in particular jobs.

Publishers want to attract the right kind of reader to each title. They attract readers in a number of ways. Firstly, they give their magazines clear names. Secondly, they choose the pictures for the front cover very carefully. Finally, they choose the best articles for the magazine.

Why do magazine publishers want to attract a particular market sector?

Because they do not make their money from the sales of the magazine. They make their money, in a way, from the sales of their readers. Advertisers want to reach particular readers. A magazine for one sector of the market is an excellent way to achieve this aim.

Nowadays, magazines do not contain titbits of information for everybody. Each title appeals to a particular market sector. A successful magazine attracts a demographic group, an interest group or a business sector group. Then it can sell advertising space to companies who want to reach that sector.

So magazines reflect their readers' interests in a very clear way. Do they also *influence* their readers? Perhaps they persuade them to have certain attitudes and values. This persuasion may help the advertisers to sell them particular products.

Next week:
Teen magazines – are they selling a lifestyle?

A Reviewing vocabulary

Make phrases with one word from each column.

1.	mass	☐	sector
2.	front	☐	society
3.	specialist	☐	space
4.	demographic	1	media
5.	advertising	☐	magazine
6.	market	☐	beliefs
7.	material	☐	lifestyle
8.	modern	☐	cover
9.	religious	☐	group
10.	celebrity	☐	success

B Identifying a new skill

1. Put these extracts from the article in Lesson 3.12 into two groups. Explain your choice.

In 2008, there were about 2,800 magazine titles in the UK alone. ☐

Magazines target particular groups. ☐

We have magazines for teens, for the elderly, etc. ☐

This persuasion may help the advertisers to sell them particular products. ☐

They attract readers in a number of ways. ☐

In 1881, the first real magazine in the world appeared. ☐

2. Read the Skills Check and check your answer.

C Practising a new skill

Read these statements about the mass media. Find and underline the possibility word(s).

1. Perhaps TV presenters have an influence on our clothes and our speech.

2. TV advertisements may have a bad effect on children.

3. It is possible that some TV channels will introduce longer advert breaks next month.

4. You may be able to complain about adverts online.

5. Some parents might not agree with advertisements for junk food and drinks.

Skills Check

Fact or possibility?

A **fact** is true. It is a piece of information which everyone agrees about.

Examples:

In 1881, the first real magazine in the world appeared.

In 2008, there were about 2,800 magazine titles in the UK alone.

Magazines target particular groups.

We have magazines for teens, for the elderly, etc.

A **possibility** is an idea. It may be true. It may not be true.

In many cases, writers help the reader to distinguish between fact and possibility.

They use special words to say to the reader: *This is a possibility.*

Examples:

***Perhaps** they persuade them to have certain attitudes and values.*

*This persuasion **may help** the advertisers to sell them particular products.*

Writers also sometimes put possibilities in question form.

Example:

Do they also influence their readers?

We can refer back to information earlier in a text in two main ways: ⑮

1. with **subject pronouns** and **object pronouns**;

2. with **possessive adjectives**.

It is very important to understand the reference of each of these words in a text.

The reference can be the **subject** or the **object** of a previous sentence.

1. Pronouns

sentences	referring back to
Magazine publishers want to attract the right kind of reader … They give their magazines very clear names.	the **subject**
In 1881, a man called George Newnes published the first real magazine. He called it *Titbits*.	the **object**
Magazines reflect their readers in a very clear way. Perhaps they persuade them to buy certain things.	the **subject** and the **object**

2. Possessive adjectives

Magazine publishers want to attract the right kind of reader … … they give their magazines very clear names.	= *the publishers of the magazines*
The production of a magazine is paid for by the advertising in the magazine and not by its sales.	= *the sales of the magazine*

A **Understanding pronouns and possessive adjectives**

Read this text. Then underline the correct noun (phrase) reference for each numbered item.

Publishers made money from the first magazines by selling a lot of **①** them. However, towards the end of the 19th century, they started to make **②** their money from advertising. If a publisher sold a lot of copies of a magazine, **③** he could charge a lot for advertisements in **④** it. Then he could lower the price so more readers bought **⑤** it. Publishers showed advertisers the sales figures, but **⑥** they often did not believe **⑦** them. So the publishers set up an organization to check **⑧** them, called the *Audit Bureau of Circulation* (or ABC). Nowadays, there are ABC figures for all magazines, and the publishers use **⑨** them to set **⑩** their prices for advertisements.

1. Publishers *or* the first magazines
2. Publishers' *or* the first magazines'
3. A publisher *or* a magazine
4. Advertisements *or* a magazine
5. The price *or* the magazine

6. Publishers *or* advertisers
7. Advertisers *or* the sales figures
8. Publishers *or* the sales figures
9. The Audit Bureau of Circulation *or* ABC figures
10. Publishers' *or* advertisers'

A Reviewing vocabulary

Complete each sentence with a verb from the box in the correct form.

> appeal   attract   feature   match   pay for
> persuade   ~~publish~~   sell   target   influence

1. In 1881, a man called George Newnes ....published.... the first real magazine.

2. In recent years, publishers .... particular groups with their magazines.

3. Some magazines nowadays .... to people in particular jobs.

4. Publishers hope their magazines .... a particular market sector.

5. Then they .... advertising space in the magazine.

6. The production of a magazine .... by the advertising.

7. The appearance of each magazine and its contents .... the interests of the target audience.

8. Magazines .... their readers in a very powerful way.

9. It is possible that they .... them to buy certain things.

10. Do people want a lifestyle because their magazine .... it every month?

B Understanding a text

1. Read the research questions below. Then read the article on the opposite page and find answers.
   a. How many copies did teen magazines sell in 1998? .... ☐
   b. How many female teenagers were there in the UK in 1998? .... ☐
   c. What has happened to sales of teen magazines in the UK recently? .... ☐
   d. Why have sales of teen magazines in the UK changed? .... ☐
   e. How influential are teen magazines? .... ☐
   f. What do teen magazines try to 'sell' to teenagers? .... ☐

2. Are your answers *facts* or *possibilities*? Put ✓ or ? in the final column above.

C Understanding new words in context

Read the text on the opposite page. Find the words on the left below. Match each one with its meaning in this context.

1. space   ☐ highest point
2. peak   ☐ say something is good
3. decline   ☐ caused by
4. due to   ☐ having a strong effect
5. influential   ☐1 area of a magazine
6. flip   ☐ how a person sees him/herself
7. promote   ☐ fall
8. self-image   ☐ look quickly

This week:

Teen magazines

– are they selling a lifestyle?

In the first part of this series, we saw that publishers do not make their money from the sales of the magazine. They make it from the sales of advertising space. What effect does this fact have on the appearance and contents of teen magazines for girls?

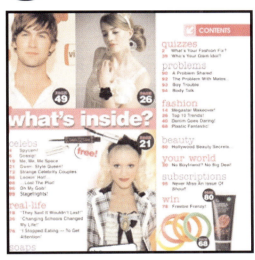

The teen magazine for girls is one of the most popular types in the Western world. At its peak in 1998, this type of magazine sold over 2.5 million copies a month in Britain. That is one for every British female teenager at the time. Sales of teen magazines have fallen since then, but this decline may be due to the rise in electronic magazines – or e-zines – on the Internet. Teenagers are probably reading as much, but with different media.

So teen magazines and e-zines for girls are very popular. Researchers in media studies think that they are also very influential. They think there is persuasion in these magazines. They believe that they persuade their readers to buy certain products, live in a certain way and have certain attitudes and values.

Some teen magazines reflect self-image, but some try to promote a particular kind of self-image. You can do some research yourself. Buy a teen magazine and flip through it. Does the magazine reflect your experience of being a teenager? Or does it try to persuade you to be a certain kind of person? It may be saying: *Teenagers like these things. Teenagers behave this way. Teenagers have these opinions and values.* But perhaps it is actually saying: *Teenagers **should** like these things, they **should** behave this way and they **should** have these values.*

Why do magazines try to persuade teenage girls to have certain values and a particular lifestyle? Because they want to sell advertising space to companies with certain products.

A   Cover the final column. Try to answer each question.

1. What is the singular of *media*?	A demographic group, or an interest group, or a group of people in the same occupation.
2. What does the *mass media* consist of?	Broadcast media such as television and radio, and print media such as newspapers and magazines.
3. What can you *broadcast*?	A group of people, usually in the same location, who live and/or work together, or have similar interests.
4. What is a *live* news event?	By making them want a particular product or lifestyle.
5. Who invented *printing*?	The Ancient Chinese.
6. What do printers use a *press* for?	A group of people of a certain age, gender, occupation, level of income, etc.
7. What can a *literate* person do?	Read and write.
8. What is a *stereotype*?	By showing them in low-status jobs, e.g., secretary, or only as housewives.
9. What are *cosmetics*?	Buy this product and your child will love you.
10. What is the *message* of a soap powder advertisement with a happy mother and a happy child?	It is an electronic magazine.
11. How might an advertisement be *sexist* against women?	1 Medium.
12. How might a news item on a TV channel be *biased*?	Things which are important to a person.
13. What are *values*?	By showing only one point of view, or by exaggerating events.
14. How does a person become a *celebrity*?	To make a newspaper, magazine or book.
15. What does a particular magazine *target*?	Something happening at the time of transmission.
16. What is a *demographic* group?	Things to make a person look more attractive, e.g., make-up.
17. What is a *community*?	By appearing on television or in films.
18. How do magazines *reflect* the interests of their readers?	A generalization about a type of person, e.g., a teenager.
19. How can magazines *influence* their readers?	A television programme or a radio programme.
20. What is an *e-zine*?	By having photographs and articles which they will like.

B   Uncover the final column. Match the questions and answers above.

3.16 Vocabulary for writing   A research report flow chart

A   Building vocabulary and knowledge

1. Match the beginnings and endings of the sentences below. What does each word in italics mean?

a. Students on university courses often have to … ☐   this kind of research *effectively*.

b. One common type of research *investigates* … ☐   the best way to conduct a survey.

c. This kind of research is called … ☐   conduct primary research.

d. A list of questions, called a *questionnaire*, is … ☐   people's habits or their opinions.

e. Follow the flow chart in Figure 1 to conduct … ☐   a *survey*.

2. Complete the flow chart (Figure 1) with a word from the right in each case. Make any necessary changes.

B   Developing critical thinking

Read the advice below about conducting surveys. Choose a reason for each piece of advice. There are two extra reasons.

1. You should choose participants carefully because …

2. You should convert the raw data into percentages because …

3. You should put the extra information in an appendix at the end because …

a. it is easier to see the relationship between answers.

b. people may want to see the detailed information.

c. the results are very interesting.

d. you need a good sample of people.

e. you will have a lot of raw data.

Select a research topic

⬇

_____ a questionnaire

⬇

Choose the _____ carefully

⬇

Conduct the _____

⬇

Record the _____ data

⬇

_____ the raw data to percentages

⬇

Display the results as figures (graphs or _____)

⬇

Analyze the responses

⬇

Write the report

⬇

Add an _____ at the end

(with the questionnaire, the raw data and the figures)

Figure 1: *A survey flow chart*

appendix (*n*)
category (*n*)
common (*adj*)
conduct (*v*)
convert (*v*)
design (*v*)
effectively (*adv*)
entertainment (*n*)
findings (*n*)
formula (*n*)
habit (*n*)
mainly (*adj*)
majority (*n*)
medium (*n*)
minority (*n*)
on average
participant (*n*)
per cent (*n*)
percentage (*n*)
pie chart (*n*)
questionnaire (*n*)
raw data (*n*)
record (*v*)
relationship (*n*)
   [= percentage, etc.]
research (*n* and *v*)
response (*n*)
result (*n*)
sample (*n*)
something else
survey (*n*)
tally chart (*n*)
usage (*n*)
while (*adv*)
   [= at the same time as]

_____

_____

_____

_____

_____

_____

3.17 Real-time writing   A research report on TV usage

A   Activating ideas

1. Study the questionnaire (Appendix 1) on the right. Complete each question.
2. Ask and answer the questions in pairs.

B   Pie charts

Write a question from Exercise A as a caption for each pie chart on the opposite page.

C   Questionnaires

Study the questionnaire on the right. Is each statement below true (*T*) or false (*F*)? Correct the false statements.

1. _F_   There are four questions.
   there are six

2. _____   All of the questions have four categories.

3. _____   Twenty participants took part in this survey.

4. _____   Twelve participants use television for entertainment.

5. _____   The majority of the participants mainly watch television in their bedrooms.

6. _____   Television usage has stayed the same in the last year for most of the participants.

D   Research reports

Study the research report on the opposite page.

1. Complete the first three sections. Write a suitable verb in the correct form in each space. Use some of the verbs in the box below.

   ┌───┐
   │ analyze   be   choose   convert   design │
   │ display   investigate   look at   record │
   └───┘

2. Complete the **Findings** section of the report with information from the questionnaire and Appendix 2. Use numbers, percentages and some of the words in the box below.

   ┌───┐
   │ a few   all   half   many   most   none │
   │   some   the majority   │
   └───┘

Appendix 1:
Questionnaire with results

1. On average, how _many hours a week do you spend_ watching television?

a. less than 10 hours	5
b. 10–20 hours	3
c. 21–30 hours	2
d. more than 30 hours	10

2. _____ mainly use television for?

a. entertainment	12
b. news	3
c. education	1
d. music	4

3. _____ mainly watch television?

a. in my bedroom	13
b. in my living room	3
c. at a friend's house	4

4. _____ while you are watching television?

a. nothing	8
b. study	2
c. listen to music	4
d. use the Internet	6

5. _____ mainly watch television with?

a. no one	14
b. with my family	2
c. with one friend	3
d. with more than one friend	1

6. _____ to your usage of this medium in the last year?

a. it has risen	1
b. it has stayed the same	18
c. it has declined	1

Appendix 2: Results

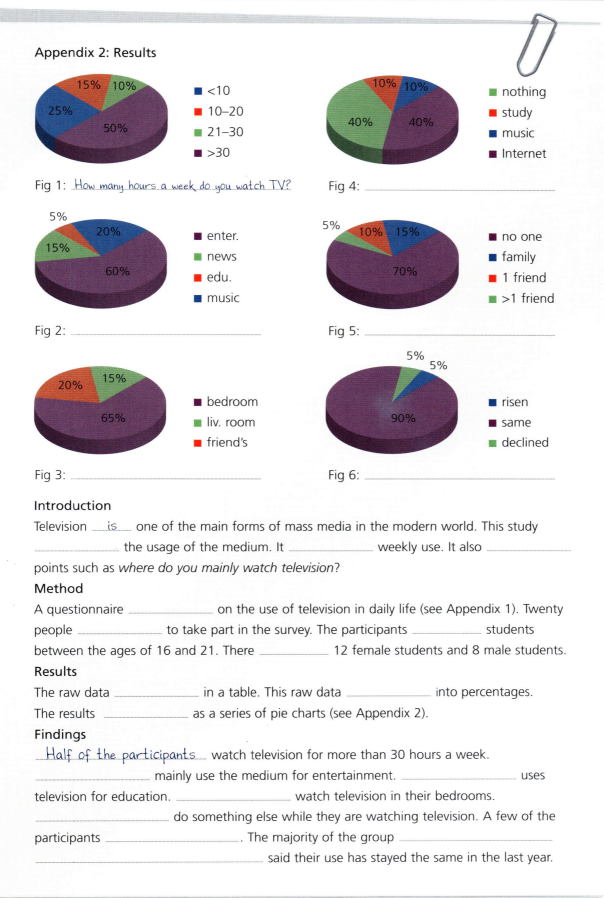

Fig 1: How many hours a week do you watch TV?

Fig 2:

Fig 3:

Fig 4:

Fig 5:

Fig 6:

Introduction

Television ___is___ one of the main forms of mass media in the modern world. This study _____ the usage of the medium. It _____ weekly use. It also _____ points such as *where do you mainly watch television*?

Method

A questionnaire _____ on the use of television in daily life (see Appendix 1). Twenty people _____ to take part in the survey. The participants _____ students between the ages of 16 and 21. There _____ 12 female students and 8 male students.

Results

The raw data _____ in a table. This raw data _____ into percentages. The results _____ as a series of pie charts (see Appendix 2).

Findings

   Half of the participants   watch television for more than 30 hours a week. _____ mainly use the medium for entertainment. _____ uses television for education. _____ watch television in their bedrooms. _____ do something else while they are watching television. A few of the participants _____. The majority of the group _____ _____ said their use has stayed the same in the last year.

A Reviewing vocabulary

1. Number the expressions below in order.
2. Write a percentage for each expression.

A few of the participants		
All of the participants	1	100%
Half of the participants		
Most of the participants		
None of the participants		
Some of the participants		

B Identifying a new skill (1)

Study these extracts from questionnaires.
What is wrong with each of them?

1. How much television do you watch?
    Quite a lot.

2. What sort of programmes do you prefer?
    Not sure. Comedy?

3. How old are you?

16–20	20–30	30–40	40–50
✓			

Read Skills Check 1 and check.

C Practising a new skill (1)

Study the survey questions below.

Which of the mass media do you use?

How do you access the Internet?

Do you check the world news on the mass media?

Make each question more specific, and decide on the categories for each question. Each participant must be able to answer, and must give only one answer.

D Identifying a new skill (2)

How can you:
*   record the results of a questionnaire?
*   display the results of a questionnaire?

Read Skills Check 2 and check.

E Practising a new skill (2)

Study the raw data on page 168.
Turn the data into percentages.

Skills Check 1

Designing a questionnaire

A written questionnaire is a good way to collect information for research. Follow these tips to design good questionnaires.

1. **Ask specific questions**

    Do not ask, e.g., *How much television do you watch?* Ask: *How many hours a week do you watch television?*

2. **Collect information into categories**

    Imagine you ask the question in #1 above. The participants may answer, e.g., *Quite a lot. About 5 or 6.* It is difficult to use information in this form. Give the participants a choice:

<10	
10–20	
>20	

3. **Make a category for every answer**

    Every participant must fit into a category. So if you ask *How old are you?* have categories for all ages including, e.g., >65; <15.

Skills Check 2

Recording and displaying results

1. **Record answers onto a tally chart**

    Put a / for each answer. After four /, put a line across the four slashes ⫿⫼ = 5. Start again with /.

<10	///
10–15	////
15–20	⫿⫼ /

2. **Turn raw data into percentages**

    Imagine you ask 20 people a question. The formula for a percentage is:
    Number divided by total number x 100
    So, for example, 10 / 20 = .5 x 100 = 50%

Yes	10		50%
No	6		30%
Maybe	4		20%

3. **Display percentages as a pie chart**

    Pie charts show the relationship between the categories. This is the most important information.

Percentages and fractions

subject		
Over	65 per cent	
Exactly	50 per cent	of the participants …
Nearly	20 per cent	
About	a third	

Quantifiers ⑯

subject		
All		
Many		of the participants …
Some		
A few		

A Understanding sentences with quantity and relationship

Study each pair of sentences below. What are the differences in form? What are the differences in meaning?

1. Over 60 per cent of the participants watch television in their bedrooms.
   Nearly 60 per cent of the participants watch television in their bedrooms.

2. All students watch television more than 30 hours a week.
   All of the students watch television more than 30 hours a week.

3. Many of the participants use the television for entertainment.
   Many of the participants mainly use the television for entertainment.

B Writing complex sentences

Complete each sentence below with a word from the box.

few majority of a one over the participants

1. _____ of the participants mainly uses television for education.
2. Many of _____ men mainly watch sport on television.
3. A _____ of the children mainly play games on the Internet.
4. The _____ of the people mainly get their news from television.
5. Nearly half _____ the women mainly listen to the news on the radio.
6. _____ 75 per cent of the students mainly watch television alone.
7. Exactly _____ third of the students use their computer for entertainment.
8. Just over 80 per cent of the _____ listen to music on their computer.

C Writing about results

Write four sentences about the information in Figure 1. Use a range of patterns from Exercise B.

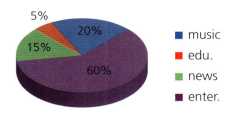

5%
20%
15%
60%

- music
- edu.
- news
- enter.

Figure 1: *What do you mainly use television for?*

A Developing vocabulary

1. Which vowel sound is missing from each column of words?
2. How is the sound spelt in each case?

A
f_____ndings
decl_____ne
f_____ve
anal_____ze
h_____t
r_____t
des_____n
_____ther

B
m_____n
c_____se
st_____
d_____ly
d_____ta
surv_____
expl_____n
_____t

3. Read the Skills Check and check.

B Thinking and organizing

You are going to do a survey into Internet usage. You are then going to write a research report.

1. **Design** the questionnaire. Complete the questions on the right.
2. **Choose** up to four categories for each question. Write them in the spaces on the right. Remember: every participant must be able to give a response to every question.
3. **Conduct** the survey. Choose at least ten participants.
4. **Record** the results. Use a tally chart.
5. **Convert** the raw data into percentages. Remember: number / total number x 100 = %.
6. **Display** the results as pie charts.

C Writing

Write the research report. You must write four sections:
- Introduction
- Method
- Results
- Findings

D Editing

Exchange reports with a partner. Read his/her report. Mark the report with ?, S, G and P.

E Rewriting

Read your essay again. Look at the ?, S, G and P on your first draft. Rewrite the report.

Skills Check

Spelling the sounds /aɪ/ and /eɪ/

The sound in *find* is written in different ways.
Examples: *five, high, die, analyze, design*
The sound in *main* is written in different ways.
Examples: *data, way, same, explain, eight*

Questionnaire

1. On average, how many hours per week ..do you spend.. on the Internet?
   a. <5 _____
   b. _____
   c. _____
   d. _____

2. _____ use the Internet for?
   a. _____
   b. _____
   c. _____
   d. _____

3. Where _____?
   a. _____
   b. _____
   c. _____
   d. _____

4. _____ while you are using the Internet?
   a. _____
   b. _____
   c. _____
   d. _____

5. How _____?
   a. _____
   b. _____
   c. _____
   d. _____

6. _____ to your use of the Internet in the last year?
   a. _____
   b. _____
   c. _____
   d. _____

Portfolio Mass-media usage

A Activating ideas

Look at the photographs of mass-media usage on the right.

1. What is happening in each picture?
2. Why are the people using the mass media in this way?

B Choosing a research topic

Study the research topics below.

Investigate the usage of mass-media radio

Why do the participants listen to the radio?

Where do the participants listen?

Investigate the news in the mass media

Which is the most popular news media for the participants?

Do the participants trust the news?

1. Choose one of the topics.
2. Think of at least three more questions for each topic.

C Designing a questionnaire

Choose up to four categories for each question.
Make your questionnaire.

3. Where do you mainly listen to the radio?
   a. in the car
   b. in the bedroom
   c. in the living room
   d. in the kitchen

D Conducting a survey

1. Choose at least ten participants. You can use your classmates, friends, members of your family or a mixture.
2. Record the results. Use a tally chart.

car	ⅢⅢ
bedroom	ⅢⅢ /
living room	////
kitchen	ⅢⅢ

3. Convert the raw data into percentages.
4. Display the results as pie charts.

E Writing

Write the report. You must write four sections:

- Introduction
- Method
- Results
- Findings

F Giving a talk

Write a three-minute talk to describe your research and findings.
Make slides to go with your talk.

Theme 4

Sports and leisure

- Classifying sports

- Sports in education

- Board games

- For and against

4.1 Vocabulary for listening   Competitive or non-competitive?

A   Reviewing vocabulary

Discuss these questions.

1. Which sports do you play?
2. Which sports do you watch?

B   Understanding vocabulary in context

🎧 4.1 Listen to a text. Number the words in the order that you hear them.

> 1. Why is physical education, or PE, compulsory in most schools?

	aerobics
	competitive
	cooperate
	loser
	PE

1	physical
	sporty
	swimming
	team
	winners

C   Using new vocabulary

1. Which verb do we use with each activity? Tick in the correct column.

	play	do	go
football	✓		
dance			
rugby			
swimming			
aerobics			
basketball			
cycling			

2. 🎧 4.2 Listen to some sentences. Check your ideas.
3. Can you see any patterns?

D   Developing critical thinking

What is your opinion of these statements? Use *I (don't) think ...*

> Children should participate in competitive sports.

> PE lessons should be compulsory at secondary school.

achievable (*adj*)
achieve (*v*)
achievement (*n*)
aerobics (*n*)
allow (*v*)
balance (*v*)
bat (*n*)
build up (*v*)
class (*n*) [= group]
classification (*n*)
classify (*v*)
club (*n*) [= stick]
competitive (*adj*)
compulsory (*adj*)
cooperate (*v*)
co-ordination (*n*)
deal with (*v*)
develop (*v*)
discuss (*v*)
kick (*v*)
knock over (*v*)
loser (*n*)
non-competitive (*adj*)
opponent (*n*)
PE (*n*)
physical education (*n*)
racket (*n*) (*or* racquet)
react (*v*)
riding (*n*)
rowing (*n*)
sporty (*adj*)
team (*n*)
tool (*n*)
touch (*v*)
trampolining (*n*)
winner (*n*)

A Activating ideas

Look at the sports on the opposite page.

1. Which of these sports do you like?

2. 🔊 **4.3** Listen. Number the sports in the order that you hear them.

> 1. These children have just finished a swimming race.

B Understanding the organization of a lecture

You are going to watch a lecture on sports.

🔊 **4.4** [DVD] **9.A** Watch the first part of the lecture. What is the lecturer going to talk about? Write the topics in order.

<u>Classifying sports</u>

1. _____

2. _____

3. _____

C Understanding a lecture

1. 🔊 **4.5** [DVD] **9.B** Watch the rest of the lecture. Is each statement true (*T*) or false (*F*)? Correct the false statements.

   a. There are four groups of sports.

   b. The three groups of sports are racing, opponent and level.

   c. We can divide racing sports into Human body and Machine.

   d. Cycling is a racing sport in the Human body category.

   e. Tennis and football are both opponent sports.

   f. Golf is a target sport.

   g. Long jump is an achievement sport, but high jump isn't.

   h. Children learn to deal with pain when they are racing.

   i. Children learn to react quickly in achievement sports.

   F   There are three.

2. Study the diagram under the photographs on the opposite page. Check your answers.

D Transferring information to the real world

1. Look at the photographs again. Which category does each sport fit into?

2. Write some more sports as examples of each sub-category.

E Identifying vowel sounds

1. All these words from the lecture contain the vowel letter *a*. But what is the sound in each word? Tick the correct vowel sound for each word.

2. 🔊 **4.6** Listen and check.

	/æ/	/e/	/ɒ/	/iː/	/ɑː/	/ɔː/	/ɜː/	/eɪ/
ag<u>ai</u>nst		✓						
b<u>a</u>ll								
cl<u>a</u>ss								
cl<u>a</u>ssify								
classific<u>a</u>tion								
h<u>ea</u>rd								
q<u>ua</u>ntity								
r<u>a</u>cing								
r<u>ea</u>ch								
t<u>a</u>rget								
t<u>ea</u>m								
t<u>a</u>ble								

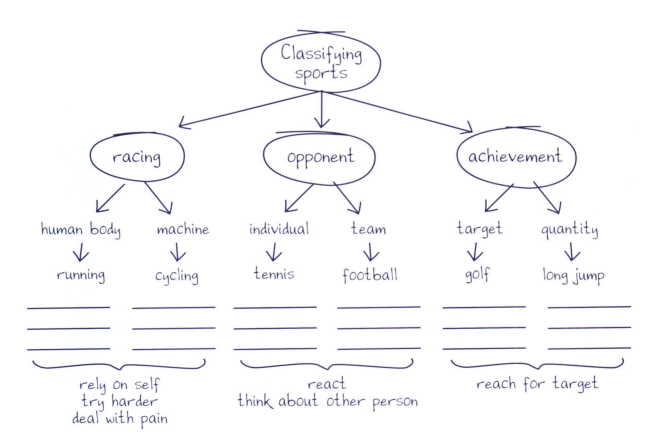

rely on self
try harder
deal with pain

react
think about other person

reach for target

A. Reviewing vocabulary

🔊 **4.7** Listen to some sentences. Tick the best way to complete each sentence.

#				
1.	☐ say		✓ know	
2.	☐ sports		☐ sport	
3.	☐ it		☐ them	
4.	☐ groups		☐ sports	
5.	☐ person		☐ time	
6.	☐ swimming		☐ winning	
7.	☐ people		☐ team	
8.	☐ football		☐ golf	
9.	☐ level		☐ result	
10.	☐ jump		☐ game	

B. Identifying a new skill

1. 🔊 **4.8** Listen to the start of a lecture about sports.
2. How can you organize your notes for this lecture?
3. Read the Skills Check and check your ideas.
4. 🔊 **4.9** Listen to the start of some more lectures on different subjects. Organize your notes in each case.

   Lecture A: *Classifying literature*
   Lecture B: *Classifying the mass media*
   Lecture C: *Classifying the elements in chemistry*
   Lecture D: *Classifying living things*

C. Identifying vowel sounds

Look at these words from the course so far.

1. Read the Pronunciation Check.
2. 🔊 **4.10** Listen and tick the correct column.

	/əʊ/	/aʊ/
al<u>o</u>ne	✓	
alth<u>ough</u>		
fl<u>o</u>wer		
m<u>o</u>st		
m<u>ou</u>ntain		
opp<u>o</u>nent		
p<u>o</u>wer		
sm<u>o</u>ke		

Skills Check

Making notes of classification

Lecturers often classify items into categories. **Branching diagrams** are the best way to record notes of classification.

Example:

Lecturers often say, e.g., *There are two / three / four kinds of …*

So you can make a diagram with the correct number of branches and complete each branch as the lecturer names it.

Lecturers often say, e.g., *An example of this kind is …*

Add the example under the category.

After the lecture, try to think of more examples of your own.

Pronunciation Check

Hearing vowels: /əʊ/ and /aʊ/

These two diphthongs are very similar. They both end with a sound like /uː/.

Examples:

/əʊ/: *no, go, also, OK, hole, row*
/aʊ/: *now, how, found*

Prepositions after the verb

A small number of verbs in English are **always** followed by a preposition.
You should learn to recognize the sound of the whole phrase – verb + preposition. ⑰

The first group	consists	of	racing sports.
Children learn to	rely	on	themselves.
So, to	sum	up,	…
Some teenagers	listen	to	music all the time.

Many verbs can be followed by different prepositions, with **a change in meaning**.

We're going to	talk	about	categories of sport.	introduces the topic
I want to		to	the director.	introduces a person or people

Let's	look	at	the first group.	use your eyes, or consider
You can		up	the words in your dictionary.	find in a reference book
Scientists		for	the reason for an event.	try to find

If the preposition changes the meaning, learn to recognize the kind of information that will come next.

A Recognizing prepositions

1. 🔊 **4.11** Listen and number the verb + preposition phrases.

	die out		reach for
	go into		rely on
	hear about		sum up
1	look at		take off
	put in		write down

1. look at

2. 🔊 **4.12** Listen to some more verb + preposition phrases. These verbs are probably new to you.
Can you hear the preposition in each case? Number the prepositions.

	into		off
	for		on
	in		out
1	about		down
	at		up

1. come about

B Predicting content from prepositions

🔊 **4.13** Listen to the start of some sentences.
Choose the correct phrase to complete each sentence.

	… a good reason for the result.
	… at yesterday's lecture.
1	… opponent sports.
	… the details after the lecture.
	… to festivals.
	… very young children.

First, we're going to look at …

4.5 Applying new listening skills   Classifying ball games

A **Previewing vocabulary**

Match the verbs and prepositions on the right to make common verb phrases.

> talk about

1.	talk		to
2.	consist		into
3.	look		from
4.	put	1	about
5.	turn		at
6.	come		of
7.	build		over
8.	deal		out
9.	knock		with
10.	work		up

B **Preparing to listen**

1. Name the game for each ball in the picture.

> D is football.

2. ● 4.14 Listen. Which game is the speaker talking about?

This is one of the oldest games in the world. People started kicking balls in China over 2,000 years ago.

> football

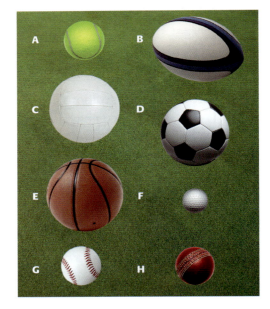

C **Listening and note-taking (1)**

You are going to watch another lecture about sports.
● 4.15 [DVD] 9.C Watch the first part of the lecture. While you watch, remember to:

- write the main topic at the top of your notes.
- draw lines to show the classification.
- add examples as the lecturer gives them.

D **Listening and note-taking (2)**

● 4.16 [DVD] 9.D Watch the last part of the lecture. Why is it important to classify ball games? Add information about each type of game to your diagram.

4.6 Vocabulary for speaking   **Sports terminology**

A   Reviewing vocabulary

How many sports can you name in one minute?

B   Understanding new vocabulary

Complete the table with words from the list on the right. You can use the same word more than once. Make any necessary changes.

Table 1: *Popular ball games*

game	Where do you play?	What do you score?	What do you hit or pass the ball with?	What special equipment do you need?
football	*pitch*	*goals*	*feet (head)*	*goals*
tennis				
basketball				
golf				
ice hockey				
handball				
rugby				

C   Practising new vocabulary

Work in pairs.

Student A

Choose one of the games from Table 1.

Answer B's questions.

Do you play the game on a court?

Yes, you do.

Student B

Which game has your partner chosen? Ask A questions with a *yes* or *no* answer.

Work out the game.

Do you score points?

Yes, you do.

Is it tennis?

Yes, it is.

attacker (*n*)
badminton (*n*)
basket (*n*)
club (*n*) [= stick]
competitive (*adj*)
co-ordination (*n*)
course (*n*)
court (*n*)
defender (*n*)
divide (*v*)
equipment (*n*)
flag (*n*)
goalkeeper (*n*)
hole (*n*) [= in golf]
hopeless (*adj*)
ice hockey (*n*)
in (*adj*) [tennis]
measure (*n*)
midfield (*n*)
net (*n*)
opponent (*n*)
out (*adj*) [tennis]
partner (*n*)
pitch (*n*)
point (*n*)
position (*n*)
post (*n*)
racket (*n*)
receiver (*n*)
rink (*n*)
role (*n*)
rugby (*n*)
rule (*n*)
score (*n* and *v*)
server (*n*)
shape (*n*)
shot (*n*)
size (*n*)
slide (*v*)
speed (*n*)
versus (*prep*)

A Previewing vocabulary

Find pairs of words in the box below. Explain the connection.

> attackers   feet   goal   hands   long   role
> score   short   tall   team   wide   defenders

> *attackers / defenders = they are opposites*

B Activating ideas

Discuss this question.

Why do schools play team games?

C Studying a model

You are going to watch several parts of a talk.

1. 🔊 **4.17** [DVD] **9.E** Watch the first part of the talk.
Then complete the speaker's words below. Use slides
A, B and C on the right to help you.

> Today, I'm going to talk about _ball games for PE_.
> There are many good ball games _____.
> Here are _____. Firstly, there's _____.
> Secondly, we _____ rugby. Next, _____.
> Then we've _____ volleyball and, finally, there's
> _____.

> First of _____, I'm going to talk about
> _____ because it is the most popular game
> _____.

> What _____ of game is football? Well, it's a
> _____, of course. It is played by
> _____. Each team has _____.

2. 🔊 **4.18** [DVD] **9.F** Watch the next part of the talk. Look at
slide D. Add notes to the slide.

D Practising a model

Talk about each bullet point in slide D. Use your notes.

> *OK. So let's look at the value of football in PE.*
> *Firstly, it's good exercise and it's enjoyable.*

Ball games for PE

A

Ball games for PE

- football
- rugby
- tennis
- volleyball
- hockey

B

Football: type

- team game
- two teams
- 11 players

C

Football: value in PE

- exercise
  good, enjoyable
- co-ordination

- roles in a team

- all shapes and sizes

- winning and losing

D

Everyday English   **Talking about games**

A   B   C   D   E   F

A   Activating ideas

Look at the photographs. Which sports words from the box can you find?

> fan   supporter   player   winner   loser   line   ball   net   bat   court

B   Studying models

1. Which question below goes with each conversation?
2. 🔊 **4.19** Listen and check. Practise the conversations.

Do you know how to play this game? How did you get on? Same time next week?
Was that in or out? What are you watching? What's wrong?

1 A: _____
  B: It's Brazil versus Germany.
  A: Who's winning?
  B: We are. We just scored.

2 A: _____
  B: I was hopeless.
  A: You weren't. You played very well.
  B: But we still lost.

3 A: _____
  B: Sure. Great game.
  A: Yes, that was a brilliant shot just now.
  B: I think it was just luck, really.

4 A: _____
  B: It landed on the line.
  A: I wasn't sure. My point, then.
  B: Yes, well played!

5 A: _____
  B: Great! We won!
  A: What was the score?
  B: Three–one.

6 A: _____
  B: Not really.
  A: Do you want to learn?
  B: OK. How do we start?

C   Showing you don't understand

1. Make two conversations from the sentences in the box. 🔊 **4.20** Listen and check your ideas.
2. Practise the conversations in pairs.

A: I'll meet you outside the sports centre at seven, OK?   B: Sorry, did you say the 30th?
A: Yes, that's right.   B: Sorry, did you say 7.00 or 7.30?
A: Seven. Is that OK?   B: Fine. I'll be there.
A: Don't forget there's a match on the 30th.   B: Yes, great. Seven o'clock outside the sports centre.

D   Practising the models

Have similar conversations using the following ideas.

- TV programme – time, date, channel
- lecture or tutorial – time, date, room, topic
- assignment – deadline, topic
- social arrangement – time, date, place

4.8 Learning new speaking skills — Speaking with slides

A Saying diphthongs

Tick the odd one out in each row. Listen and check your answers.

1. no ☐   do ☐   go ✓   so ☐
2. how ☐   row ☐   know ☐   low ☐
3. hole ☐   doll ☐   roll ☐   role ☐
4. town ☐   down ☐   brown ☐   own ☐
5. now ☐   show ☐   grow ☐   flow ☐
6. phone ☐   alone ☐   done ☐   stone ☐
7. boat ☐   board ☐   float ☐   goal ☐
8. found ☐   noun ☐   out ☐   bought ☐

B Identifying a new skill

1. Study the slide below. How can a speaker talk about this slide? Read Skills Check 1.

> **Classifying sports**
> - Racing
> - Opponent
> - Achievement

2. What are the rules for talking with slides? Read Skills Check 2.

C Practising a new skill

1. Study the slide in Exercise B. Give a short talk about the slide.

2. Study each slide below. Give a short talk about each one.

A
> **Mass media**
> - Broadcast
> - Print

B
> **Study of the mind**
> - Psychology
> - Sociology

C
> **Selecting people for jobs**
> - Qualifications
> - Experience
> - Attitude

D
> **Types of UK school**
> - Nursery
> - Primary
> - Secondary
> - Sixth form college

E
> **Analyzing advertisements**
> - Source
> - Audience
> - Purpose
> - Reaction

F
> **Types of literature**
> - Novels
> - Plays
> - Poetry
> - Biography/Autobiography

Skills Check 1

Giving a talk with slides (1)

Introduce each slide

Now	I'm going to talk about	sports.
	let's look at	
	we turn to	

Introduce the contents of each slide

There are three	types	of sport.
	kinds	
	branches	

Firstly,	there are	racing sports.
Next,	we have	opponent sports.
Finally,	...	achievement sports.

Give extra information about each point

Racing sports include running and swimming. Opponents can be individuals or teams. Achievements are sometimes targets ...

Skills Check 2

Giving a talk with slides (2)

Some **Dos** and **Don'ts**.
- Don't stand in front of the screen!
- Don't speak too fast!
- Speak to the audience, not to the slide!
- Leave the slide on the screen for a few moments at the end. Your audience wants to think about your words.

114   Theme 4: Speaking

We use the modal *must* for obligation, e.g., to talk about the rules of a sport.   ⑱
We use the modal *should* for advice, e.g., to talk about the best way to play a game.

subject	modal	negative	infinitive	other information
The pitch	must	n't	measure	at least 90 metres by 45 metres.
Players			use	their hands.
Attackers	should		stay	in the opponents' half most of the time.
Defenders			try	to score goals all the time.

A   Explaining the rules (1)

1. Complete these rules from football with *must* or *mustn't* and a suitable verb from the box.

> allow   ~~be~~   cross   last   push   throw   touch   wear

  a. There ___must be___ an area around the goal which is called the penalty area.
  b. The goalkeeper _____ the ball with his/her hands outside the goal area.
  c. The goalkeeper _____ clothes of a different colour from the opponents' clothes.
  d. The interval between the two halves _____ more than 15 minutes.
  e. The ball _____ the whole of the goal line to score.
  f. When the ball goes out of play at the sides of the pitch, a player _____ the ball in.
  g. A player _____ another player with his/her hands.
  h. The referee _____ extra time for injuries and substitutions.

2. 🔊 **4.21** Listen and check your answers. Notice the pronunciation of *must / mustn't* in each sentence.

B   Explaining the rules (2)

Work in pairs. Study some rules for a game below. Then cover the rules and explain them to your partner.

TENNIS: RULES
• each point begins with a serve
• each hits ball to receiver
• ball must not hit net – serve again
• ball must land in service court
• receiver must allow ball to bounce once
• ball must not bounce more than once
• players must not touch net with rackets

BADMINTON: RULES
• each point begins with a serve
• server hits shuttlecock to receiver
• serve must be underarm
• shuttlecock must be below waist height
• receiver must not let shuttlecock touch ground
• shuttlecock must stay in court
• players must not touch net with rackets

C   Giving advice about slides

1. What should you do to give a good presentation with slides? Make sentences about each point.

2. 🔊 **4.22** Listen and check your answers. Notice the pronunciation of *should / shouldn't*.

> You shouldn't use many coloured backgrounds.

• use many coloured backgrounds
• use a lot of effects, e.g., flashing words
• write full sentences on the slide
• read out the slide word for word
• stand in front of the screen
• talk to the slide
• talk to the audience
• speak quickly
• pause between sentences
• wait a few moments between slides

A   Reviewing sounds

Find another word from the box below with the same (underlined) vowel sound as in the table. Listen and practise the words.

bar   teach   pitch   union   help   post
have   shape   size   called

1.	score	ball	supp<u>o</u>rt	*called*
2.	hand	match	back	
3.	goal	role	opp<u>o</u>nent	
4.	eye	try	side	
5.	chest	head	m<u>ea</u>sure	
6.	use	too	you	
7.	large	ap<u>a</u>rt	halves	
8.	each	team	m<u>e</u>tres	
9.	game	place	take	
10.	pitch	kick	in	

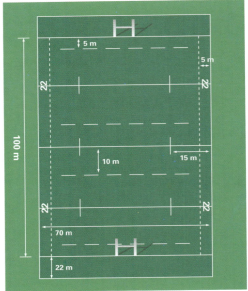

Figure 1: *A rugby pitch*

B   Researching information and making slides

Work in groups.

1. Each person will receive one or two pieces of information about rugby union (from page 173). Underline the important information for a presentation slide.

2. Make a slide for your part(s) of the talk.

C   Using a key skill

1. Give the talk in your group. Remember to:
   - introduce each slide.
   - introduce the contents of each slide.
   - give extra information about the contents.
   - leave the slide on the screen for a few moments.

2. Complete the feedback form at the bottom of the page while you listen.

Feedback form			
The speaker ...	all of the time	most of the time	some of the time
looked at the audience.			
spoke at the correct speed.			
paused between sentences.			
made sure the audience could read the slide.			
used clear slides.			
added extra information.			

4.11 Vocabulary for reading   Simple board games

A Reviewing vocabulary

Circle the correct form to complete each sentence.

1. Many schools make *competitive* / *competition* sport compulsory.
2. Team games help in the physical *develop* / *development* of children.
3. Children learn to *co-ordinate* / *co-ordination* different parts of the body.
4. They also improve their *cooperate* / *cooperation* with other children.
5. Team games teach children about different *role* / *roles*.
6. For example, *defends* / *defenders* should not try to score goals all the time.
7. They can also help children to deal with winning and *lose* / *losing*.
8. They are certainly very useful for *sport* / *sporty* children.
9. But other activities, like *aerobic* / *aerobics*, can also be valuable.
10. Perhaps schools should *allowed* / *allow* children to choose between different types of physical activity.

B Understanding vocabulary in context

Complete this information about the game ludo. Use a word or words from the list on the right in each case. Make any necessary changes.

Ludo

The game is played by two, three or four __players__.

It is played on a _____ with four coloured areas.

Each player has four coloured _____. The players

take _____. Each player throws the _____.

He/she moves the same number of _____. Then

one of the opponents has a _____. Sometimes, a

piece _____ a square which has an opponent's piece

on it. The opponent must move his/her piece back to the start.

You must throw the exact number of squares to get _____.

The _____ of the game is to get all your playing pieces to the centre of

the board. Are board games _____? Psychologists say that even simple

games like ludo teach children to _____ their actions in real life.

C Developing critical thinking

Do you know the rules of ludo in the situations below? If you don't know, guess.

What happens:

- if you throw a six and then another six?
- if you land on a square which has your own piece on it?
- if there are three squares between your piece and home, and you throw a four?

---

advance (*v*)
board (*n*)
capture (*v*)
checkmate (*n*)
critical thinking (*n*)
dice (*n*)
disk (*n*)
  [= playing piece]
educational (*adj*)
engage in (*v*)
estimate (*n* and *v*)
home (*n*)
  [= target in game]
land (*v*)
land on (*v*)
man / men (*n*)
  [= piece/s]
mention (*v*)
move (*n* and *v*)
objective (*n*)
pastime (*n*)
pawn (*n*)
piece (*n*)
plan (*n* and *v*)
play (*n*)
player (*n*)
problem-solving (*n*)
ruins (*n*)
spread (*v*)
  [= move outwards]
square (*n*)
trap (*v*)
turn (*n*)
version (*n*)

A   Activating ideas

Study the three illustrations in the text opposite. What will the text be about?

B   Predicting content

Study the section headings in the text. Which section will each sentence below appear in?

Eight of the men are called *pawns*. ☐

From India, it was taken to Persia in the 6th century. ☐

It is estimated that there are now 300 million players worldwide. ☐

One player moves, then the other player moves. ☐

The objective of the game is to capture the king. ☐

C   Understanding a text

Read the questions below. Then read the first four sections of the text opposite and tick the best answer.

1. Where does this game come from?
   a. ☐ Sanskrit.
   b. ✓ India.
   c. ☐ Persia.

2. When did the game first appear?
   a. ☐ Around 1000 BCE.
   b. ☐ Around 2000 BCE.
   c. ☐ Around 0 BCE.

3. How did the game reach Europe?
   a. ☐ Through Persia to Arabia, then to Spain.
   b. ☐ Through Persia to China, then Japan.
   c. ☐ Through Persia to China, then to Spain.

4. Where do the names of the pieces come from?
   a. ☐ From Spanish.
   b. ☐ From Persian.
   c. ☐ From several languages.

5. How do you play the game?
   a. ☐ Players take it in turns.
   b. ☐ Players reach the opposite side of the board.
   c. ☐ Players land on the same square.

6. How do you win the game?
   a. ☐ You say 'checkmate'.
   b. ☐ You get to somewhere on the board.
   c. ☐ You stop your opponent's king from moving.

D   Predicting information from prepositions

1. What *sort of information* do you expect to follow each preposition?

2. What is the *actual information* in each case?
   a. The game was first played in …
   b. From India, it was taken to …
   c. The game is for …
   d. The name *rook* comes from …
   e. The game is now on …

E   Researching

1. Read the assignment task.

2. Read the final section of the text opposite. What information in this section will help you with the assignment?

Education Faculty
Assignment 4
_____

Board games such as chess and draughts help with child development.

To what extent do you agree with the statement above? Do some research into the educational value of board games.

Can you play four army groups?

1 History

This game was first played in India over 2,000 years ago. Real soldiers were used then, and real horses pulling chariots. It was called *Chaturanga*, which means 'four army groups' in the ancient Indian language of Sanskrit. This Sanskrit word is the origin of the modern name in Arabic.

From India, it was taken to Persia in the 6th century. Arab traders learnt the pastime there. The Arabs took the game back to their own countries in the 7th century. It spread to China shortly after then, and from there to Korea and Japan. Arabs also carried it to Spain. People played it there by the 12th century. From Spain, it spread to the rest of Europe.

2 The playing pieces

The names of the pieces indicate the history of the game. For example, the name of the main piece in English is *king*. In Persia, this piece was called *shah*, which means 'king'. The name of another piece in English is *rook*. This name comes from the word *roka*, which is 'ship' in Sanskrit. Eight of the men are called *pawns*. This word comes from a Spanish word for 'farm worker'.

3 How to play

The game is for two players. Play starts with all the pieces in two lines on opposite sides of the board. One player moves, then the other player moves. Some pieces must move horizontally and/or vertically. Other pieces must move diagonally. A player takes an opponent's piece if he/she lands on the same square. A player gets a piece back if one of his/her pawns reaches the opposite side of the board. The most important piece is the king.

4 How to win

The objective of the game is to capture the king. One player must trap the opponent's king somewhere on the board so he/she cannot move. If a player gets close to that position, he/she says 'check'. The word is a form of the Persian word *shah*. If the opponent's king cannot move, the player says 'checkmate'. This word comes from a sentence in Persian, *shah mat*, which means 'The king is dead.'

5 The game today

The game is now one of the most popular in the world. It is estimated that there are now 300 million players worldwide. In 2006, 147 countries participated in the annual Olympiad. Educationalists believe the game develops children's critical thinking and problem-solving skills. It is now on the curriculum of primary schools in over 30 countries around the world. In a recent survey in the United States, it was reported that children's 'test scores improved by 17.3 per cent for students regularly engaged in' the game, compared with under 5 per cent for children participating in other games.

4.13 Learning new reading skills Referring back

A Reviewing vocabulary

What will come next in each case?

1. This game was first played in India over …
   = period / 2,000 years ago.
2. It was called …
3. From India, it was taken to …
4. The name of the main piece in English is …
5. The game is for …
6. A player takes an opponent's piece if …
7. The most important piece is …
8. The objective of the game is …
9. One player must …
10. If the opponent's king cannot move, …

B Identifying a key skill

1. Study these sections of the text from Lesson 4.12. What do the underlined words mean?

> The Arabs took the game back to their own countries in the 7th century. It spread to China shortly after <u>then</u>, and from <u>there</u> to Korea and Japan.

> One player moves, then the other player moves.

> … there are now 300 million players worldwide.

2. Read the Skills Check and check your ideas.

C Practising a new skill

Find and underline the words *there* and *then* in the following text. What does each word refer to?

Skills Check

Referring back

Writers refer back in a text with the words *then* and *there*:

then = back to a date or time

there = back to a place

Examples:

*Real soldiers were used **then**.*
= 2,000 years ago

*Arab traders learnt the pastime **there**.*
= in Persia

But be careful!

then   can also introduce the next action

there   can also introduce a new piece of information

Examples:

*One player moves, **then** the other player moves.*

***There** are now 300 million players worldwide.*

Researchers believe that the game of polo first appeared in the area of modern-day Iran. Persian tribes played the game there, perhaps to give their horses some exercise. The game was called *Chogan* then. The first recorded polo match occurred in 600 BCE between the Turkomans and the Persians. From Persia, the game spread to India. In 1859, two British soldiers saw a polo match there and shortly after then, they formed the famous Calcutta Polo Club. The club is still active today. From India, the game spread around the world. There are even polo teams in South America. In fact, the current world champions are from there. Argentina have held the title since 1949.

Study these two sentences about chess. They describe a situation which is **always true**. ⑲

Event 1: *A player lands on the same square as an opponent's piece.*

Event 2: *He/she takes the opponent's piece.*

We can join these two sentences with *if* or with *when*. Study the tables below.

	event 1		event 2
If	a player lands on the same square	**,**	he/she takes the opponent's piece.
When			

event 2		event 1
A player takes an opponent's piece	**if**	he/she lands on the same square.
	when	

Where do we put *if / when*?

Where do we put Event 1? What about Event 2?

What tense do we use for Event 1? What about Event 2?

A Understanding sentences with *if* and *when*

1.	If a player lands on the same square as an opponent's piece …		he/she says 'Check'.
2.	When a pawn reaches the opposite side of the board …		they get better at critical thinking.
3.	The game is over when …		the opponent's king can't move.
4.	If a player gets close to trapping the opponent's king …		he/she takes the piece.
5.	A player says 'Checkmate' when …		the player gets another piece.
6.	If children play chess regularly …		a player traps the opponent's king.

B Predicting information in sentences with *if* and *when*

Complete these sentences about situations which are always true.

1. If you heat water to 100°C, … it boils.
2. Water freezes when …
3. Metal expands if …
4. When ice is put into water, …
5. If you drop a glass, …
6. People get thirsty if …
7. If you don't eat, …
8. Many metals rust if …
9. If plants aren't watered, …
10. You get the colour orange …

4.15 Applying new reading skills   Quirkat

A Reviewing vocabulary

Choose a word or phrase from the box for each space.

> capture   engage in   estimate   men
> objective   ~~pastime~~   spread   trap

1. Chess is a very popular ___pastime___ .

2. It has now _____ all over the world.

3. People _____ that there are 40 million players in Russia alone.

4. Each player starts with 16 _____ .

5. The _____ of the game is …

6. … to _____ the opponent's king.

7. You must _____ the king so he cannot move.

8. Researchers say that if children regularly _____ the game, they do better on tests.

B Activating ideas

Study the photographs on this page.

1. Which game(s) can you play on each board?

2. Scan the text on the opposite page. Which game is it about?

C Understanding a text

1. Read the topic sentences below. They are all from the text opposite. Which section does each sentence come from? Write the number of the section.

   a. The objective of the game is very simple.   _____

   b. You play the game on a normal chessboard, which has 64 black and white squares.   _____

   c. The game continues to be popular all over the world.   _____

   d. Archaeologists discovered a form of this game in the ruins of the ancient city of Ur in Iraq.   _____

   e. The game is for two players.   _____

2. Read the text opposite. What does each of the highlighted words refer to?
   Archaeologists discovered a form of this … ==They== dated the game = archaeologists

D Understanding new words in context

Tick the correct meaning in context of each of these words from the text.

1. form (line 2)	✓	kind	☐	make
2. ruins (line 2)	☐	destroys	☐	old damaged buildings
3. mentioned (line 5)	☐	written about	☐	said
4. version (line 12)	☐	form	☐	translation
5. disk (line 18)	☐	CD	☐	circle
6. men (line 25)	☐	pieces	☐	male people

E Developing critical thinking

Which game is more valuable in child development, chess or draughts?

Can you play Quirkat?

1 History

Archaeologists discovered a form of this game in the ruins of the ancient city of Ur in Iraq. They dated the game to about 3000 BCE. However, it did not start there. Five hundred years before then, it began in Egypt. We do not know the name then, but later it was called *Quirkat*.

5 The game is mentioned in the Arabic book *Kitab-al Aghani,* which appeared sometime in the 10th century. The Arabs took the game to Spain, and from there it travelled to southern France around 1200. The people there renamed it *Alquerque*.

10 Around 1535 in France, a new rule appeared. A player had to take an opponent's piece when he/she had a chance. The first book about this new version appeared in Spain in 1547. Shortly after then, the game arrived in England. There it was called *draughts*.

2 The playing pieces

15 You play the game on a normal chessboard, which has 64 black and white squares. Each player starts with 12 pieces, which are all disks. One player has black disks and one has white. They all start on the white squares.

3 How to play

20 The game is for two players. A piece can move one square, diagonally, forward. A piece can only move to an empty square. Players take turns to move their pieces. A player takes an opponent's piece by jumping over it onto an
25 empty square. A player can take several men in one move. When a piece arrives at the opponent's edge of the board, it becomes a king. A king is two disks, one on top of the other. A king can only move one square, like any other piece. However, it can move backwards as well as forwards.

4 How to win

30 The objective of the game is very simple. One player must take all of the opponent's pieces.

5 The game today

The game continues to be popular all over the world. It is estimated that there are now 40 million players worldwide. In October 2008, 160 players from 37 countries competed in a tournament in Beijing.
35 Educationalists say that draughts can help children develop skills of spatial awareness. In other words, they become aware of the position of things and the physical relationship between things. Draughts can also help older children to plan their actions. It helps them see that there is a good time to advance and a good time to wait in any situation.

A (Circle) the odd one out. Find the correct reason underneath.

1. gymnastics	dance	(tennis)	aerobics
2. running	swimming	rowing	football
3. rugby	high jump	karate	basketball
4. football	handball	tennis	volleyball
5. goal	club	stick	racket
6. hand	head	chest	foot
7. attacker	defender	scorer	midfielder
8. hall	court	course	pitch
9. chess	badminton	ludo	draughts
10. king	pawn	piece	check

☐ It is not a board game. It's a sport.
☐ It is not one of the three types of player in football.
☐ It is a general word. The others are all connected with chess.
☐ It is an opponent sport. The others are racing sports.
☐ It is not a bat. The others are things you hit the ball with.
☐ It is an achievement sport. The others are opponent sports.
☐ It is a bat sport. The others all use part of the human body.
☐ It is not a special word for the playing area in a particular sport.
☐ It is a part of the body which you must not use in football (unless you are a goalkeeper).
☐1 It is a competitive sport. The others can be non-competitive.

B Match the opposites.

1. attack	☐ often
2. winner	☐ hide
3. land	☐1 defend
4. majority	☐ partly
5. achieve	☐ group
6. individual	☐ female
7. display	☐ minority
8. male	☐ loser
9. mainly	☐ fail
10. rarely	☐ take off
11. trap	☐ calculate
12. move	☐ job
13. pastime	☐ release
14. opponent	☐ stay
15. estimate	☐ teammate

C Match the words and phrases with similar meanings.

1. capture	☐ injure
2. objective	☐ leisure activity
3. advance	☐ go forward
4. piece	☐ ethnic group
5. cooperate	☐ version
6. show	☐ demonstrate
7. form	☐ way
8. generalization	☐ stereotype
9. method	☐ broadcast
10. race	☐1 take
11. pastime	☐ aim
12. transmit	☐ job
13. wound	☐ take part in
14. task	☐ work together
15. participate	☐ man

4.16 Vocabulary for writing — Physical activity or electronic games?

A Reviewing vocabulary

Complete these words from Theme 4 with the correct vowel(s) in each space.

1. a ch i e v e
2. cl____ss____fy
3. c____mp____t____t____v____
4. c____p____r____t____
5. c____rd____n____t____n

6. d____v____l____p
7. ____q____pm____nt
8. ____st____m____t
9. ____bj____ct____v____
10. spr____d

B Building vocabulary

Read the first paragraph of the text. Then write the numbers for the extra pieces of information in the correct place. Do the same with the second paragraph.

Fifty years ago, all children played physical games _____. They got exercise from the games _____. They learnt motor skills _____. They learnt social skills _____. They learnt mental skills _____. In many cases, the physical games made the children feel better about themselves _____.

1. and raised their self-esteem
2. and they also learnt skills
3. like concentration and focus on a particular task
4. like cooperation with other people
5. like hand and eye co-ordination
6. when they were out of school

In 1961, the first electronic game was developed _____. Fifty years later, sales of electronic games reached $5 billion _____. Many children do not get physical exercise _____. They spend most of their leisure time playing computer games _____. They do not get physical activity _____. They do not develop their social skills _____. They do not improve their mental skills _____.

7. and now every teenager plays computer games
8. because the tasks are too simple
9. because they are on their own
10. by Steve Russell at MIT in the United States
11. except pressing buttons with their fingers
12. in their bedroom
13. when they are out of school

C Developing critical thinking

Should physical education be compulsory in secondary schools?

---

against (*prep*)
allow (*v*)
button (*n*)
cause (*n* and *v*)
character (*n*)
  [= in video game]
concentration (*n*)
copy (*n* and *v*)
educational (*adj*)
electronic (*adj*)
encourage (*v*)
exercise (*n* and *v*)
finger (*n*)
focus (*n* and *v*)
handwriting (*n*)
humiliate (*v*)
in favour [of]
lead to (*v*)
leisure (*n*)
let (*v*)
mental skills
motor skills
oppose (*v*)
out of school
recent (*adj*)
restrict (*v*)
screen (*n*)
self-esteem (*n*)
simple (*adj*)
social skills
support (*n* and *v*)
violent (*adj*)

A Reviewing vocabulary

1. What are:
   - social skills?   • motor skills?   • mental skills?
2. How can you develop each kind of skill?

B Activating ideas

Study the assignment at the bottom of the page.

1. Give three reasons in support of the idea.
2. Give three reasons to oppose the idea.

C Gathering information

1. Study the notes for the assignment at the top of the opposite page.

   Which column has:
   - examples?
   - explanations?
   - general points?
2. Read the two paragraphs below the notes. Complete the notes with information from the paragraphs.

D Writing an opinion

1. Study the opinions below. Which one do you agree with more?

   Parents should allow their children to play computer games.

   Parents should not allow their children to play computer games.
2. Give a more specific opinion. Add some of the words from the box below to one of the sentences above.
3. Write the final paragraph of the essay for the assignment. Give your own opinion.

> with their friends   violent
> only a few hours per week   all the time
> educational   on their own   young

Faculty of Education
Assignment 1

Computer games:
dangerous ... or educational?

Parents should allow their children to play computer games without any restrictions.

Discuss.

Parents should allow their children to play computer games without any restrictions.

for		
1. educational	learn about world	e.g., geog.; hist.; based on quizzes
2. improve social skills	must play with 2 / 3 people	
3. improve mental skills		

against		
1.	only simple task against computer	e.g., Downhill Racer – turn character left or right on screen
2. show violence		
3. do not develop social skills		e.g., survey: 82% play games on own some of time

There are many reasons to support the idea. Firstly, some games are educational. Children can learn about the world from the games. For example, there are geography games and history games. There are also games which are based on quizzes. Secondly, some games improve social skills. You must play some games with two or three people. A recent survey says that 76 per cent of teenagers play games with their friends most of the time. Finally, some games improve mental skills. There are many games which involve problem-solving. For example, in *My Town*, children build and manage a town and deal with its problems.

There are also many reasons to oppose the idea. Firstly, some games do not teach useful information. Players only complete a simple task against the computer. For example, in the game *Downhill Racer*, players only turn a character left or right on the screen. Secondly, some games show violence. In fact, the aim of some games is violent behaviour, which children may copy in real life. In March 2009, a teenager killed 12 people in his school in Germany. The teenager played a violent computer game the night before. Finally, some games do not develop social skills. Children play the games alone in their bedrooms. A recent survey says 82 per cent of teenagers play games on their own some of the time.

A   Spelling key words

Rewrite each word with the correct vowel letter in each space. Then read Skills Check 1.

1. activ_____ty   _activity_
2. reas_____n
3. devel_____p
4. rec_____nt
5. education_____l
6. s_____pport
7. fing_____r
8. usef_____l
9. ment_____l
10. viol_____nt
11. fin_____lly
12. childr_____n

B   Identifying a new skill

1. Read Skills Check 2.
2. Study the extract below from the essay in Lesson 4.17. Mark the sentences *P*, *EXP* and *EG*.

Firstly, some games do not teach useful information. Players only complete a simple task against the computer. For example, in the game *Downhill Racer*, players only turn a character left or right on the screen.

Skills Check 1

Spelling schwa /ə/

Schwa is the most common sound in English. You can hear it in almost every word with more than one syllable.

But how do you spell it? The simple answer is … there are no rules. You must learn the spelling of each word with schwa.

a	educational, alone, about, mental
e	violent, problem, different, finger, children
i	activity
o	develop, button, reason
u	suggest, actually, useful, support

C   Practising a key skill

The sentences below come from two different paragraphs. One paragraph is *for* computer games (✓). One is *against* (✗).

1. Mark each sentence ✓ or ✗.
2. Mark the *P*, *EXP* and *EG* in each paragraph.
3. Cover the sentences. Write the paragraphs.

Skills Check 2

PEXPEG

Many paragraphs in academic English have the PEXPEG structure.

P	point	*This is one of my ideas.*
EXP	explain	*Explain the idea.*
EG	example	*An example of this point.*

In *Beat the Clock*, the player must use six different keys to get a good score.		
Some games require very fast and complicated finger movements.		
Computer games do not develop motor skills.		
In *Monkey Business*, the player only presses two buttons.		
Computer games improve motor skills.	✓	P
Some games involve very little physical activity.		

4.19 Grammar for writing — Articles: *the* vs zero

Every time you write **a noun**, you must ask one or two questions. ⑳

1. Do I need an **article** with this noun?

2. If I need an article, which article do I need?

Read this text. Study the purple nouns.

*A teenager killed some students in his school. **The teenager** played computer **games**. The aim of **the games** was **violence**. It seems that some people are strongly influenced by **the pictures** on **the screen**. Of course, some computer games do not show **violence**.*

Here are some reasons for using *the* or no article with nouns.

article	reason		example
the	the second, etc., mention	1	… a teenager *killed* … **The teenager** *played* …
	with *of*	2	… **the aim** of …
	the reference is clear from the context	3	… on **the screen** (of the computer)
zero	with plural nouns = *all*	4	*The teenager played computer **games**.*
	with uncountable nouns	5	… *some games do not show **violence**.*

A Choosing articles

1. Tick the correct article in each case.
2. Write the number of the reason from the table above.

Do [the / – ✓4] violent **games** cause [the / – ✓5] **violence** in [the ✓3 / –] real **world**?

Some psychologists think that they do. A psychologist, Albert Bandura, conducted a famous experiment in 1961. He put several children into a room. There was a doll in [the / –] corner of [the / –] room. An adult came into [the / –] room. [the / –] half of the time, [the / –] adult hit [the / –] doll and half of the time he did not. So [the / –] 50 per cent of [the / –] children saw [the / –] violence and 50 per cent did not. [the / –] children in [the / –] first group became violent. They hit [the / –] doll when [the / –] adult left [the / –] room. [the / –] children in [the / –] second group did not show [the / –] violence. Bandura said: '[the / –] children who see [the / –] violence often become violent.'

B Understanding the use of *the* and zero article

Study the first paragraph of the essay in 4.17.

1. Underline the nouns with *the*. Give a reason for using *the* in each case.
2. Circle the nouns with zero article. Give a reason for using no article in each case.

4.20 Applying new writing skills — Compulsory PE at secondary schools

A Reviewing vocabulary

Complete each sentence with a suitable word.

1. Computer games are now the most popular ____leisure____ activity for teenagers.
2. Many children nowadays do not get much physical _____ .
3. Children need to improve hand and eye _____ .
4. Team games teach children to _____ with other children.
5. Many teenagers do not like _____ sport because they are not interested in winning.
6. Games need concentration and _____ .
7. Some children have very little confidence and low _____ .
8. Many teachers do not _____ the idea of compulsory PE at secondary school.

B Thinking

You are going to do the assignment on the right.
Think of three points *for* and three points *against* the idea.

C Organizing

1. Study the points (P) in the notes at the bottom of the page *for* and *against* the idea.
   - Write notes to **explain** (EXP) each point.
   - Think of an **example** (EG) for each point.
   - Add extra **points, explanations** and **examples**.
2. Write notes for your opinion.

> ### Faculty of Sports Science
> Assignment 1
> _____
> **The role of physical education**
>
> *Physical education should be compulsory in secondary schools.*
>
> Discuss.

D Writing

Write your essay. Think carefully about the use of *the* and no article.

E Editing and rewriting

Follow the final stages of the TOWER process.

Physical education should be compulsory in secondary schools.		
for		
1. not much exercise out of school	modern lifestyles = no physical activity	parents drive children, etc.
2. helps develop motor skills		
3. helps develop mental skills		
4. helps develop social skills		
5.		
against		
1. not conducted well		
2. sporty children enjoy but other children don't		
3. lower self-esteem		
4.		

My opinion

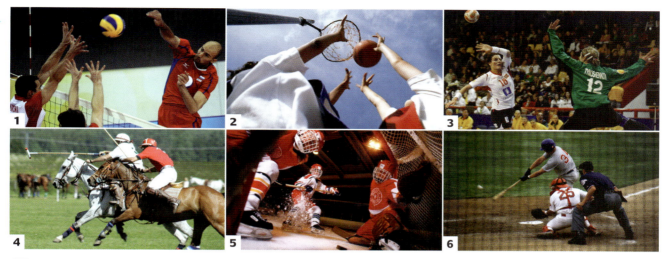

Portfolio   **Team games**

A   Activating ideas

Look at the photographs of sports above.

1. What is the name of each sport?
2. How do you play each sport?

B   Gathering information (1)

1. Divide into three groups. Group A: 🔊 **4.23**, Group B: 🔊 **4.24**, Group C: 🔊 **4.25**. Listen to the information about one of these three sports – *polo*, *baseball* and *netball*. Make notes to answer these questions.
   - Where does this game come from?
   - When did it first appear?
   - How did the game reach Europe?
   - Where do the names of the game / equipment come from?
   - What equipment do you need to play the game?
   - How do you play the game?
   - How do you win the game?
2. Work in groups of three, one student for each sport. Exchange information about your sport. Make notes.

C   Gathering information (2)

1. Work in pairs. Each student reads one of the texts about sports on pages 132/133 – *Can you play crosse, shinty or hurling?* or *Can you play baggataway or lacrosse?* Make notes.
2. Explain the information you read about to your partner. Your partner should make notes.

D   Giving a talk

Choose one of the sports from your portfolio notes – *polo, baseball, netball, hockey* or *lacrosse*.
Write a short talk. Make two or three slides for your talk. Give your talk in a small group.

E   Writing

Choose a sport you know well. Write notes, then write a short article.

Can you play *crosse, shinty* or *hurling?*

History

The Ancient Egyptians, the Romans, the Greeks and the Persians all have records of a game very similar to modern hockey. The earliest record is around 2050 BCE. Hockey has been recorded under many different names in many different countries, for example, *crosse* in France, *shinty* in Scotland and *hurling* in Ireland.

There are many ideas about the origins of the name *hockey*. Some sources say it comes from the French *hoquet*, which means a curved stick. Other sources say it comes from the American Indians playing their version of hockey, which is called *lacrosse*. Apparently, they shouted *hoo-ee* when they scored a point. A few sources say the game is named after a Colonel Hockey from England.

The first hockey club, Blackheath, was founded in 1861 in England. Hockey became a very popular sport at British schools in the 19th century. The English Hockey Association started in 1875.

The equipment

Players wear guards on their shins and ankles. They also wear mouth guards to protect their teeth because the ball is very heavy. Each player has a curved wooden stick. The goalkeeper wears a lot more protection. He/she wears a helmet with a face mask, shoulder pads, elbow pads, padded gloves, padded leg guards and 'kickers', which protect the feet when kicking the hard ball.

How to play

It is a game for two teams. There are 11 people on each team. They try to shoot a ball with the stick into the other team's goal. You can only score a goal if you shoot from within the shooting circle. You can only hit the ball with the flat side of the stick. If the ball touches your foot, it is a foul.

How to win

The objective of the game is simple. You must score more goals than the other team.

Can you play baggataway or lacrosse?

History

There are records of a game called *baggataway* dated 1492 CE. Iriquois Indians in North America played the game. The modern game of lacrosse developed from this game in about 1630.

French explorers in Canada saw the Indians playing the game in the 1600s and took it back to Europe.

The name comes from the French phrase *la crosse*, which means 'the curved stick'. In its early days, the game was played with a curved stick, like hockey.

The game was originally very violent, with many people dying from injuries in the game. However, by the 1800s, there were many rules and fewer serious injuries.

The equipment

There are two versions of the modern game. In the male version, there is a lot of protective clothing, because players try to hit members of the other team with the ball. In the female version, players do not have to wear protection, because hitting the other team is against the rules. Only the goalkeeper wears a mask. In both versions, each player has a stick with a piece of net at one end.

How to play

There are either ten people on each team (men) or twelve people (women). Each player uses a cross – the netted stick – to pass and catch a rubber ball. The stick is also used to throw the ball into the other team's goal. When the ball goes out of play, the player closest to the ball restarts. Players must not touch the ball with their hands.

How to win

The aim of the game is simple. You must score more goals than the other team.

Theme 5

Nutrition and health

- **A balanced diet**

- **Portions**

- **How to eat healthily**

- **Obesity**

Listening: A balanced diet

5.1 Vocabulary for listening   Why do we eat?

1   2   3   4

A   Reviewing vocabulary

1. How many foods can you name from each category in the chart below?
2. 🔊 **5.1** Listen and write the names of foods in the correct category.

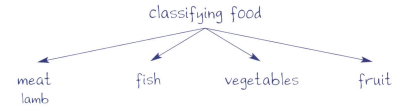

classifying food

meat   fish   vegetables   fruit
lamb

B   Understanding new vocabulary in context

🔊 **5.2** Listen and choose the best way to complete each sentence.

Part 1	Part 2
Why do we eat?	How does the body keep the energy?
We eat because ...	It stores it ...
.... do we feel hungry?	.... a healthy diet.
.... from food.	.... *amount* of food.
.... the body keeps it.	1 as fat.
1 we are hungry.	.... *kind* of food as well.
.... the body needs more energy.	.... our diet.
.... to do work.	.... the energy in fat.
.... to operate correctly.	.... the extra energy.

C   Using new vocabulary

What is your normal diet?
What do you normally eat for breakfast, for lunch and for dinner?

balance (*n*)
basically (*adv*)
carbohydrate (*n*)
chemical (*n*)
dairy product (*n*)
damaged (*adj*)
diet (*n*)
energy (*n*)
exercise (*n*) [= physical]
explorer (*n*)
fat (*adj* and *n*)
health (*n*)
healthy (*adj*)
hungry (*adj*)
ill (*adj*)
medicine (*n*)
mineral (*n*)
normally (*adv*)
nutrient (*n*)
portion (*n*)
protein (*n*)
pyramid (*n*)
recommend (*v*)
store (*v*)
unhealthy (*adj*)
vegetable (*n*)
vitamin (*n*)
voyage (*n*)

5.2 Listening review (1) Nutrients

A Reviewing vocabulary

Match the verbs and nouns or adjectives.

1. classify ☐ exercise
2. define ☐ careful
3. feel ☐ energy
4. eat ☐1☐ foods
5. get ☐ a healthy diet
6. take ☐ a word
7. be ☐ food
8. have ☐ hungry

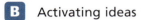

B Activating ideas

Study the photograph on the opposite page. How many items can you name in one minute?

C Understanding the organization of a lecture

🔊 5.3 DVD 10.A Watch the introduction to a lecture from Food Sciences. What is the lecturer going to talk about this week? In what order? Number the points correctly on the right.

	classification of nutrients
	definition of *nutrient*
	food groups
	energy
	examples of food with each nutrient
	food quantity

D Understanding a lecture (1)

🔊 5.4 DVD 10.B Watch the first part of the lecture. Answer the questions.

1. What are nutrients?
   a. ☐ energy
   b. ☐ chemicals
   c. ☐ energy and chemicals
2. What is energy in the human body?
   a. ☐ the ability to do work
   b. ☐ electricity
   c. ☐ many things
3. What happens if you have too much of a particular type of nutrient?
   a. ☐ nothing
   b. ☐ you get fat
   c. ☐ you get ill

E Understanding a lecture (2)

🔊 5.5 DVD 10.C Watch the second part of the lecture. Complete the diagram below.

nutrients

carbohydrates

F Developing critical thinking

Discuss these questions.

1. Why are the foods on the opposite page arranged in a triangle?
2. How else could you arrange the information to show the same idea?

The food pyramid

5.3 Listening review (2)   Vitamins

A   Reviewing vocabulary

In this course, you have learnt to recognize a number of fixed expressions.

🔊 **5.6** Listen and number the expressions in order.

.... a long time ago	.... in the past
.... after that,	.... let's look at
.... as you know	.... so, there are several
.... at that time	.... these days
__1__ going to talk about	.... to sum up, then
.... I've told you	.... we have heard about
.... in my opinion	.... what about
.... in other words	.... you can see why

B   Waiting for definitions

In this course, you have learnt to wait for definitions.

🔊 **5.7** Listen to some more information about nutrition. Match the words and the definitions.

1. molecule   ☐ it is essential for healing skin wounds
2. solvent   ☐ it makes collagen
3. dissolving   ☐ changing from solid to liquid
4. enzymes   ☐ they help the human body to carry out chemical reactions
5. praline hydroloxase ☐1 a compound of different elements
6. collagen   ☐ a liquid

C   Recognizing important words

In this course, you have learnt to recognize important words.

🔊 **5.8** Listen. Complete the notes with the important words from each sentence.

vitamin C = most important vitamin?
_____
_____
_____
_____

D   Understanding a sequence

In this course, you have learnt to hear dates in context.

🔊 **5.9** Listen. Write the correct year in each space.

3000 BCE	Deaths from scurvy in Ancient Egypt.
	Deaths from scurvy in Ancient Greece.
	Deaths from scurvy in Ancient Rome.
	American Indians gave medicine to a French explorer.
	James Lind: 'We need lemons on long voyages.'
	James Cook gave lime juice to his sailors.
	Charles King proved the connection between vitamin C and scurvy.

5.4 Grammar review (1) Predicting; past and present, positive and negative, singular and plural

A Predicting the next information

In this course, you have learnt to predict the next information from the structure of the sentence. Study the sentences. What will come next in each case? 🔊 **5.10** Listen and find the information that comes next.

1. A festival is	☐	1949.
2. *Celebrate* means	☐	14ᵗʰ December 1926.
3. I made a hypothesis, then	☐	any lakes.
4. There's a mountain range	☐	I did an experiment.
5. There aren't	☐	forests and lakes.
6. There is a river in the south.	1	a special event in one country or several countries.
7. The first flight took place on	☐	It is very long.
8. She was born in	☐	remember a happy event.
9. The area consists of	☐	about the history of mass media.
10. First, I'm going to talk	☐	in the north of the country.

B Recognizing present and past

In this course, you have learnt to recognize the present and the past in context.
🔊 **5.11** Listen. Tick in the correct column for each sentence.

	present	past			present	past
1.	✓			7.		
2.				8.		
3.				9.		
4.				10.		
5.				11.		
6.				12.		

C Recognizing positive and negative

In this course, you have learnt to recognize positive and negative sentences in context.
🔊 **5.12** Listen. Tick the sentence you hear.

1.	The human body needs vitamins.	✓	The human body doesn't need vitamins.	☐
2.	The human body can make vitamins.	☐	The human body can't make vitamins.	☐
3.	It gets them from fruit and vegetables.	☐	It doesn't get them from fruit and vegetables.	☐
4.	Cooking can destroy vitamins.	☐	Cooking can't destroy vitamins.	☐
5.	Boiled vegetables have a lot of vitamins.	☐	Boiled vegetables don't have a lot of vitamins.	☐
6.	You should eat raw fruit.	☐	You shouldn't eat raw fruit.	☐
7.	Washing fruit removes vitamins.	☐	Washing fruit doesn't remove vitamins.	☐
8.	Washing fruit removes most germs.	☐	Washing fruit doesn't remove germs.	☐

D Recognizing singular and plural subjects

In this course, you have learnt to recognize singular and plural subjects in context.
🔊 **5.13** Listen. Is the subject of each sentence singular or plural?

1.	fat	✓	fats	☐	6. festival ☐	festivals ☐
2.	fat	☐	fats	☐	7. manager ☐	managers ☐
3.	vitamin	☐	vitamins	☐	8. bank ☐	banks ☐
4.	meeting	☐	meetings	☐	9. river ☐	rivers ☐
5.	researcher	☐	researchers	☐	10. mountain ☐	mountains ☐

A Reviewing vocabulary

1. 🔊 **5.14** Listen to each sound. It is the stressed syllable of a word connected with food. Can you identify the word?

2. 🔊 **5.15** Listen and check your ideas.

a. pro   *protein*

b. new

c. high

d. die

e. vit

f. min

g. pair

h. dam

i. ness

j. lees

B Activating ideas

What is a healthy diet?
Number the types of food in the table in order.

1 = *you should eat very little of this*

6 = *you should eat a lot of this*

	fats
	meat and fish
	eggs, milk, cheese
	vegetables
	fruit
	carbohydrates

Food groups

Groups are:

1. fats

2.

3.

4.

5.

6.

C Listening and note-taking

You are going to watch another lecture from the Food Sciences course.

1. 🔊 **5.16** DVD **10.D** Watch the introduction. What is the lecturer going to talk about this week? Complete the list of topics.

2. 🔊 **5.17** DVD **10.E** Watch the first part of the lecture. Complete the notes.

3. 🔊 **5.18** DVD **10.F** Watch the second part of the lecture. Complete Figure 1. Shade or colour in the squares.

4. 🔊 **5.19** DVD **10.G** Watch the last part of the lecture. What does the lecturer want you to do?

fats											
dairy products											meat and fish
vegetables											fruit
carbohydrates											

Figure 1: *The balanced diet pyramid*

Speaking: Portions

5.6 Vocabulary for speaking — Portions

A Reviewing vocabulary

Look at the quiz.

1. Ask and answer in pairs. Make a note of your partner's responses.
2. Read the marking guide on page 171. Work out your partner's score.
3. Tell your partner his/her score. Do you agree with the score given?

Section A

1 How much butter do you have on bread?
   a. Lots
   b. A little
   c. None / I don't eat bread

2 How often do you eat biscuits or cakes in a week?
   a. 5 or more times
   b. 2–4 times
   c. Sometimes or never

3 How often do you eat sweets or chocolate in a week?
   a. 5 or more times
   b. 2–4 times
   c. Sometimes or never

4 How often do you eat chips or crisps in a week?
   a. 5 or more times
   b. 2–4 times
   c. Sometimes or never

5 How often do you eat burgers in a week?
   a. 5 or more times
   b. 2–4 times
   c. Sometimes or never

Section B

1 How many slices of bread (or equivalent) do you eat most days?
   a. 5 or more
   b. 2–4
   c. 1 or none

2 How often do you eat rice or pasta in a week?
   a. 5 or more times
   b. 2–4 times
   c. Sometimes or never

3 How many potatoes do you usually have at a meal?
   a. 5 or more
   b. 2–4
   c. 1 or none

4 How many times a week do you eat cereal for breakfast?
   a. 5 or more times
   b. 2–4 times
   c. Sometimes or never

5 How many portions of fruit and vegetables do you eat every day?
   a. 5 or more
   b. 2–4
   c. 1 or none

B Understanding new vocabulary

🔊 **5.20** Listen and complete the text. Use words from the list on the right. Make any necessary changes.

We are often told to eat three portions of meat, or five portions of vegetables, etc. But what is a portion? Here is a guide to portion size for a number of common foods.

- a _____ of bread
- a _____ of pasta or rice
- a small _____ of cereal
- two small potatoes
- one large egg
- three thin _____ of meat
- one _____ of fish
- half a _____ of beans or peas
- a handful of _____
- a small _____ of cheese
- a small _____ of yoghurt
- a _____ of milk

---

a little (n)
a lot (n)
biscuit (n)
bowl (n)
burger (n)
cake (n)
can (n)
carton (n)
cereal (n)
chip (n)
fewer (adj)
glass (n)
handful (n)
intake (n)
juice (n)
less (adj)
lots (n)
nut (n)
pasta (n)
piece (n)
queue (n)
receipt (n)
sauce (n)
slice (n)
snack (n)
spoonful (n)
sweets (n)
take-away (n)
teaspoon (n)
tray (n)
typical (adj)
yoghurt (n)

A Activating ideas

Study Figure 1 on the right.

1. What does it show?
2. Do you have a balanced diet?

B Studying a model

You are going to hear a student giving a talk about diet.

1. 🔊 **5.21** Listen and look at the tables and figures.
2. Study the start of each sentence below. Complete it in a logical way. Use information from the tables and the figures.

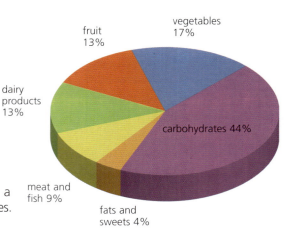

Figure 1: *A balanced diet by category*

Introduction

a. According to nutritionists, …
   we should eat a balanced diet.

Figure 1

b. We can see a balanced diet …
c. I wanted to find out …
d. Firstly, let me tell you …

Table 1

e. I recorded …
f. You can see the results …
g. For breakfast, …
h. For lunch, …
i. For dinner, …
j. I also had …
k. Now, I'm going to explain …

Table 2

l. I put …
m. I estimated …
n. Here are the results …
o. I converted …

Figure 2

p. Then I drew this …
q. We can compare …

Conclusion

r. I had almost the correct amount …
s. I also ate …
t. However, …
u. I am going to change …
v. I don't think …

Table 1: *My food intake for one day*

meal	intake				
breakfast	2 slices toast	1 piece butter	1 spoonful sugar		
lunch	1 burger	lots of chips	peas	1 carton yoghurt	1 glass orange juice
dinner	pasta	tomato sauce			
snacks	chocolate bar				

Table 2: *Classifying my food intake with portions*

food type	intake		
carbohydrates	toast (2)	chips (2)	pasta (1)
vegetables	peas (1)	tomato sauce (1)	
dairy products	yoghurt (1)		
fruit	orange juice (1)		
meat and fish	burger (1)		
fats and sweets	butter (1)	chocolate bar (1)	

C Practising a model

Cover the sentence openers above. Practise giving the talk. Use the information in the tables and figures.

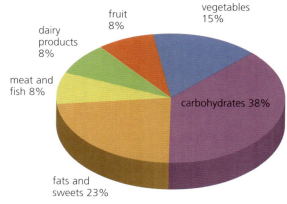

Figure 2: *My daily intake by category*

A   **Activating ideas**

| restaurant   canteen   supermarket   coffee shop   vending machine   take-away |

1. Look at the photographs. Match each one to a word or phrase above.
2. Where would you go to for:
   - a three-course meal?
   - a snack?
   - breakfast?
   - a quick lunch?
   - a coffee?
   - a healthy meal?

B   **Studying models**

1. Look at the conversations. Who are A and B in each case? Where are they?
2. Choose the correct phrase. 🔊 **5.22** Listen and check your ideas.
3. Practise the conversations. Add more lines to each conversation.

1
A: Are you ready to order / for order?
B: Yes. I'll have the chicken with noodles.
A: Anything to drink?
B: Just tap water, please.

4
A: What can I get / I can get you?
B: Two coffees, please.
A: With milk?
B: Yes, please.

2
A: What would you like to have / to take?
B: The curry, please.
A: Rice or chips?
B: Umm, rice please.

5
A: What do you want / like?
B: A cheese sandwich, I think.
A: OK. Put the money in here. Press G-1-2.
B: Thanks. I think I've got the right coins.

3
A: That's £7.38 all together, please.
B: Could I have / to have a bag?
A: Certainly. Here you are.
B: Thanks.

6
A: Good evening. Pizza Rapida.
B: Oh, hi. Can I order a pizza for / with delivery, please?
A: It will be about 45 minutes. Is that OK?
B: That will be fine.

C   **Practising a model**

1. Write a new conversation for one of these places.
   - a juice bar
   - an Internet café
   - a Chinese take-away
   - a coffee shop
   - a self-service restaurant
2. Practise the conversation with a partner.

A Pronouncing vowels correctly

1. In this course, you have learnt to pronounce key vowels.
2. Say each word in the left-hand column. Find another word in the right-hand column with the same vowel sound. Choose five words. Use each word in a sentence.

Short vowels

1.	mix	/ɪ/		friend
2.	flat	/æ/		lot
3.	job	/ɒ/		luck
4.	dust	/ʌ/		pitch
5.	net	/e/		snack

Long vowels and diphthongs

1.	fee	/iː/		burst
2.	smart	/ɑː/		brake
3.	court	/ɔː/		fall
4.	rude	/uː/		noise
5.	worst	/ɜː/		role
6.	plain	/eɪ/		keep
7.	own	/əʊ/		far
8.	shy	/aɪ/		group
9.	cloud	/aʊ/		sound
10.	boy	/ɔɪ/		tide

B Stressing words correctly

In this course, you have learnt to stress multi-syllable words correctly.

1. Say each word in the box below. Write the word in the correct column of the table.
2. Choose five words. Use each word in a sentence.

> atmosphere behaviour between career customer difference
> impression influence lightning persuade predict primary recruitment
> reward semester substance symbol tertiary vacation vapour

Oo	oO	Ooo	oOo
		atmosphere	

C Using fixed phrases

In this course, you have learnt to use a number of fixed phrases.
Complete each phrase with one word. Choose five phrases. Use each phrase in a sentence.

1. I'm __going__ to talk about …
2. First of _____, I will …
3. Then I'll _____ you about …
4. Finally, I _____ mention some of the …
5. It's every year on the 30th. Sorry. _____ you say the 30th?
6. I don't understand. _____ you repeat that?
7. Did you _____ that …
8. _____, the first powered flight happened in …
9. _____ to research in the USA …
10. It says _____ that …
11. I _____ that children watch too much TV.
12. Now we _____ to …
13. Firstly, _____ are …
14. Next we _____ …

Closed and open questions

A Making closed questions

Complete each closed question with one word in each space.
Then ask and answer in pairs.

1. _Is_ your house near here?

2. _____ you like football?

3. _____ you got a car?

4. _____ you play tennis?

5. _____ you like to go abroad?

6. _____ you do homework last night?

7. _____ you from Italy?

8. _____ you good at Maths at school?

9. _____ you tell me the time?

10. _____ you going to be a teacher?

B Making open questions

Make a question for each answer.

1. _Where are you from? / Where do you come from?_   Japan.

2. _____   I'm 18.

3. _____   I'm a student.

4. _____   It's $5.

5. _____   On the second floor.

6. _____   At 10.00 a.m.

7. _____   Two hours.

8. _____   About 20.

9. _____   Once or twice a week.

10. _____   Mrs Johnson.

C Reviewing key patterns

There is a mistake in each sentence or question below. Find the mistake and correct it.

1. I think it isn't a good idea.   _I don't think it's a good idea._

2. We do not celebrate very much birthdays.

3. Goalkeepers can to touch the ball with their hands.

4. I'm going to make the examination next month.

5. Who did invent the bicycle?

6. When Karl Benz invented the motor car?

7. I'd like having tea.

8. Would you mind to open the window?

9. It was sunny because I went for a walk.

10. My city is on the Nile that is the longest river in the world.

5.10 Speaking review (3)   My diet

A Reviewing vocabulary
Match each portion expression with a food type.

1. a slice of ☐ cereal
2. a piece of ☐ potatoes
3. a carton of ☐ egg
4. a spoonful of ☐1 orange juice
5. a glass of ☐ bread
6. a can of ☐ sugar
7. a handful of ☐ yoghurt
8. a large ☐ beans
9. a bowl of ☐ pasta
10. two small ☐ cheese

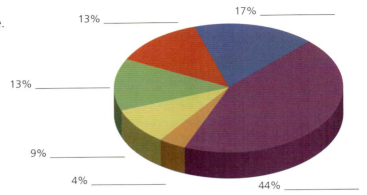

13% _____   17% _____

13% _____

9% _____

4% _____

44% _____

B Activating ideas
What is a balanced diet?

1. Name each section of the pie chart on the right.
2. Name some foods which go in each section.

C Researching
Complete Table 1 with information about your food intake yesterday.

Table 1: *My food intake for one day*

meal	intake						
breakfast							
lunch							
dinner							
snacks							

D Analyzing

1. Analyze your intake in Table 2. Write the portions in brackets after each item.
2. Convert the raw data into percentages and make a pie chart of the results.

Table 2: *Classifying my food intake with portions*

food type	items					
carbohydrates						
vegetables						
dairy products						
fruit						
meat and fish						
fats and sweets						

E Giving a talk
Give a talk about your diet. Talk about:

- the idea of a balanced diet.
- your research.
- your analysis.
- your diet compared with a balanced diet.
- changes you are going to make …
  and things you won't change.

5.11 Vocabulary for reading   Three square meals a day

A Reviewing vocabulary

Find pairs of words in the box below. Explain the connection.

apple / orange – they are both kinds of fruit

> apple bottle bowl carbohydrate carrot cereal fruit
> hungry less milk more orange potatoes protein rice
> spoonful sugar thirsty tomato vegetables

B Understanding new vocabulary

Study each word or phrase below. Find an opposite word or phrase in the list.

1. lose (weight) *put on*
2. stop _____
3. increase _____
4. eat _____
5. healthy (food) _____
6. slow down _____
7. problem _____
8. use _____

C Understanding new vocabulary in context

Read the sentences below. What do the words in italics mean in each case?

1. You should *chew* your food many times before you *swallow* it.
2. You can buy yoghurt in a *low-fat* form.
3. Do you like plain *peanuts* or ones with salt on them?
4. Can you give me the *recipe* for this cake? It's delicious.
5. You should keep cold meat in the *fridge*. If you don't, it may go bad.
6. I bought a *bar* of chocolate, but I only ate one piece.

D Using new vocabulary

Complete each sentence with a word or phrase from Exercise B or Exercise C. Make any necessary changes.

1. The car slowed down, then it *speeded up* again.
2. You should try to _____ your intake of fatty foods.
3. You shouldn't eat so many burgers and chips. All that _____ is not good for you.
4. Some people _____ themselves. They hardly eat anything.
5. The human body _____ energy in the form of fat.
6. You don't have to turn off the television. You can _____ watching it.
7. If you don't do enough exercise, you _____ weight.
8. I can't follow this _____ for a chocolate cake. It's too complicated.

---

bar (*n*) [= piece]
bar (*n*)
  [= serving counter]
blood pressure (*n*)
body rate (*n*)
canned (*adj*)
carry on (*v*)
chew (*v*)
chocolate (*n*)
dried (*adj*)
fatty (*adj*)
fill up on (*v*)
fridge (*n*)
frozen (*adj*)
heart attack (*n*)
junk food (*n*)
low-fat (*adj*)
peanut (*n*)
preservation (*n*)
preserve (*v*)
put on (*v*)
recipe (*n*)
reduce (*v*)
salt (*n*)
saturated (*adj*)
slow down (*v*)
solution (*n*)
speed up (*v*)
starve (*v*)
store (*v*)
stroke (*n*) [= medical]
swallow (*v*)
unhealthy (*adj*)
variety (*n*)

A   Reviewing vocabulary
Which is the odd one out? Why?

1. apples	potatoes	lemons	oranges
2. meat	juice	tea	coffee
3. chocolate	pasta	cake	sweets
4. ice-cream	butter	cheese	rice
5. potatoes	eggs	crisps	chips
6. carrots	peas	cabbage	chicken

B   Activating ideas
You are going to read an article about healthy eating. Read the title opposite.
Which of these sentences will be in the text? Tick one or more. Explain your answers.

1. ☐ Don't drink anything while you are eating.
2. ☐ I had a good meal in a restaurant last week.
3. ☐ I love eating burger and chips.
4. ☐ I will try to eat in a more healthy way in future.
5. ☐ You must eat many different kinds of food each week.
6. ☐ You should eat fruit every day.

C   Understanding a text
Read the text opposite. Find a good answer for each question.

1. Why should you eat breakfast?   ☐ Because it will reduce your intake at the next meal.
2. Why should you eat snacks?   ☐ Because it helps you to eat food very quickly.
3. Why should you drink water?   ☐ Because it actually leads to fatness.
4. Why should you eat a variety of foods?   ☐ Because you must meet all the needs of your body.
5. Why shouldn't you shop when you are hungry? ☐ Because you may buy sweets then.
6. Why shouldn't you eat in front of the TV? ☒ Because it will wake up your body.
7. Why shouldn't you starve?   ☐ Because you may eat too fast.
8. Why shouldn't you drink while you are eating? ☐ Because it will fill up your stomach.

D   Showing comprehension with conditional sentences
You can complete each of these conditional sentences with information from the text.
Read the *If …* clause in each case. Complete the sentence in a logical way.

1. If you eat healthy snacks, …
2. If you don't eat breakfast, …
3. If you drink water after your meal, …
4. If you shop when you are hungry, …
5. If you eat a variety of foods, …
6. If you don't eat in front of the TV, …
7. If you don't eat for a long time, …
8. If you don't drink with your food, …

E   Reading and reacting
Are you going to follow any of the advice in the text?

The dos and don'ts of healthy eating

Eat breakfast

Even if you are not very hungry, eat something. Have a piece of bread or fruit. Your body slows down at night. It speeds up again when you eat something. If you wait until lunchtime to eat, that is four or five more hours of slow body rate.

Eat snacks

If you don't eat anything for several hours, you will eat much more at the next meal. Eat healthy, low-fat snacks between meals.

Drink water

Drink at least two glasses of water after your meal. You will feel fuller and not go back for seconds.

Think FAT!

When you want to eat fatty foods, think about three things:

frequency	Don't eat them so often.
amount	Don't eat so much.
type	Don't eat saturated fats – check food labels.

Eat a variety of foods

Your body needs more than 40 different nutrients for good health. That means you must eat many different kinds of food each week. Every day, you should eat bread and fruit, vegetables, dairy products, meat or fish.

Don't shop when you are hungry

Eat something before you go to the shops. If you don't, you will buy a bar of chocolate or some junk food while you are there.

Don't eat in front of the TV

Firstly, you will enjoy your meal better. Secondly, you will take longer to eat it, and that is good for your body. Thirdly, you will not eat as much.

Don't give up foods

If you like a particular food a lot, carry on eating it. Reduce the portions or the number of times you eat the food each week.

Don't starve

Starving makes you fat. It is strange but true – well, almost! If you don't eat for long periods of time, you may put on weight. On the one hand, while you are starving, your body slows down and stores fat. On the other hand, when you eat again, you will eat more than normal.

Don't drink and eat

Don't drink anything while you are eating. Any liquid encourages you to swallow before you have finished chewing. If you don't drink, you will chew more and enjoy the food more.

A   Reviewing vocabulary

In this course, you have learnt to recognize words quickly. What is the full word in each case? The words are not connected with food.

1. acc... *urate / ept / ommodation*
2. aff...
3. comb...
4. cont...
5. demo...
6. est...
7. inf...
8. prin...
9. requ...
10. sit...

B   Predicting information

In this course, you have learnt to predict information in a text.

1. Study the extracts on the right. What will the full text be about?
2. What advice will the text give about:
   a. salt?
   b. fatty foods?
   c. labels on supermarket foods?
   d. calories?
   e. home-cooked food?
   f. sugars, like fructose and sucrose?
   g. recommended intakes?

C   Dealing with new words

In this course you have learnt to deal with new words.

Study the highlighted words.

1. What part of speech is each word?
2. Guess the meaning from context.

D   Reading tables

In this course, you have learnt to read tables.

1. Find and explain each of these numbers from the tables.
   a. 2
   b. 70 (F)
   c. 2,110
2. Work in pairs and test your partner on other numbers.

The hidden dangers in food

Have you stopped putting salt on your chips and sugar in your tea? Have you given up fatty foods like butter? Unfortunately, you will find these items are in most processed foods on supermarket shelves, but you have to look carefully.

Salt

Salt is found in most processed foods because it is addictive and it makes people want to eat more.

Table 1: *Recommended daily salt intake*

age	grams
0–1 years	<1
1–3 years	2
4–6 years	3
7–10 years	5
11+	6

Fat

The human body needs a small amount of fat every day, but too much can harm your health.

Table 2: *Recommended daily fat intake*

age	grams
2–3 years	40
4–8 years	50
9–13 years	70
adult males	70 (F) 80 (M)

Sugar

Sugar is found in high quantities in processed foods, even savoury items like spaghetti.

Table 3: *Recommended daily calorie intake*

age	males	females
1–3 years	1,230	1,165
4–6 years	1,715	1,545
7–10 years	1,970	1,740
11–14 years	2,220	1,845
15–18 years	2,755	2,110
adults	2,550	1,940

5.14 Grammar review (3)   Salt

Salt is very important for health. The brain needs salt for messages to the hands and feet. The heart needs salt to work correctly. If people do not have enough salt, they sometimes die. Salt is also useful for preserving food or keeping it fresh. In the past, salting was the main way to preserve meat. But nowadays, we do not need salt for this purpose. There are other ways of preserving food, like freezing, drying and canning.

However, salt can also be very dangerous for young children and old people. If people have too much salt, they can develop high blood pressure. People with high blood pressure often have a heart attack or a stroke. Around 300,000 people in Britain die of heart attacks and strokes every year.

According to recent research, most people eat too much salt every day. In 2001, people in Britain consumed 9.5 grams of salt each day. Nowadays, the average person in Britain eats 8.6 grams of salt each day, but the figure is still too high. People only need about six grams, or a teaspoon. What is the answer? First, stop putting salt on your food. Secondly, don't buy ready-meals from supermarkets. Processed food contains a lot of salt.

frozen

dried

canned

A **Recognizing parts of speech**

1. Study the first sentence of the text above. Find:

    a. two nouns   _salt,_

    b. one verb

    c. one adjective

    d. one preposition

    e. one adverb

2. Study the second sentence in the text. Find:

    a. the subject

    b. the verb

    c. the object

B **Recognizing information in a text**

Read the text. Find:

1. two pieces of advice
2. two past facts
3. two statements of frequency

C **Recognizing extra information**

Find the extra information in each case.

1. Why is salt important?   _for health_
2. Why does the brain need salt?
3. Why does the heart need salt?
4. What happens if people do not have enough salt?
5. What other ways of preserving food are there?
6. Who can salt be dangerous for?
7. What happens if people have too much salt?
8. How much is six grams of salt?

A   Reviewing vocabulary

What word or phrase do you expect to follow each word or phrase below?

1. a piece of ... *bread, cheese, meat*
2. a bar of ...
3. a glass of ...
4. saturated ...
5. low-fat ...

6. fatty ...
7. junk ...
8. eat between ...
9. reduce ...
10. store ...

B   Activating ideas

You are going to read the text on the opposite page. It is about healthy eating.

1. Look at the heading and subheading. What will the main idea of this article be?
2. Look at the two section headings. Which heading will each sentence below be in? Write *P* (problem) or *S* (solution).
    a. Go to the shops regularly ...   ___S___
    b. You get home at 3.00 p.m. and you're starving.   ....
    c. Plan to have ten-minute meals.   ....
    d. You are a complete failure, aren't you?   ....
    e. You must make an eating plan ...   .
    f. You plan a healthy meal, but it's a complicated recipe.   ....

C   Understanding a text

Read the text on the opposite page. Complete Table 1.

Table 1: *How to plan for healthy eating*

	the problems	the solutions
1.	no healthy things in fridge	go shopping regularly; buy healthy things
2.		
3.		
4.		
5.		

D   Using a key skill

What does each pronoun and adverb below refer to?

1. Then (line 3)   _after the plan_
2. there (line 5)   ....
3. Then (line 7)   ....
4. It (line 8)   ....
5. then (line 12)   ....

6. it (line 14)   ....
7. it (line 20)   ....
8. them (line 23)   ....
9. them (line 26)   ....
10. then (line 30)   ....

E   Reading and reacting

1. Are you going to follow any of the advice in the text?
2. Look back at the text in Lesson 5.12. Which piece of advice in the two texts is the most important, in your opinion?

Plan for your life
(Don't live for your plan)

The problems

Is this your problem? You want to eat in a healthy way. You plan to
eat in a healthy way. Then something goes wrong.

You forget to go shopping and, when you go to the fridge, the only
5 thing there is … peanut butter.
OR
You make yourself a healthy sandwich for lunch. Then all your
friends go to the burger bar. Well, you can't say no, can you? It's rude.
OR
10 You say to yourself: 'Today, I'm not going to eat anything until
6.00 p.m.' You get home at 3.00 p.m. and you're starving. You decide
to have a quick snack then. Peanut butter sandwiches again …
OR
You plan a healthy meal, but it's a complicated recipe. It's going to
15 take hours to prepare, but you are really looking forward to doing it.
Then you get an extra assignment from college and there just isn't
time. What else is in the fridge …?

You are a complete failure, aren't you?

The solutions

20 You can't change your life to match your eating plan. It won't work.
You must make an eating plan that actually works for you and your
lifestyle.

Firstly, how can you eat healthy snacks if you don't buy them? Go to
the shops regularly and buy fruit and vegetables for a quick meal.

25 Secondly, why must meals with friends be *unhealthy* meals? You
shouldn't use them as an excuse for bad eating habits. In most
restaurants nowadays, you can have a healthy choice. You don't have
to fill up on burgers and chips.

Thirdly, when do you *actually* get hungry? If you are starving at
30 3.00 p.m. , you must have a healthy snack then.

Fourthly, how long do you *really* have to prepare meals? If you only
have ten minutes during the week, plan to have ten-minute meals.

Finally, remember that you are not a failure because you have one
unhealthy meal every now and then. If you end up eating peanut
35 butter sandwiches once a month, well, you're only human.

1. What is *gender equality*?

2. What is the *social distance* for colleagues in Britain?

3. What is a *subject portal*?

4. What do *sociologists* study?

5. What is *bullying*?

6. What are Jung's *personality extremes*?

7. What are the points on Leary's *interpersonal circle*?

8. How can you make a *good impression* at the start of an interview?

9. What do *architects* do?

10. Why should you draw up a *short list* of candidates for a job?

11. What is the first stage of the *scientific method*?

12. Where can you find lines of *longitude* and *latitude*?

13. Why it is hotter at the *Equator* than at the *Poles*?

14. Where is *Nicaragua*?

15. How many countries *border* China?

16. What do they *race* in Bali?

17. What is the *Palio*?

18. What did Russia *launch* in 1957?

19. What was *published* for the first time in Britain in 1881?

20. What is an *e-zine*?

21. Where did the game of *chess* originate?

22. What is the *objective* of football?

23. What is a *peninsula*?

24. What is a *parade*?

25. What does working *shifts* mean?

26. Who invented a *rocket* in 1934 which used liquid oxygen?

27. Who developed *gunpowder* in about 800 BCE?

28. When did the Wright brothers make the first *powered* flight?

29. When was the board game *chess* invented?

30. When do you say *checkmate*?

5.16 Vocabulary for writing   A global problem

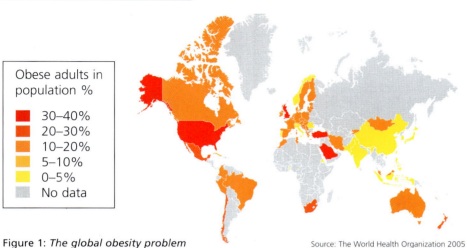

Obese adults in population %

- 🟥 30–40%
- 🟧 20–30%
- 🟧 10–20%
- 🟨 5–10%
- 🟨 0–5%
- ⬜ No data

Figure 1: *The global obesity problem*

Source: The World Health Organization 2005

A Extending a text

Read the text. Copy extra information from the box to complete each sentence.

Nowadays, *obesity* is an increasing problem in many parts of the world, _as we can see in Figure 1._ .

At one time, only a few rich people *suffered* from the condition, _____ .

Now, it is a *significant* factor in the main causes of natural death.
Researchers believe that people in many countries must change their lifestyles.
Firstly, they need to change their attitude to food. *Nutritionists* say we should eat at regular times, _____ .
Secondly, we should eat the correct type of food. We should not *snack* on baked foods _____ .
We should think about the *ingredients* in our food, especially processed food.
We should eat *lean* meat, like chicken, _____ .
Finally, of course, we should take exercise, _____ .

- and we should not *consume* food as quickly as possible.
- ~~as we can see in Figure 1.~~
- or become *vegetarians*.
- or sweets, like chocolate.
- so researchers did not even measure obesity.
- for example, walk to the shops.

B Building vocabulary

Explain the meaning of the words in italics in the text.

obesity = being very fat

actual (*adj*)
condition (*n*) [medical]
consume (*v*)
deliver (*v*)
diabetes (*n*)
even (*adv*)
examine (*v*)
fast food (*n*)
flour (*n*)
heart disease (*n*)
hunter-gatherer (*n*)
ingredient (*n*)
instead of (*prep*)
lean (*adj*)
lemonade (*n*)
natural death (*n*)
nutrient (*n*)
nutritionist (*n*)
obesity (*n*)
particularly (*adv*)
potato (*n*)
raw (*adj*)
salad (*n*)
seed (*n*)
significant (*adj*)
snack (*n* and *v*)
suffer from (*v*)
sugary (*adj*)
trend (*n*)
vegetarian (*n*)
wheat (*n*)

A Reviewing vocabulary

The words below are from phrases in Lesson 5.16.
Complete each phrase with a suitable word.

1. an increasing …   *problem*
2. a significant …   ....
3. main …   ....
4. correct …   ....
5. baked …   ....
6. lean …   ....
7. regular …   ....
8. processed …   ....

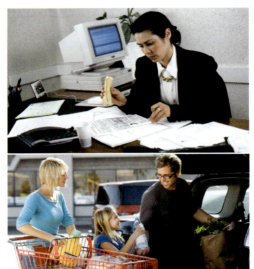

B Activating ideas

1. Look at the assignment on the right. What does *identify* mean?
2. Discuss these questions. Do most people in Britain:
   a. have regular mealtimes?
   b. spend a long time on the main meal of the day?
   c. eat snacks between meals?
   d. eat processed food most of the time?
   e. consume a lot of sugary drinks?
   f. eat large portions at mealtimes?
   g. walk to the shops or the market?
3. Look at the notes in the diagram at the top of the opposite page and check your answers to B2.

Faculty of Biomedicine
Assignment 5: *Obesity*

The problem of obesity has many causes. Some causes are medical, some causes are psychological, but some causes are social.

Identify some of the social reasons for obesity in a country that you know well.

C Studying a model

Study the essay under the notes on the opposite page.

1. How many paragraphs are there? What information is in each paragraph?
2. Decide what sort of information can complete each sentence. Then find and copy the correct information from below into each space.

noun / noun phrase	verb + other information	preposition + other information	sentence
cola or lemonade. fast-food restaurants. the day. the amount of sugar and fat.	continue working. do not even leave their houses. is processed.	to the market. at their desks. of processed food.	many people do not have meals at regular times. food is consumed very quickly. it is delivered to their home.

D Practising a model

1. Look again at the questions in B2 above. Give answers for your country.
2. Make notes about food habits in your country. Use the diagram structure from the opposite page.
3. Write a five-paragraph essay.

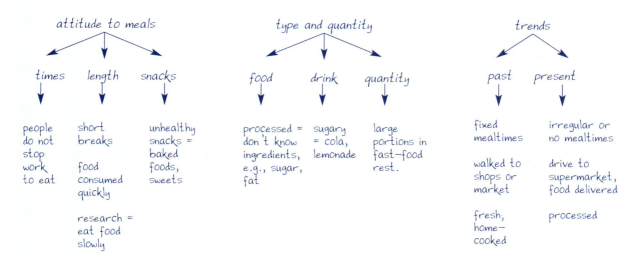

Obesity in Britain

The rate of obesity in Britain is 24.2 per cent (OECD statistics 2005), and it is rising. This study looks at some of the social reasons for obesity in Britain. It examines attitudes to meals in society. It also looks at the food which is consumed. Finally, it considers changes in the country.

The attitude to meals in a society is a significant factor in obesity. Firstly, many people do not stop work to eat. For example, they have sandwiches _____, or a take-away, and _____. Secondly, meal breaks are often very short, and _____. Research shows that it is better to eat food slowly. Finally, many people have unhealthy snacks of baked foods and sweets throughout _____.

The type of food and drink in a society affects obesity. The quantity is also important. Many people in Britain eat a lot _____. They do not know the actual ingredients, particularly _____. Many people consume large amounts of sugary drinks, like _____. Portions are often very large in _____.

The changes in food habits in Britain are very worrying. In the past, there were fixed times for meals, but nowadays, _____. At one time, people in Britain walked to the shops or _____. Nowadays, most people drive to a supermarket, but some people _____. They order food on the Internet and _____. People used to eat a lot of fresh, home-cooked food, but now a lot of food in Britain _____.

In conclusion, people in Britain must make some changes if they want to reduce obesity. Firstly, they must change their attitude to food. Secondly, they must change the type of food and quantity of food. Finally, they must take regular exercise.

5.18 Writing review (2) — Spelling vowels; collocations; fixed phrases

A Reviewing vocabulary

In this course, you have learnt to spell a large number of key words.
Complete each word with one vowel in each space. Write one sentence each for five of the words.

1. a d v a n t a g e — There are many advantages to this location.
2. c___m p___t___t___v___
3. v___l___m___
4. ___c___n___m___c
5. p r___s s___r___
6. ___n v___r___n m___n t___l
7. r___j___c t
8. d___m___n s t r___t___

B Using collocations

In this course, you have learnt to put verbs and nouns together.
Match each verb with a noun or noun phrase. Write one sentence each for five of the verb + noun collocations.

1. apply _____ a survey
2. make _____ an idea
3. do _____ data
4. record __1__ to a university — I applied to university to study Engineering.
5. convert _____ skills
6. conduct _____ a hypothesis
7. support _____ an experiment
8. improve _____ the results

C Using fixed phrases

In this course, you have learnt to use a large number of fixed phrases.
Complete each sentence or phrase with something suitable.

1. I am particularly interested in _working with children_.
2. After leaving university, I would like _____.
3. According to research at Manchester University, _____.
4. In this study, we look at _____.
5. As we can see from Table 1, _____.
6. There are several disadvantages to _____.
7. In some countries, _____.
8. Some people believe that _____.
9. At one time, _____.
10. Nowadays, _____.

5.19 Grammar review (4)   Present and past tenses; modifying nouns

A   Reviewing verbs

Write the past tense and past participle of each verb.

	infinitive	past	past participle
1.	begin	began	begun
2.	come		
3.	do		
4.	eat		
5.	find		
6.	give		
7.	go		

	infinitive	past	past participle
8.	hide		
9.	know		
10.	let		
11.	lose		
12.	make		
13.	put		
14.	take		

B   Modifying nouns and joining sentences

1. Study each set of sentences below. Modify the nouns with information from the box beside each set.

2. Rewrite each set of sentences as one sentence.

a. Humans hunted animals.
    Humans gathered fruit.

> early   from trees
> for food

b. They developed tools.
    They found roots.

> like   for digging
> under the ground   potatoes

c. They planted crops.
    They kept animals.

> like   wheat   cows
> rice   sheep   like

C   Group dictation

You are going to write a text about the history of the human diet.

Work in groups of six. Each person will receive one paragraph from the text (page 169). You must not show your paragraph to the other people in the group.

1. Read out your paragraph. As a group, decide the order of the paragraphs.

2. Read each paragraph in order. The rest of the group write the paragraph.

A   Reviewing vocabulary

There is one mistake in each sentence. Find it and correct it.

1. Scientists say that societies must change their lifestyles if
    they want *to* ⋏ reduce obesity.

2. This study is examining attitudes to meals in different societies.

3. It also looks at the types of food which consumed.

4. The attitude to meals in a society is for health very important.

5. Many people in the USA and Britain not have meals at regular times.

6. In the past, there was fixed times for meals.

7. Nowadays, many people do not stop actually to eat.

8. At a time, people in the USA and Britain used fresh ingredients.

9. But nowadays, most people buy the processed foods.

10. Many people consume large amounts of sugary drinks, as cola or lemonade.

B   Thinking and organizing

You are going to write about obesity in Italy.

1. Study the diagram. Predict the notes for each sub-category.
2. Work in groups of three. Read your research notes (page 170). Work with the other members of your group to complete the diagram.

Obesity in Italy
8.5% (OECD 2005) / rising

attitude to meals

times   length   snacks

type and quantity

food   drink   quantity

trends

past   present

C   Writing

Write the essay. Remember to:

- use the correct tense: present, past or future.
- use the correct form: active or passive.
- modify nouns.
- join sentences with *and*, *but*, *because*, *so.*

D   Editing and rewriting

1. Exchange essays with a partner. Read his/her essay. Mark the essay with *?*, *S*, *G* and *P*.
2. Read your essay again. Correct the mistakes and rewrite it.

1   2   3   4   5   6

A   Activating ideas

Look at the photographs of fast food.

1. How many items can you name?
2. Which food above has the most calories?
3. Do you like fast food? Why (not)?

B   Gathering information (1)

Work in two groups, A and B.

Read the menu from *Presto Pizza* or *Bob's Burger Bar* on pages 164–165.

1. Check the dishes on your menu. Check the meaning and pronunciation of new words.
2. One person is the waiter/waitress. The rest are customers. The waiter/waitress must take the orders from the rest of the group, then choose his/her own meals.
3. Work out the most popular and the least popular food with your group.

C   Gathering information (2)

1. Check the nutritional analysis on page 166 for your meal in Exercise B. Complete Table 1 below.
2. Talk to the people in your group. Which person had the healthiest meal? Explain your answer.
3. Check the recommended daily allowance for each nutrient. What percentage of your daily allowance did you consume with the meal?

Table 1: *Nutritional analysis of a complete meal*

dish	calories	fat	protein	carbohydrate	salt
totals					
percentage of RDA					

D   Doing research

Collect menus from two or three local fast-food restaurants.

Do they give nutritional information on the menu? If so, do a nutritional analysis on one meal from each restaurant. If not, check average values from information on the Internet.

Presto Pizza

Starters/side dishes

Garlic bread

Potato wedges and sour cream

Nachos – tortilla chips covered in cheese, peppers and salsa

Main courses

Margherita – cheese and tomato pizza

Pepperoni – beef pepperoni, cheese and tomato pizza

Spicy – spicy sausage, chillies, onions, cheese and tomato pizza

Vegetarian – onions, black olives, peppers, mushrooms, sweetcorn, cheese and tomato pizza

Desserts

Chocolate cheesecake – served with cream or vanilla ice–cream

Apple pie – served with cream, custard or vanilla ice–cream

Burgers

Beefburger
– beefburger in a burger bun with lettuce, tomatoes, mayonnaise, relish and ketchup

Cheeseburger
– beefburger in a burger bun with melted cheese, lettuce, tomatoes, mayonnaise, relish and ketchup

Chicken burger
– chicken in a burger bun with lettuce, tomatoes, mayonnaise, relish and ketchup

Vegetarian burger
– vegetable burger, melted cheese, lettuce, tomatoes, mayonnaise, relish and ketchup in a burger bun

Other
Chips

Salad

Chicken nuggets

Milkshake – vanilla-flavoured

Bob's Burger Bar

Table 2: *Nutritional analysis of Presto Pizza*

dish	calories	fat (g)	protein (g)	carbohydrate (g)	salt (g)
garlic bread	407	16	10	56	0.4
potato wedges	328	13	4	46	0.6
nachos	434	22	15	42	0.4
margherita pizza	217	8	10	25	2.0
pepperoni pizza	259	12	13	24	2.3
spicy pizza	213	8	10	25	2.3
vegetarian pizza	188	5	7	26	2.0
chocolate cheesecake	440	19	9	60	0.4
apple pie	249	12	2	34	0.4

Table 3: *Nutritional analysis of Bob's Burger Bar*

dish	calories	fat (g)	protein (g)	carbohydrate (g)	salt (g)
beefburger	254	9	13	31	1.0
cheeseburger	299	13	16	31	1.0
chicken burger	537	31	24	40	2.0
vegetarian burger	485	27	10	50	1.0
chips	210	10	3	26	0.6
salad	118	8	8	4	0.2
chicken nuggets	310	13	10	12	2.0
milkshake	570	16	14	89	0.1

Table 4: *Recommended daily allowance (RDA) (in grams)*

nutrient	calories	fat (g)	protein (g)	carbohydrate (g)	salt (g)
RDA	2,000 (F) 2,500 (M)	50–60	50–60	300	6

Note: Nutritional analysis on food often shows **sodium** content. You must multiply this by 2.5 to get the **salt** content.

Resources

Survey of 100 people

1	<10	10–20	21–30	>30	Total
	10	50	15	25	100
2	enter.	news	edu.	mus.	
	40	30	10	20	100

Survey of 50 people

3	bedroom	liv. room	friend's		
	20	15	15		50
4	nothing	studying	music	Internet	
	10	5	15	20	50

Survey of 1,000 people

5	alone	family	1 friend	>1 friend	
	500	250	100	150	1,000
6	up	same	down		
	750	200	50		1,000

A	About 30,000 years ago, humans learnt to control fire. Humans in Africa developed tools for digging and found roots like potatoes under the ground. They made the tools from pieces of wood and stone.
B	In the last 2,000 years, humans have invented methods of preserving food. The invention of food preservation resulted in significant changes in food consumption. The ingredients in your main meal today probably came from many countries.
C	This study investigates the development of food in human history. It describes five stages, from early humans to the present day.
D	According to anthropologists, the diet of humans has passed through five main periods. Two million years ago, early humans were hunter-gatherers. They moved to a place with food. They hunted or gathered the food, then moved on. Early humans ate raw meat and fish, and fruits and seeds from the trees.
E	After about 20,000 years, the cooking pot was invented. Humans also began to use stones to make flour from wheat.
F	About 2,000 years ago, people stopped moving from place to place. Crops like wheat and rice were planted and animals like cows and sheep were farmed.

Theme 1: Writing 1.17

Group B

Origins (1)
• 624 CE – Prophet Muhammad (PBUH) + friends and relatives
• celebrates battle – Jang e Badr – in war between Mecca and Medina

PBUH = peace be upon him

attitude: times	Mealtimes in Italy are very regular. Lunch is the main meal of the day at 1.00 p.m.
attitude: length	Lunch can take up to three hours. Lunch is a family meal because children do not go to school in the afternoon. Shops and small businesses are closed in the afternoon.
attitude: snacks	Italians eat snacks, but the main ones are home-made ice cream and small squares of pizza. They walk to the shops to buy the snacks so they get exercise.
type and quantity: food	Food must be fresh. Most food is from the local area. Italians eat a lot of vegetables and lean meat, like chicken. They do not eat fatty foods at any meal.
type and quantity: drink	Many Italians, even young people, drink water instead of sugary drinks.
type and quantity: quantity	Italians eat a lot of food, but it is mostly vegetables and pasta. They do not eat much meat. They eat fish more than meat.
trends: past	1. People bought food fresh every day. 2. They ate home-cooked food. 3. The Italian diet was healthy.
trends: present	1. Some people, particularly teenagers, buy processed food. 2. Teenagers eat a lot of fast food. 3. Eating habits are changing, particularly the habits of young people.

Theme 1: Writing 1.17

Group C

Origins (2)
- 624 CE Prophet Muhammad (PBUH) + friends / relatives
- celebrates end of holy month of Ramadan
- Holy Koran revealed to Prophet (PBUH) in Ramadan

PBUH = peace be upon him

Theme 1: Speaking 1.10

Group B

Holi

Holi is the Festival of Colours. It is a Hindu festival, and it is about 4,000 years old. It began in India originally. Holi usually lasts for two days, and it celebrates the start of spring each year.

On the first day there is a bonfire, which is a symbol of the death of the evil spirit Holika. There is traditional music, Holi songs and dancing.

On the second day, it's best to wear your old clothes. There is a ritual of throwing coloured water and powder at everybody in the street. It continues all day. By the end of the day, you are covered in all the colours of the rainbow.

Theme 5: Speaking 5.6

Food quiz
Marking guide

Give your partner points for each answer as follows:

a = 5 points
b = 3 points
c = 1 point

Add up the score for each section.

What do the scores mean?

You need a low score for Section A.

A score below 10 is very good. If you get a score of 20 or more, you need to reduce the amount of sugar and fat in your diet.

You need a high score for Section B. A score of 20 or over is very good. If you get a score of 10 or less, you need to increase the amount of bread, cereals, potatoes, fruit and vegetables in your diet.

Overall, your score in A must be *lower* than your score in B.

Theme 1: Writing 1.17

Group A

Introduction
- celebrated in Muslim countries throughout the world
- name = 'breaking of fast'
- at end of Ramadan
- Muslims fast during Ramadan — sunrise to sunset
- 3 days

Theme 1: Speaking 1.10

Group A

San Fermin

From 6th to 14th July in the northwest of Spain, the festival of Saint Fermin is celebrated. It is for all the people of the region. Saint Fermin is their guide and protector. It began in about the 13th century. The original event was a market every September. It was moved to July in about 1591. The main event of the week is a procession through the streets with a huge statue of the saint. Every day, there is music and dancing. There is also a race between the local young men and six bulls. The men dress in red and white.

Theme 2: Speaking 2.10

Group B

Invention	the motorcar
Date	1885
Inventor	Karl Benz
Nationality	German
Born	1844
Facts	called his first car a 'motor carriage'; produced and sold the cars himself; continued to work in his own company until 1903, when he retired
Died	1929

A	Rugby union is a team game. It is played by two teams of 15 players. The players mainly use their hands, but all the players can use their feet, too.
B	Matches take place on a pitch which must measure 100 metres long by 70 metres wide. There must be goals at each end. Each goalpost must be at least seven metres high. The posts must be 5.6 metres apart. There must be a bar across the goal at three metres.
C	A rugby match lasts 80 minutes. It is divided into two halves of 40 minutes each.
D	Each side tries to score by putting the ball down behind the other team's goal. This is called a try, which is worth three points. A team can also score points by kicking the ball between the opponents' goalposts.
E	There are two types of player. The *forwards* try to get the ball. The *backs* take the ball from the forwards and try to score points.
F	Firstly, rugby is very good exercise. Secondly, it helps with hand and eye co-ordination. Thirdly, it teaches children to play a role in a team. Players should not try to score on their own. They should work with other players to get into good positions. Fourthly, children of different shapes and sizes can participate. Forwards are often large and strong. Backs are often small and fast. Finally, it helps to teach children about winning and losing.

Theme 2: Speaking 2.10

Group A

Invention	the helicopter
Date	1939
Inventor	Igor Sikorsky
Nationality	Russian, but worked in America for a large part of his life
Born	1889
Facts	began work on helicopters in 1910; started his own company in 1923; from 1925 to 1939, built flying boats (planes that could land on water)
Died	1972

Theme 1: Writing 1.17

Group D

Eid al-Fitr today
- before:
  - decorate houses
  - special food, e.g., Malaysia = cake 'ketupat'
- on day ...
  - up v. early
  - new clothes
  - pray – special place
  - special prayers
  - home – breakfast
  - money to children, e.g., Malaysia = new coins in coloured envelopes

🎵 1.1

Presenter: **1.1. Theme 1: Culture and civilization**
Lesson 1.1. Vocabulary for listening: Coming of age

Exercise B1. Listen to a talk about births, marriages and deaths, and check your ideas.

Lecturer: People who study *modern* society are called sociologists. But people who study *primitive* societies, or societies in the past, are called anthropologists. According to anthropologists, all societies past and present have celebrated the happy things in life, like births and marriages, with special events. All societies have remembered the sad things in life, like deaths. These events are called rituals. The events have procedures and people follow them exactly.

What are the origins of rituals? Anthropologists say that rituals are a way of talking to God (or the gods). People come together to celebrate or remember something. For example, there are harvest festivals at the end of the summer in many countries. They thank God for the harvest. They want God to send the sun and the rain. Then they will have a good harvest the next year, too.

Are traditional festivals dying in your country? In the past, parents taught their children about the procedures. They were passed down from one generation to the next. But nowadays, modern societies in some countries are losing the rituals of the past.

🎵 1.2

Presenter: **1.2. Lesson 1.2. Real-time listening: *Seijin no hi***

Exercise C1. Listen to the talk once. Juri pauses a few times during her talk. Guess the next word on each occasion.

Juri: I'm going to talk to you today about a festival in [PAUSE]. The festival is called *Seijin no hi*, which is spelt S-E-I-J-I-N, N-O, H-I. The name means 'the coming of age festival'. It is a very old [PAUSE]. It started at least 800 years [PAUSE].

Coming of age is celebrated all around the [PAUSE]. Coming of age means a child becomes an [PAUSE]. In some countries, it is only for boys or only for [PAUSE]. But in Japan, the festival is for boys *and* [PAUSE]. In some countries, children come of age at 18 or 16 or even 14, but in Japan, coming of age happens at 20 years [PAUSE].

The festival takes place on the second Monday of January each [PAUSE]. So all boys and girls who become 20 that year can take part in the *Seijin no hi*.

Coming of age means different things in different [PAUSE]. In some countries, it means you can drive a [PAUSE]. In other countries, it means you can get [PAUSE]. In Japan, it means you can vote … and [PAUSE]!

The day starts with a ceremony in the local town hall. Town halls are local government offices. The ceremony is called *seijin shiki*. First, a government official makes a [PAUSE]. Then he gives each boy and girl a small [PAUSE].

Before going to the [PAUSE], the girls put on traditional dresses called kimonos. The word is spelt K-I-M-O-N-O. They usually rent the kimonos because these special dresses can cost as much as a [PAUSE]. The boys used to wear dark kimonos too, but now most of them wear business [PAUSE].

After attending the ceremony, the new adults go to special [PAUSE]. Finally, the young people go [PAUSE]. It is usually very late at [PAUSE]. They went out in the morning as children. They go home as [PAUSE].

🎵 1.3

Presenter: **1.3. Exercise C2. Listen again and check your ideas.**

Juri: I'm going to talk to you today about a festival in Japan. The festival is called *Seijin no hi*, which is spelt S-E-I-J-I-N, N-O, H-I. The name means 'the coming of age festival'. It is a very old festival. It started at least 800 years ago.

Coming of age is celebrated all around the world. Coming of age means a child becomes an adult. In some countries, it is only for boys or only for girls. But in Japan, the festival is for boys *and* girls. In some countries, children come of age at 18 or 16 or even 14, but in Japan, coming of age happens at 20 years old.

The festival takes place on the second Monday of January each year. So all boys and girls who become 20 that year can take part in the *Seijin no hi*.

Coming of age means different things in different countries. In some countries, it means you can drive a car. In other countries, it means you can get married. In Japan, it means you can vote… and smoke!

The day starts with a ceremony in the local town hall. Town halls are local government offices. The ceremony is called *seijin shiki*. First, a government official makes a speech. Then he gives each boy and girl a small present.

Before going to the ceremony, the girls put on traditional dresses called kimonos. The word is spelt K-I-M-O-N-O. They usually rent the kimonos because these special dresses can cost as much as a car. The boys used to wear dark kimonos too, but now most of them wear business suits. After attending the ceremony, the new adults go to special parties. Finally, the young people go home. It is usually very late at night. They went out in the morning as children. They go home as adults.

🌐 1.4

Presenter: **1.4. Exercise F2. Listen to some sentences. Number the words above in order.**

Voice:
1. I'm going to talk to you today about a festival.
2. An official makes a speech.
3. There is a ceremony at the town hall.
4. Each boy and girl receives a present.
5. Coming of age is when a child becomes an adult.
6. All the young men and women attend.
7. After that, there are special parties.
8. This is a traditional event in Japan.
9. Coming of age is celebrated all around the world.
10. Town halls are local government offices.

🌐 1.5

Presenter: **1.5. Lesson 1.3. Learning new listening skills: Following a sequence of events**

Exercise A2. Listen. Tick the word you hear in each case.

Voice:
1. First of all, I'm going to talk about coming of age in general.
2. People celebrate festivals all over the world.
3. At the start of the ceremony, everyone sings a song.
4. She got a present from her friends.
5. There is always a ritual involved in a festival.
6. We have a big party after the ceremony.
7. Everybody eats a traditional meal.
8. The main event is in the morning.
9. Parents pass rituals on to their children.
10. There is an official dinner in the evening.

🌐 1.6

Presenter: **1.6. Exercise C. Listen and number the events in order.**

Voice 1: Sweet Sixteen is a coming of age ceremony for girls in the United States of America. It is for girls who have reached the age of 16. On the day of the ceremony, first, the girl lights 16 candles. The candles represent 16 important people in her life. Then, she sits in a chair. Her father helps her take off flat shoes and put on shoes with high heels. Next, the father and daughter dance. Finally, everybody watches a video of the girl from babyhood to the present day.

Voice 2: *Goyuje* is a coming of age ceremony for boys in Korea. It is for boys who have reached the age of 20. Before going to the ceremony, the boy visits the grave of one of his ancestors. At the ceremony, the boy changes his clothes three times. After changing his clothes each time, he listens to advice from the guests. After the third time, the guests wish him health, good luck and a long life. Next, the boy drinks from a special cup and bows to the guests. Then, the boy is given a new name. Finally, the boy is congratulated on becoming an adult.

🌐 1.7

Presenter: **1.7. Lesson 1.4. Grammar for listening: Identifying singular and plural; *after* or *before* + gerund**

Exercise A. Listen. Is each subject singular or plural?

Voice:
1. The house is very interesting.
2. The houses are very interesting.
3. The rituals are very strange.
4. The festival is very old.
5. The main event happens in the morning.
6. The parties happen in the evening.
7. The girls sit on the floor.
8. The father dances with his daughter.
9. The mother gives presents to her son.
10. The officials make speeches.
11. The day starts early.
12. The guests watch a video.

🌐 1.8

Presenter: **1.8. Exercise B. Listen. Number the subjects in order. There are extra subjects you do not need.**

Voice:
1. After getting money from the bank, the man goes to the supermarket.
2. Before leaving home, the woman always turns off all the lights.
3. After playing football on Wednesday evening, the boy is very tired.
4. Before going to the ceremony, the girls make special presents.

5. After making speeches, the officials shake hands with the guests.
6. After listening to the speech, the students leave the hall.
7. After checking all the application forms, the manager makes a shortlist.
8. Before attending the interview, the candidates research the company.
9. After interviewing all the candidates, the interviewer chose the best one.
10. After hitting the rain droplets, the light splits into the colours of the rainbow.

🌐 **1.9**

Presenter: **1.9. Lesson 1.5. Applying new listening skills: Quinceañera**

                               Exercise B. Listen to her talk. Make notes of the important points.

Adriana: I'm going to talk to you this morning about a festival in Mexico. It is called *Quinceañera*, spelt Q-U-I-N-C-E-A-N-E-R-A. The name means '15 years'. The festival is for girls and it happens when a girl becomes 15 years old. It is a coming of age celebration.

                               It is a very old ritual. It may come from the Aztecs, people who lived in Mexico 1,000 years ago. In the past in Mexico, parents expected a daughter to get married after she was 15, but today it just means the end of childhood. It means the child has become an adult.

                               The girl usually wears a long pink or a long white dress. She wears flat shoes – in other words, shoes with no heels. She wears these shoes at the beginning of the ceremony but changes them to shoes with high heels during the ceremony. The shoes with high heels are another sign. She is not a child any more. She is a woman.

                               On the girl's 15th birthday, there are several special events.

                               First, the girl's family and friends go to a ceremony. The ceremony is in a church. There are speeches in the church. Then, a number of people walk with the birthday girl. There are 14 couples – one couple for each year of her life.

                               Next, the girl gives a small doll to her younger sister. Once again, this represents the end of childhood. The girl played with dolls. But she is an adult now. She will not play with dolls any more.

                               After that, the girl gets special presents. For example, she gets a tiara for her head. Princesses wear tiaras, so this means she is a princess in the eyes of God. It also means she has lived through childhood.

                               Finally, after attending the ceremony, the guests go to a party in a local hall, or at the home of the girl's parents.

🌐 **1.10**

Presenter: **1.10. Lesson 1.6. Vocabulary for speaking: Birthdays**

                               Exercise A2. Listen and repeat each word.

Voice: ritual, traditional, symbol, modern, event, origin, adult, official, celebrate, death, marriage, light, wear

🌐 **1.11**

Presenter: **1.11. Exercise C1. Listen to four short talks about birthday traditions: presents, parties, candles and cards. Make one or two notes about each topic.**

Voice 1:   In British culture, birthdays are important. People give presents to friends and relatives on their birthday. They often have parties for the lucky person. The presents are covered with colourful paper.

Voice 2:   People often sing a special song for birthdays. The song 'Happy Birthday' was originally written by two sisters in 1893. Today it is sung at all birthday parties.

Voice 3:   Birthday cakes usually have candles on them. There are two original meanings of the candles. They are a symbol of good spirits against evil spirits. They are also a symbol of the time that passes each year.

Voice 4:   In British culture, people send a lot of cards. The average person sends between 30 and 60 cards every year. They are not all for birthdays. They can be to say, for example, *Good luck!* or *Congratulations!*

🌐 **1.12**

Presenter: **1.12. Exercise C2. Listen to some words from the talk. How many syllables are there in each?**

Voice: culture, lucky, relative, birth, evil, originally, birthday, symbol, colourful, card

🔊 **1.13**

Presenter: **1.13. Lesson 1.7. Real-time speaking: Local festivals**

Exercise B2. Listen to the conversation. Complete A's questions.

Voice A: Are there any traditional festivals in your country?
Voice B: Yes, we have one in the summer. It's called *Noc Swietojanska* in Polish. I like it a lot.
Voice A: Sorry? Did you say *Noc*?
Voice B: Yes. It means 'night'. Saint John's Night. We celebrate the longest day of the year, and the shortest night. It's on the 23rd of June.
Voice A: We celebrate that in my country too. What do you do exactly?
Voice B: Well, people dress in colourful traditional clothes. There is music, dancing and fireworks. The young women make wreaths of flowers with candles on them.
Voice A: Sorry? Could you repeat that?
Voice B: If a woman is single, she makes a wreath – a ring of flowers. Then she puts the flowers on a lake or river. When a young man finds it, he falls in love with the girl – that's the tradition.
Voice A: Ah, OK. Do the men give flowers to the girls?
Voice B: No, they don't. In some places they make a fire and jump over it.
Voice A: Why do they do that?
Voice B: Because it shows that they are strong and brave.
Voice A: How do you prepare for the celebration?
Voice B: We make the food during the day, too. The men prepare the music and the lights outside.
Voice A: When does it start?
Voice B: It starts at about 8.00 p.m. We dance and talk and eat. The party continues all night – it doesn't stop until sunrise.
Voice A: Sunrise? Does everybody work the next day?
Voice B: Yes, they do. But they're very tired!

🔊 **1.14**

Presenter: **1.14. Exercise C1. Listen to the conversation again. What do you notice about the intonation of the questions?**

[REPEAT OF SCRIPT FROM 🔊 **1.13**]

🔊 **1.15**

Presenter: **1.15. Everyday English: The right thing to say**

Exercise B1. Listen and match each phrase with one of the conversations.

Presenter: Conversation 1.

Voice A: What's wrong?
Voice B: Oh, I didn't get the job.
Voice A: Bad luck. I'm sorry.
Voice B: Thanks.

Presenter: Conversation 2.

Voice A: Hi, there! Happy birthday!
Voice B: Oh, thanks!
Voice A: And here's a card.
Voice B: That's really nice of you. Thank you!

Presenter: Conversation 3.

Voice A: What's the matter? Has something happened?
Voice B: Yes. My grandmother has died.
Voice A: Oh, I'm so sorry.
Voice B: Thanks. We were really close.

Presenter: Conversation 4.

Voice A: Are you tired?
Voice B: Yes, I am. We've just had a new baby.
Voice A: Congratulations! Is it a girl or boy?
Voice B: A boy.

Presenter: Conversation 5.

Voice A: You look a bit stressed.
Voice B: Yes. I've got an important exam tomorrow.
Voice A: Well, good luck. I'm sure you'll be fine.
Voice B: Thanks. I hope so.

Presenter:	Conversation 6.
Voice A:	I passed my test!
Voice B:	Sorry? Which test?
Voice A:	My driving test.
Voice B:	Well done! That's great!

🔊 1.16

Presenter: **1.16. Lesson 1.8. Learning new speaking skills: Echoing and commenting**

Exercise B3. Listen and check. Say the words.

Voice:
a. club	c. come	e. few	g. rude	i. colour
b. cool	d. two	f. useful	h. run	j. cut

🔊 1.17

Presenter: **1.17. Exercise C2. Listen. Tick the reply you hear.**

Voice A:	My cousin got married last week.
Voice B:	Your cousin? Did you go?

Voice A:	I got a present today.
Voice B:	That is not interesting for me.

Voice A:	I'm taking my exam tomorrow.
Voice B:	Tomorrow? Are you going to pass?

🔊 1.18

Presenter: **1.18. Exercise D1. Listen to some sentences about traditional events.**

Voice:
a. We eat delicious cakes at New Year.
b. It's my birthday next month.
c. In my country, we have spring cleaning.
d. In my country, a married woman wears a ring on her right hand.

🔊 1.19

Presenter: **1.19. Portfolio: Festivals around the world**

Presenter: Exercise B1. Group A: Novruz.

Voice: I'm going to talk to you today about a festival in Turkey. The festival is called Novruz – N-O-V-R-U-Z. As I say, it takes place in Turkey but there are similar festivals in Iran and many other countries including Uzbekistan. The name comes from two Turkish words, *nev* meaning 'new' and *ruz* which means 'day'.

It happens on the 22nd of March every year. It is a very, very old festival. People celebrated the end of winter on this day because, on the 22nd of March, the hours of daytime and night time are equal. From this day on, the days are longer than the nights.

People prepare for the event for many days or even weeks before. They buy new clothes. They clean their houses and their gardens. On the day, people put on their new clothes. Some people travel to high areas of land, mountains and hills. Other people visit the graves of their relatives. Some people fire guns into the air.

People have a special meal for the festival of Novruz. The meal has seven foods and all the foods begin with the letter *S*. There is *samsa*, *seb*, *sümelek*, *sebzi* (or vegetables), *sedena*, *serya* and *süt* (which is milk).

🔊 1.20

Presenter: **1.20. Exercise B1. Group B: Nooruz.**

Voice: I'm going to talk to you today about a festival in Iran. The festival is called Nooruz – N-O-O-R-U-Z. The name comes from two Farsi words, *noo* meaning 'new' and *ruz* which means 'day'.

It starts on the last Wednesday of the month. This is called *Chahar Shanbeh Soori* – that's spelt C-H-A-H-A-R, S-H-A-N-B-E-H, S-O-O-R-I. It means 'Wednesday fire'.

The festival is probably thousands of years old. Some people say a Persian ruler, Jamshid, gave it the name *Nooroz* over 8,000 years ago. It celebrates the start of a new year.

People prepare for the event for many days or even weeks before. They buy new clothes. They clean their houses and their gardens. They build bonfires. Every family brings several piles of wood.

On the day, people put on their new clothes. Singers dress up as a character called Haji Firoz, with black faces and bright red, blue, yellow or purple clothes. They sing and dance and parade through the streets.

Just after sunset, someone lights the bonfire. Everybody jumps over it. Some people believe that the fire takes away illness and gives health. There are fireworks in the country areas. Children go from house to house asking for sweets or money.

People eat seven foods. Firstly, there is vinegar, which is called *serkeh*, then apple which is *seeb*, garlic – *seer*, wild olive – *senjed*, berries – *sumac*, and the juice of germinating wheat which is called *samanu*. Finally, there are vegetables, called *sabzeh*.

🔊 1.21

Presenter: **1.21. Exercise B1. Group C: Seezdah Bedar.**

Voice: I'm going to talk to you today about a festival in Iran. The festival is called Seezdah Bedar. That's S-E-E-Z-D-A-H, B-E-D-A-R. It means 'getting rid of 13'. It happens on the 13th day of the new year. The festival is probably thousands of years old. Some people say it is connected with the 12 signs of the Zodiac. Each sign, they say, will rule the earth for 1,000 years and then the world will end, so 13 is an unlucky number in Iran.

People prepare for the event for many weeks before. They put grains of wheat or barley into a dish to grow the *sabzee*. The grains produce green shoots in time for the new year.

On the day, families get up early in the morning and go to parks, hills and mountains. They have a picnic and play games. At the end of the picnic, the family throws the *sabzee*, or green vegetables, into a stream. These vegetables are supposed to contain all the bad luck of the family for the next year.

In the picnic, they eat sandwiches and special snacks called *ajil*. *Ajil* are nuts, seeds and dried fruit.

🔊 2.1

Presenter: **2.1. Theme 2: Technology**
Lesson 2.1. Vocabulary for listening: Power sources for travel

Exercise B2. Listen and check your ideas.

Lecturer: Hundreds of thousands of years ago, there was only one way to travel from one place to another – walking. The only power source for travel was the human body.

Then, many thousands of years ago, some people started to ride horses. So they used animal power for travel. Around the same time, some people started to use boats. Sometimes they used the power of the wind. They put up a sail. Sometimes they used the power of the human body. They rowed the boat or even the ship.

These power sources – human, animal and wind – were the only sources for travel for thousands of years. Then, in 1765, James Watt invented the steam engine. Ten years later, steam was used to power a ship. In 1825, a man called Stephenson used steam power to move a train along a track. There were even steam cars for a few years.

In the next 150 years, many power sources appeared for travel. There was the petrol engine for cars and planes. There was electricity for trains. In the 20th century, scientists invented the rocket for spacecraft and the jet engine for planes.

🔊 2.2 [DVD] 7.A

Presenter: **2.2. Lesson 2.2. Real-time listening: Transport inventions (1)**

Lecturer: I'm going to talk to you today about inventions – that is, new ways of doing something. All the inventions are in the field, or area, of transport. First, I'm going to talk about different methods or types of transport. After that, I'll tell you when each method was invented. Finally, I'm going to say which invention was the most important, as far as I'm concerned … I mean, in my opinion.

🔊 2.3 [DVD] 7.B

Lecturer: OK. So, first, what are the main methods of transport that we use today? We can, of course, travel on land, on sea and in the air. We use cars and bicycles, trains, small boats and big ships and, of course, planes. OK. So, there are several methods of transport. But when was each method invented?

The first method of transport was, of course, walking. But about 40,000 years ago – yes, that's right, 40,000 – some Indonesian natives made a boat and sailed from one island to another.

For centuries man sailed the seas, using only the power of the wind. Then, in 1775, J. C. Perier – that's P-E-R-I-E-R – invented the steam ship. Steam also powered the first train. In 1830, James Stephenson drove his engine, called the Rocket, along a track and the railway age began. Just nine years later, in 1839, a man called Macmillan invented the bicycle. Fifty years after that, in 1888, Karl Benz – that's B-E-N-Z, invented the motor car. So now man could move quickly on land and on the sea.

Finally, at the beginning of the 20th century, the Wright brothers conquered the air. That's *Wright* with a silent W. On the 17th of December in 1903, they flew their plane, called Flyer, a distance of 1,000 kilometres, and went down in history.

Lecturer:	So we have heard about the main inventions in the field of transport. But which invention was the most important? In my opinion, it was the last invention, the plane. This invention has made the world into a much smaller place. People can travel right to the other side of the world in a day. Why is that important? Because the more we travel, the more we understand other people and other cultures.

🔵 2.5

Presenter:	**2.5. Exercise E2. Listen and check your answers.**
Voice:	because, engine, history, jet, petrol, rocket, that, track, transport, was, went, what, when, which, wind

🔵 2.6

Presenter:	**2.6. Exercise F2. Listen and check your answers.**
Voice:	after, called, concerned, course, each, far, flew, last, more, move, people, source, steam, transport, use, world

🔵 2.7

Presenter:	**2.7. Lesson 2.3. Learning new listening skills: Recognizing change of topic**
	Exercise A. Listen to some sentences. Tick the best way to complete each sentence.
Lecturer:	1. I'm going to talk to you today about … 2. All the inventions are in the field of … 3. We can, of course, travel on … 4. When was each method … 5. Sailing boats use the power of the … 6. In 1830, James Stephenson drove his engine, called the Rocket, along a … 7. In 1903 the Wright brothers conquered the … 8. The plane was the most important invention, in my … 9. The plane has made the world a much smaller … 10. The more we travel, the more we understand other people and other …

🔵 2.8

Presenter:	**2.8. Exercise B1. Listen to the first part of the lecture in Lesson 2.2. What is the lecturer doing in this part?**

[REPEAT OF SCRIPT FROM 🔵 2.2]

🔵 2.9

Presenter:	**2.9. Exercise B3. Listen to the introductions to some more lectures. Organize your notes.**
Presenter:	Introduction 1.
Lecturer 1:	I'm going to talk to you today about festivals. First, I'm going to explain the origins of festivals in general. How does a particular festival start? After that, I'll tell you about some of the most important festivals in the world. Finally, I'm going to say which festivals are good tourist attractions as far as I am concerned … I mean, in my opinion.
Presenter:	Introduction 2.
Lecturer 2:	The topic of today's lecture is Turkey. I'll begin by giving you some basic facts about the country – size, population, etc. Then I'll describe the main natural features of the country. After that, I'll tell you a few things about the modern history of Turkey. Finally, I'll give you some ideas about the future for Turkey.
Presenter:	Introduction 3.
Lecturer 3:	Today we're going to talk about the weather. Firstly, I'll mention briefly the main weather conditions. Then I'll explain how each weather condition comes about – what causes rain, for example, or snow. Next, I'll say a few words about damage which can be caused by weather – floods, landslides, hurricanes. Finally, the big topic: climate change. What is happening to our weather?

🔵 2.10

Presenter:	**2.10. Exercise C1. Read Skills Check 2 and listen to the extracts. What is the lecturer doing in each extract?**
Presenter:	Extract 1.
Lecturer:	So, first, what are the main methods of transport …

Presenter:	Extract 2.
Lecturer:	So, there are several methods of transport. But when …
Presenter:	Extract 3.
Lecturer:	So we've heard about the main inventions in the field of transport. But which invention …
Presenter:	Extract 4.
Lecturer:	In my opinion …

🔊 2.11

Presenter:	**2.11. Exercise C2. Listen to some extracts from the lectures in Exercise B. How does the lecturer signal the change of topic in each case? Number the phrases.**
Lecturer 1 (2.9):	Finally, I'm going to say which festivals are good tourist attractions as far as I am concerned … I mean, in my opinion. So first, how does a festival start?
Lecturer 3 (2.9):	The most destructive weather condition is the hurricane, in general, although of course tsunamis sometimes kill huge numbers of people. So we have heard about natural disasters. Now, climate change …
Lecturer 2 (2.9):	Perhaps the most important recent event is the application by Turkey to join the EU. The other countries are still considering the application. So we have seen some important events in recent history. But what does the future hold for the country?
Lecturer 1 (2.9):	So all festivals begin with an event and modern rituals often remember something about that event. Right, that's origins. What about today? What are the most important festivals in the modern world?
Lecturer 2 (2.9):	As you can see, Turkey is a big country in terms of population and quite big in terms of area. OK, now let's look at the main natural features – mountains, lakes, and so on.

🔊 2.12

Presenter:	**2.12. Exercise C3. Listen and check your ideas.**
Voice:	a. fresh c. relationship e. shuttle g. research i. which
	b. each d. match f. much h. change j. chec<

🔊 2.13

Presenter:	**2.13. Lesson 2.4. Grammar for listening: years and dates**
	Exercise A1. Listen and write the year.
Voice:	1. in 1762 6. in 2010 (twenty ten)
	2. around 1543 7. in 1033
	3. in 2004 (two thousand and four) 8. in 1914
	4. around 1691 9. in 1940
	5. in 1938 10. in 1802 (eighteen hundred and two)

🔊 2.14

Presenter:	**2.14. Exercise A2. Listen and write the date.**
Voice:	1. on the first of February
	2. on the tenth of December
	3. on May sixteenth
	4. on November the ninth
	5. on October the thirty-first
	6. on the seventh of September
	7. on the nineteenth of August
	8. on June eleventh
	9. on July the second
	10. on January the thirteenth

🔊 2.15

Presenter:	**2.15. Exercise A3. Listen and complete Table 1 below.**
Lecturer:	The first carts with wheels appeared around 3500 BCE. Around 2000 BCE, horses were used for the first time for transportation. The first horse-drawn bus appeared in 1662. More than 100 years later, in 1769, the first steam-powered car was built. Fourteen years later, the Montgolfiere brothers took off in the first hot-air balloon. In 1862 the first petrol engine car appeared – before that, cars used steam. Five years later, the first motorcycle was built.

The first powered flight took place on the 17ᵗʰ of December 1903. Planes developed very quickly and on the 14ᵗʰ of October 1947, a jet plane flew faster than the speed of sound. But perhaps the greatest advance in the history of transport was the landing on the Moon. On the 21ˢᵗ of July 1969, the first man stepped from his spacecraft onto the surface of another object in our Solar System.

🔊 2.16 [DVD] 7.D

Presenter: **2.16. Lesson 2.5. Applying new listening skills: Transport inventions (2)**

Lecturer: I'm going to talk to you today about inventions. All the inventions are in the field of flying ... First, I'm going to talk about different methods of flying. After that, I'll tell you when each method was invented and who invented it. Finally, I'm going to say which invention was the most important, in my opinion.

OK. So, first, what are the main methods of flying that we use today? There is the plane itself, then the jet plane, which is much faster. For transporting large numbers of people, there is the jumbo jet.

The jumbo jet can carry more than 500 people. A very different kind of flying machine is the helicopter. It can go straight up and straight down. It can even stay in one place. Finally, there is the rocket, which takes astronauts into space. And of course, the Space Shuttle, which takes them up into space and brings them back.

OK. So, there are several methods of flying. But when was each method invented? And who invented it? The Wright brothers flew the first plane with an engine in 1903. The plane had two propellers – pieces of wood which turn to pull the plane through the air. For nearly 30 years the propeller plane was the only type, but in 1930, Whittle – spelt W-H-I-T-T-L-E – invented the jet engine. *Jet* means a very fast stream of something – in this case, air. Jet planes can go much faster than propeller planes. In 1970, the American aircraft company, Boeing – that's B-O-E-I-N-G – invented the jumbo jet. *Jumbo* means 'very big'.

Sixty years earlier, in around 1910, Sikorsky started work on a helicopter but it did not fly until 1939. So the next development was in 1926. Robert Goddard invented the rocket but it was not until 1961 that Russian scientists sent a man into space on a rocket. Finally, in 1976, NASA, which is the American Space Administration, invented a plane which could go into space and return to Earth. They called it the Space Shuttle because a shuttle is something which goes to a place and comes back. On April 12, 1981, the first Space Shuttle took off from Florida in the United States.

So we have heard about the main inventions in the field of flying. But which invention was the most important? In my opinion, it was the last invention, the Space Shuttle. This invention has helped us to reach out into space. From space we see the world as it really is – a small ball, which we must look after.

🔊 2.17

Presenter: **2.17. Lesson 2.6. Vocabulary for speaking: Automobile inventions**

     Exercise B1. Listen to a text about female inventors. Match each invention from the box to the photograph of the inventor above.

Lecturer: Is the field of automobile technology a man's world? Some people think that it is. But in fact many materials and parts of vehicles were invented by women. The inventions helped to make transport safer and faster. For example, windscreen wipers were invented by Mary Anderson. Your sports car is probably made from Kevlar. It is a very hard, very light industrial material. Stephanie Kwolek invented the product. Giuliana Tesoro produced fire-resistant materials. They have improved the safety of your car in an accident. A female computer scientist, Grace Hopper, changed the way computer programs work. Her invention led to much smaller computers. Every car now has a computer to control the engine and the brakes. The computer can even tell you if you are going to run out of petrol.

🔊 2.18

Presenter: **2.18. Lesson 2.7. Real-time speaking: Over a billion in the world**

     Exercise B2. Listen and complete the missing numbers and dates in the website.

Voice A: Look at this.
Voice B: What are you doing?
Voice A: I'm reading about transport inventions.
Voice B: Oh, you're doing research for the next lecture.
Voice A: Did you know there are over a billion bicycles in the world?
Voice B: Only a million?
Voice A: No, one billion, apparently. It says here that it was invented in the 19ᵗʰ century by Kirkpatrick Macmillan and now there are a billion.
Voice B: When was it invented?
Voice A: In 1893 … Wow!
Voice B: What?
Voice A: According to this, the speed record for a bicycle is 268 kilometres an hour. It was set in 1995. Apparently, he was riding behind a car.
Voice B: Amazing.
Voice A: But it seems that Leonardo da Vinci actually drew a picture of a bicycle more than 300 years earlier.
Voice B: Pardon? Who drew a bicycle?
Voice A: Da Vinci. D-A and V-I-N-C-I. The famous Italian painter and inventor drew a bicycle.

Voice B:	No he didn't! I read about that. Apparently someone else drew the bicycle in Leonardo's notebook in 1970.
Voice A:	Are you sure? But it says here that he did it.
Voice B:	Maybe – but you shouldn't believe everything you read on the Internet.

🔊 **2.19**

Presenter: **2.19. Exercise C2. Listen again and check.**

[REPEAT OF SCRIPT FROM 🔊 **2.18**]

🔊 **2.20**

Presenter: **2.20. Everyday English: Using technology**

Exercise B2. Listen and check.

Presenter: Conversation 1.

Voice A:	I can't get the washing machine to work.
Voice B:	Put in the powder.
Voice A:	I've done that.
Voice B:	OK. Pull this thing out. Put the coins in here. Push it in. Switch it on.

Presenter: Conversation 2.

Voice A:	How do you set the time?
Voice B:	Press the 'Menu' button and go to 'Settings'.
Voice A:	OK, and then I choose 'Date and time'?
Voice B:	That's right. We're an hour behind Berlin.

Presenter: Conversation 3.

Voice A:	How does this thing work?
Voice B:	Follow the instructions on the screen.
Voice A:	'Insert coins.' OK. 'Press Button A.'
Voice B:	When the light flashes, it takes a picture.

Presenter: Conversation 4.

Voice A:	The photocopier is broken.
Voice B:	No, it isn't. It's run out of paper.
Voice A:	How do you put more paper in?
Voice B:	It says here: 'Open cover. Insert paper. Replace cover.'

Presenter: Conversation 5.

Voice A:	Have you ever used the SPSS program?
Voice B:	Yes, I have. But I'm not very good at it.
Voice A:	Do you know how to input new data?
Voice B:	Click on 'Data view'.

Presenter: Conversation 6.

Voice A:	Do you know how to use the book checkout?
Voice B:	Just put the book on the scanner.
Voice A:	But it won't read my library card.
Voice B:	Let's ask for help.

🔊 **2.21**

Presenter: **2.21. Lesson 2.8. Learning new speaking skills: Talking about research**

Exercise A3. Listen. Say the words you hear.

Voice: sure, should, picture, switch, research, choose, inventicns, push, information

2.22

Presenter: **2.22. Exercise B1. Listen and complete the sentences.**

Voice:
  a. It seems that humans can never travel to other stars.
  b. Apparently, people from Asia sailed across the Pacific 600 years ago.
  c. It says here that the motorcycle was invented in 1885.
  d. According to this, the first cars were always black.
  e. Did you know that the scientific name for a horse is *equus caballus*?
  f. It seems that bamboo sometimes grows a metre a day.

2.23

Presenter: **2.23. Lesson 2.9. Grammar for speaking: Checking questions**

  Exercise A2. Listen and check.

Voice A: The French Revolution was in 1789.
Voice B: When was the French Revolution?

Voice A: The Incas built a city on a 2,000-metre mountain.
Voice B: Who built a city on a mountain?

Voice A: Apparently, penicillin comes from a fungus.
Voice B: Pardon? Where does it come from?

Voice A: It seems Henry the Eighth had six wives.
Voice B: Pardon? How many wives did he have?

Voice A: It says here that too much water makes you ill.
Voice B: Sorry? What makes you ill?

Voice A: Some animals sleep in winter to save energy.
Voice B: Sorry? Why do they sleep in winter?

2.24

Presenter: **2.24. Lesson 2.10. Applying new speaking skills: The helicopter and the motorcar**

  Exercise A2. Listen. Then practise saying these sentences.

Voice:
  a. Which cheese did she choose?
  b. You wash the dishes. I'll watch TV.
  c. Is that a chip shop?
  d. Was the ship near the shore?

2.25

Presenter: **2.25. Portfolio: Great transport inventions**

Presenter: **Exercise B1. Group A.**

Lecturer: I'm going to talk to you today about an invention in the field of transport. Firstly, I'm going to talk about the invention. After that, I'll tell you a little about the inventor. Finally, I'll talk about the uses of the invention. The invention is important for both transport and safety.

  OK. So first, what is the invention? It's called kevlar, that's K-E-V-L-A-R. It is a very strong material. In fact, it is five times stronger than steel.

  The inventor was an American woman called Stephanie Kwolek. That's K-W-O-L-E-K. She was born in 1923 in Pennsylvania in the USA. She studied Chemistry at university then she went to work for the chemical industry in New York. Her company wanted to improve the strength of car tyres. If a car tyre explodes at high speed, it is very dangerous.

  Kwolek succeeded in making the new material in 1965. She made it from petroleum. Kevlar was used to make tyres safer but people realized it had many other uses. It is used in sails, ropes and equipment, including parts for space rockets. However, Kevlar is now famous for stopping bullets and fighting fires! Police officers in many countries wear Kevlar bullet-proof vests. Fire officers wear Kevlar heat-proof suits. Kwolek retired in 1986 but she is still a consultant. She has won many awards for her work and inventions in chemistry.

🔊 2.26

Lecturer:　I'm going to talk to you today about an invention in the field of transport. Firstly, I'm going to talk about the invention. After that, I'll tell you a little about the inventor. Finally, I'll talk about the uses of the invention. The invention is important for both transport and safety.

OK. So first, what is the invention? It's the car windscreen made of non-reflecting glass. What does that mean? Well, the windscreen, of course, is the piece of glass in a car which the driver looks through. Glass normally reflects or sends back eight to ten per cent of the light that shines on it. But with Blodgett's glass, all the light passes straight through. This, of course, means that you can see more clearly through the glass.

The inventor of non-reflecting glass was an American woman called Katherine Blodgett, that's B-L-O-D-G-E-T-T. She was born in 1898 in New York State. She obtained a master's degree in Physics from the University of Chicago. She was only 19 years of age. She joined General Electric Company in 1917. She was its first female scientist. She left for some time to continue her studies. She became the first woman to get a PhD in Physics from Cambridge University, England, in 1926.

Blodgett then returned to General Electric Company. She worked for many years in the research laboratory. Then, in 1938, she found a way to make very thin layers of glass which did not reflect light at all. Blodgett's glass is used in all kinds of devices, including cameras, microscopes and computer screens.

Blodgett received many awards for her work. She retired in 1963 and died in 1979 in the town where she was born.

🔊 2.27

Presenter:　**2.27. Exercise B1. Group C.**

Lecturer:　I'm going to talk to you today about an invention in the field of transport. Firstly, I'm going to talk about the invention. After that, I'll tell you a little about the inventor. Finally, I'll talk about the uses of the invention.

OK. So first, what is the invention? It's the train ventilator. A ventilator is something that brings fresh air into a closed space. This invention made travelling by train much more enjoyable.

The inventor was an American woman called Olive Dennis. That's D-E-N-N-I-S. She was born in 1885 or 1895. She obtained master's degrees in Mathematics and Astronomy from Columbia University. She was only the second woman to obtain a degree in Civil Engineering from Cornell University. She found it difficult to find a job as an engineer. So she started work as a draughtsman for a train company in 1920. In 1921, she became the first female engineer for the company. She worked as a research scientist for the company for the next 30 years.

🔊 3.1

Presenter:　**3.1. Theme 3: Arts and media**
Lesson 3.1. Vocabulary for listening: The mass media

Exercise B2. Listen and check.

Lecturer:　Nowadays there are many information organizations. For example, we have television, radio, newspapers and, of course, the Internet. They all provide news and information to the general public. The word for all of these organizations is *media*. It is an unusual word because it is a plural. The singular word is *medium*. This word has different meanings in everyday English. But here it means 'a way of communicating'. For example, we can say 'The Internet is the most important medium today.'

We often talk about the *mass media*. The word *mass* means 'a large amount'. So we use the phrase for media that reaches a large number of people.

The mass media have a lot of influence on the general public. This is because modern technology can give the news very fast to millions of people. So the media have a very big influence. In television and radio, we say information is broadcast to viewers and listeners. This means it is transmitted over a very wide area, perhaps over the whole world at the same time. People in many different countries often watch the same breaking news events live on television, for example.

🔊 3.2

Presenter:　**3.2. Exercise C1. Listen. Make notes about each event.**

Lecturer:　In 1815, there was an important battle between the British and French armies at a place in Belgium called Waterloo. As a matter of fact, the small town is only about 400 kilometres from London. The battle took place on the 18th of June. However, the general public in London did not know the result of the battle for four days. Why did it take so long for the news to reach London? Firstly, because there were no reporters at the scene. Secondly, because all messages had to go slowly overland. There was no method to broadcast the news from Belgium to London.

Two hundred years later, on the 11th of September 2001, there was a major news event in New York City. The World Trade Center was attacked by terrorists. Reporters were at the scene in a few minutes. The news of the event was broadcast around the world, so hundreds of millions of people watched the breaking news live on television.

🎧 3.3

Presenter: **3.3. Lesson 3.2. Real-time listening: The early history of mass-media news**

Exercise A2. Listen and check your ideas.

Voice: Picture A: A Roman man is making an official announcement to the crowd.
Picture B: This is a very early newspaper.
Picture C: This is an example of early printing from China.
Picture D: This is an early machine for printing.
Picture E: This is one of the first newspapers in the world.
Picture F: This is one of the very first newspaper advertisements.
Picture G: The people are listening to a story from a newspaper, because some of them cannot read.
Picture H: This is a range of print media from the present day.

🎧 3.4 [DVD] 8.A

Lecturer: Today I'm going to talk about the early history of the mass media for news. I'm not going to talk about the complete history today – just the early history. And I'm not going to talk about the mass media for entertainment, just the mass media for news. We'll talk about the mass media for entertainment another day. First, I'll talk about spoken news. Then, I'll tell you about written news in Ancient Rome and Ancient China. Next, I'll describe the start of printing and the development of daily newspapers. Finally, I'll set you an assignment.

🎧 3.5 [DVD] 8.B

Lecturer: For many thousands of years in human history, there was no mass media for news because ancient people didn't have written language. Gradually, ancient people developed written language. But most people were not literate – they could not read or write their own language. People communicated news in speech. For example, in England, there were town criers. These people shouted the news in the streets. But news was not communicated to all the people in a particular area at the same time – for example, everybody in one town or city – because all communication was in speech. There was no method of transmitting speech to a large number of people. Transmission of speech to a mass audience started with the invention of the radio in the late 19ᵗʰ century.

So, there was no written news for thousands of years. Then around 60 BCE, the first written news appeared. It was called *Acta Diurna*, which means 'daily acts' or 'events'. It was not printed, it was handwritten. It appeared each day on message boards in the squares of Ancient Rome. However, as I said, most people could not read. Therefore this was not really mass media. Someone had to read the news to individuals or groups of people. At around the same time, there were daily reports in Ancient China called *Pao*. But these reports were for government officials. They were not for the general public.

So how did the mass media for news really start? In around 900 CE, the first real printing appeared. It was invented in China. There was one wooden block for each character. The printer could move these around to make text. However, the process was very slow so printing was very expensive. Then, in 1446 a German, Gutenberg, invented the first printing press. This was really the start of the mass media for news. The printing machine produced text quickly and cheaply. So the printer could make hundreds or even thousands of copies and distribute them all over the town, the area, or even the country. In 1450, book distribution was very small. There were only a few thousand books in Europe. All of them were produced by hand. By 1500, there were more than nine million books. The general public wanted to read the books. So they started to learn to read. Printing led to literacy in the general public, and literacy led to the first daily newspapers at the start of the 17ᵗʰ century.

In 1477, a tiny event occurred. However, it is very important in the history of the mass media. An Englishman, William Caxton, produced the first book with advertisements. Why is this so important? Because the mass media and advertising are very closely linked.

OK. We have heard that the mass media really began in the 15th century and newspapers in the 17ᵗʰ century. We have seen that literacy for the general public also started around then. But we have also noted that, almost from the first, there was a link between the mass media for news and advertising. What are the links today? That is your assignment. Think about the different kinds of mass media for news today. Just news, for the moment. What is the link with advertising? By the way, I'm not just thinking about advertising products and services. I'm thinking about advertising ideas and opinions as well.

🎧 3.6

Presenter: **3.6. Exercise D1. Listen to some sentences. Number the words below in order.**

Voice: 1. When did the mass media for news begin?
2. I'm going to talk about the early history of the subject.
3. At first, people could only communicate in speech.
4. So communication of the news was still through speech.
5. There was no method of transmitting speech over large distances.
6. The first newspaper appeared in Ancient Rome.
7. But most of the general public couldn't read.
8. The Gutenberg printing machine made the process much faster.
9. Newspapers were very widely distributed.
10. The ability to read is called *literacy*.

3.7

Presenter: **3.7. Lesson 3.3. Learning new listening skills: Predicting content from linking words**

Exercise A. Listen to some sentences. Tick the word you hear.

Voice:
1. I will define the word *media*.
2. I am going to talk about the news media.
3. *Medium* has two main meanings.
4. A medium is a way of communicating, too.
5. The mass media gets to or reaches a large number of people.
6. People communicated in pairs or small groups or even in large crowds.
7. In around 900 CE, the first printing appeared.
8. The *Acta Diurna* appeared on message boards.
9. However, most people could not read.
10. Therefore this was not really mass media.

3.8

Presenter: **3.8. Exercise C. Listen to some extracts from a lecture. Predict the next part from the linking word.**

Voice:
1. There are advertisements during most mass-media news programmes because … [PAUSE] the mass-media companies do not make money from the news itself.
2. In fact, … [PAUSE] one minute of TV news could cost the company $20,000.
3. Most mass-media news companies buy the pictures from other companies but … [PAUSE] they add the sound.
4. They pay a person to talk over the pictures. In addition, … [PAUSE] they employ people to link the news items.
5. It is very expensive to produce news programmes, so … [PAUSE] mass-media news companies are very big.

3.9

Presenter: **3.9. Lesson 3.4. Grammar for listening: Word-building: verbs into nouns**

Exercise A. Listen to some sentences. Each sentence contains one of each pair of words on the right. Do you hear the noun or the verb in each case?

Voice:
1. The festival is celebrated in August.
2. When you combine all the colours of the rainbow, white light appears.
3. The competition is won by the strongest man.
4. Man has always wanted to explore space.
5. It is very important to motivate people to do a good job.
6. At first, the Wright brothers made bicycles but later they changed to the production of planes.
7. You must get a person who is qualified for a job.
8. In this lecture, I'm going to talk about the natural features of the country. After this description, I will tell you a little about the history.
9. Everyone in the town participates in the festival.
10. The careful preparations of the Wright brothers helped them to succeed.

3.10

Presenter: **3.10. Exercise B. Listen to a sentence. Try to hear the important verb. Which noun do you expect the speaker to use later in the text? Say the noun.**

Voice:
1. In this talk, I'm going to tell you how to apply to university.
2. It is very important to organize your files logically.
3. You must attend every lecture.
4. During the experiment, we measured the distance for each container.
5. Marconi found a way to transmit speech over long distances.
6. First, I'm going to explain the rules.
7. You must choose the best place to advertise.
8. The country is situated in northern Europe.
9. The selection panel decides the best candidate.
10. Extroverts sometimes behave in a rude way.

3.11

Presenter: **3.11. Lesson 3.5. Applying new listening skills: Advantages and disadvantages of mass-media news**

Exercise A. Listen to each sound. It is the stressed syllable of a word connected with the mass media. Can you identify the word?

Voice:

a. me	c. chan	e. miss	g. vert	i. ven
b. tel	d. me	f. mun	h. port	j. news

🔊 3.12

Presenter: **3.12. Exercise A2. Listen and check your ideas.**

Voice:

a. media	c. channel	e. transmission	g. advertisement	i. event
b. television	d. message	f. communicate	h. report	j. newspaper

🔊 3.13 DVD 8.C

Presenter: **3.13. Lesson 3.6. Vocabulary for speaking: stereotypes.**

Lecturer: In the last lecture, we looked at the origins of mass-media news. As I said, at one time, there was no mass-media news, because people couldn't read, and because there was no transmission of speech. Nowadays, news is all around us all of the time. Is this a good thing or a bad thing? What are the advantages and disadvantages of mass-media news?

Let's look first at some advantages. There are many advantages but I'm only going to talk about three. Firstly, mass-media news reaches people very quickly because there are reporters in every country. In addition, we have very fast communications nowadays. People often watch a news event as it happens. There is even a special phrase for this. It is called 'breaking news'.

So that is one advantage: speed. Secondly, it is very cheap to receive television and radio programmes nowadays so mass-media news is very cheap. In fact, the consumer – the television viewer – does not pay for news directly at all. Advertising pays for the news.

So we have speed and cost. Finally, it is very difficult now for governments or people to hide anything. At one time, governments or people in public life could keep secrets. But nowadays mass-media reporters find out secrets and broadcast them to the world. The general public needs to know about these secrets in many cases.

What about the disadvantages? Well, once again, there are many disadvantages but I am only going to mention three. Firstly, mass-media news needs stories all the time. Some TV news channels are on 24 hours a day so they need new stories all the time. Perhaps some of these stories are not really news. Perhaps the general public don't need to know some of the stories.
So that is one disadvantage: quantity. Perhaps there is too much news nowadays. Secondly, mass-media news is cheap for the consumer but it is expensive for the mass-media company. As I mentioned in the last lecture, one minute of news can cost $20,000. So the news company has to sell advertising during the news broadcasts. Perhaps the advertisers influence the news companies in their choice of story.

OK, that's quantity and bias. Are some news companies biased because they take money from particular advertisers? Finally, nobody can keep a secret any more because there are reporters everywhere. But some secrets are good, aren't they? People need privacy sometimes, don't they? People need to be private, at home, with their children. Perhaps the mass-media news programmes tell us things which we don't need to know, about celebrities and even about ordinary people.

🔊 3.14

Presenter: **3.14. Exercise B1. Listen. Complete each conversation with a word from the list on the right. Make any necessary changes.**

Presenter: Conversation 1.

Voice A: What's a feature?
Voice B: It's the main article in a magazine.

Presenter: Conversation 2.

Voice A: What's the difference between *ad* and *advert*?
Voice B: There's no difference. They're both short for *advertisement*.

Presenter: Conversation 3.

Voice A: Does *audience* mean the people at a concert?
Voice B: Yes. And it means the people who see an advertisement.

Presenter: Conversation 4.

Voice A: Do you spell *generalize* with ~*ise* or ~*ize* at the end?
Voice B: You can use either. The pronunciation is the same.

🔊 3.15 DVD 8.D

Tutor: OK. What is a stereotype? The word means 'a typical member of a community'. Men are a community in this sense, and so are women. Foreigners in general are a community, and people from particular countries. Workers in particular industries belong to a community, too.

Stereotypes can help us to understand each other quickly. We use words or phrases to activate memories.

But we must be careful. If I say, 'My cousin is a construction worker,' you quickly form an impression of the person. You have a stereotypical construction worker in your mind. But the impression may be wrong. My cousin, the construction worker, is a woman. Does this fit the stereotype?

Stereotypes are a kind of generalization. Perhaps many people in a community fit the stereotype, but some don't. Stereotypes are useful, but they don't represent reality. Many stereotypes are negative generalizations. For example, 'All women are housewives. All teenagers are rude. All elderly people have bad memories.' Stereotypes of people from different races or religions can be particularly dangerous. As you can see, the issue is important, and difficult. So we need to use stereotypes with caution, and work hard not to use negative stereotypes.

🕐 3.16

Presenter:	**3.16. Lesson 3.7. Real-time speaking: Magazine advertisements.** **Exercise B2. Listen and check your ideas.**
Voice A:	Where do you think the first advert is from?
Voice B:	I think it comes from a women's magazine.
Voice A:	And who is the target audience?
Voice B:	Young women.
Voice C:	I agree. Maybe older women, too.
Voice A:	What is the purpose of the ad?
Voice C:	To sell cosmetics.
Voice A:	Why is the target audience interested in adverts like this?
Voice C:	Because most women want to look attractive. They feel it's important.
Voice B:	That's a stereotype!
Voice C:	Maybe. But it's true.
Voice A:	And how does the ad persuade them to buy the product?
Voice C:	The woman is very beautiful. The message is: if you use this make-up, you will look beautiful, too.
Voice A:	Do you think it's a good advert?
Voice B:	I don't like it. In my opinion, the image doesn't represent reality.
Voice A:	And how about you?
Voice C:	I don't believe it's a bad advert. It's not reality, but I think it's very effective.
Voice A:	Who created the ad? Who designed it?
Voice C:	I think an advertising agency designed the image.
Voice B:	I agree. And the cosmetics company paid for it. I think it was very expensive.

🕐 3.17

Presenter:	**3.17. Everyday English. Talking about the media**
	Exercise B2. Listen and check.
Presenter:	Conversation 1.
Voice A:	Have you seen the new *Vogue*?
Voice B:	No. The shop has run out.
Voice A:	There's an article on the Milan Fashion Week.
Voice B:	I'll get one tomorrow.
Presenter:	Conversation 2.
Voice A:	Have you read the review of the book?
Voice B:	Yes, I saw it in the literature magazine.
Voice A:	What did you think?
Voice B:	I think it was a bit biased.
Presenter:	Conversation 3.
Voice A:	Did you see that documentary last night?
Voice B:	That awful thing on Channel 7 about cinema?
Voice A:	Yes. Didn't you like it?
Voice B:	No. I didn't think much of it.
Presenter:	Conversation 4.
Voice A:	What sort of media do you work with?
Voice B:	TV and film mostly. How about you?
Voice A:	Photography.
Voice B:	That's interesting.
Presenter:	Conversation 5.
Voice A:	Do you read the papers?
Voice B:	Yes, every day.
Voice A:	Do you have a favourite?
Voice B:	No, I like to read all the different styles.

Presenter:	Conversation 6.

Voice A:	Are you going to see the Rembrandt exhibition?
Voice B:	Yes. When is it on?
Voice A:	It starts tomorrow for three months.
Voice B:	Good. I really like his stuff.

🔊 3.18

Presenter:	**3.18. Lesson 3.8. Learning new speaking skills: Taking part in a tutorial**
	Exercise A3. Listen. Say the words.

Voice:	while, my, case, way, change, otherwise, buy, maybe, always, find, fight, paper, like, they, wife

🔊 3.19

Presenter:	**3.19. Exercise D1. Listen to an extract from a tutorial. Practise the conversation.**

Voice A:	What is the most important subject at school?
Voice B:	In my opinion, Maths is the most important subject because you need it for every job. For example, in a shop or bank.
Voice C:	I agree. But I think English is also very important. It's an international language.

🔊 3.20

Presenter:	**3.20. Lesson 3.9. Grammar for speaking: Introductory phrases**
	Exercise C1. Listen and answer some questions about the advert on the right.

Voice:	1. What do you think the advert is selling?
	2. Who do you think the advert is for?
	3. Do you think there is anything strange about the advert?
	4. Do you think it gives you any information?
	5. How much influence do you think advertisers have?
	6. What do you think the role of advertising is in *your* life?

🔊 4.1

Presenter:	**4.1. Theme 4: Sports and leisure**
	Lesson 4.1. Vocabulary for listening: Competitive or non-competitive?
	Exercise B. Listen to a text. Number the words in the order that you hear them.

Speaker:	Why is physical education, or PE, compulsory in most schools? All around the world, secondary schools have two or three hours a week for some kind of physical activity. At one time, children played team games in these periods, like football or rugby. These games are competitive. In other words, there is usually a winner and a loser. According to the theory, children learn two main things from competitive sports. Firstly, they learn to co-operate with other people. Secondly, they learn to be good losers … and good winners.
	But ideas in education have changed, and, nowadays, many schools use PE periods to do non-competitive activities such as dance, aerobics or trampolining. Children also go swimming in PE lessons without taking part in races. PE teachers say that all children can do these activities and enjoy them, not just the sporty ones.

🔊 4.2

Presenter:	**4.2. Exercise C2. Listen to some sentences. Check your ideas.**

Voice:	1. Can you play football?
	2. We don't have competitive sports now. We do dance.
	3. I don't know how to play rugby.
	4. All of the children go swimming once a week.
	5. Some schools are doing aerobics now instead of team sports.
	6. I like watching basketball but I don't like playing it.
	7. At one time, I went cycling every weekend, but not now.

🔊 4.3

Presenter:	**4.3. Lesson 4.2. Real-time listening: Racing, opponent and achievement sports**
	Exercise A2. Listen. Number the sports in the order that you hear them.

Voice:	1. These children have just finished a swimming race.
	2. These boys are playing basketball. One team has just scored.
	3. These boys are rowing. They are moving very fast through the water.

4. These children are playing table tennis. It is a very fast game.
5. These children are starting a running race. It is probably a short race, a sprint.
6. This woman has just cleared the bar in the high jump.
7. This man is about to throw the discus. The sport is very old.
8. The woman is about to throw the javelin. The sport began in ancient times.
9. The girls are learning karate. It is a form of fighting.

🌐 4.4 [DVD] 9.A

Lecturer: Today I'm going to talk about sports. As you know, there are many different sports but it is possible to classify them into groups. The verb *classify* comes from the noun *class* so *classifying* means putting things into classes, or groups. So first, today, I'm going to classify sports into three groups and then give examples of each type. Then I'm going to explain the reason for classification. Why do we classify sports in Physical Education training?

🌐 4.5 [DVD] 9.B

Lecturer: OK. So first, classification. There are three groups of sports. The first group consists of racing sports. Racing, of course, means trying to go faster than another person. The second group is opponent sports. An opponent is someone you play against. Finally, there are achievement sports. Achievement means reaching a certain level, a good level.

So, we've seen that sports can be classified into three groups. Now, what sort of sports go into each category or group? Let's look at the first group: racing – trying to go faster than another person. There are two sub-categories here. Some racing sports just use the power of the human body. For example, running and swimming. Other sports in this category use the power of machines. Cycling uses bicycles, motor racing uses cars, for example.

What about the second group? Opponent sports. Once again, with opponent sports, there are two sub-categories. The opponent might be an individual or a team. For example, we usually play tennis against one person, but we play football against a team.

Finally, let's turn to achievement sports. In achievement sports, there are also two sub-categories. Sometimes we try to reach a target. For example, in golf, we try to get a white ball into a small hole. So that's a target sport. Sometimes we try to achieve a particular quantity – distance, for example, or height. In the long jump, we try to jump farther than all the other people. In the high jump, we try to jump higher.

OK. So, to sum up. We have heard about three categories of sports – racing, opponent and achievement. We have seen that each category has two sub-categories. In racing, it's human body and machine, in opponent sports, it's a person or team, and in achievement sports, it's target or quantity.

OK. I hope you have understood the classification. But why do we classify sports in this way in Physical Education training? Well, each type of sport teaches a child something different. Racing sports teach children to rely on themselves, to try harder, even if they are feeling physical pain. Opponent sports teach children to react more quickly, and to think about the actions of another person. Achievement sports teach children to reach for a target – something which is hard to achieve but achievable.

Next week, we're going to look at ball games in detail.

🌐 4.6

Presenter: **4.6. Exercise E2. Listen and check.**

Voice: against, ball, class, classify, classification, heard, quantity, racing, reach, target, team, table

🌐 4.7

Presenter: **4.7. Lesson 4.3. Learning new listening skills: Branching diagrams**

Exercise A. Listen to some sentences. Tick the best way to complete each sentence.

Voice:
1. As you …
2. … there are many different …
3. … but it is possible to classify …
4. We can classify sports into three …
5. Firstly, there are racing sports. Racing, of course, means trying to go faster than another…
6. For example, racing sports include running and …
7. The second group of sports is opponent sports. In an opponent sport, you play against an individual or a …
8. For example, tennis is an opponent sport and so is …
9. Finally there are achievement sports. In achievement sports, you try to reach a certain …
10. The high jump is an achievement sport, and so is the long …

🎧 4.8

Presenter: **4.8. Exercise B1. Listen to the start of a lecture about sports.**

Lecturer: I'm going to talk to you today about sports. I'm going to start by classifying sports into three categories. The first group consists of racing sports. Racing, of course, means trying to go faster than another person. The second group is opponent sports. An opponent is someone you play against. Finally, there are achievement sports. Achievement means reaching a certain level, a good level.

🎧 4.9

Presenter: **4.9. Exercise B4. Listen to the start of some more lectures on different subjects. Organize your notes in each case.**

Lecturer A: Today, we are looking at the classification of literature. There are four main kinds of literature. Firstly, we have novels; secondly, plays; thirdly, poetry; and, finally, of course, biography or autobiography.

Lecturer B: Firstly, in this lecture, I want to classify the mass media. I'm going to divide it into two categories. On the one hand, there is the broadcast media. On the other hand, we have the print media. Of course, we can subdivide each of these categories. Broadcast media has three sub-categories. It consists of television, radio and, nowadays, the Internet. Print media contains newspapers and magazines.

Lecturer C: We are going to look at elements in this lecture. Elements are the basic building blocks of our world. Carbon is an element. Hydrogen is an element. Oxygen is an element. But how can we classify elements? There are over 100 elements but we can classify all elements into just three groups. The first group is metals. The second group is non-metals. And the third group is gases … but not all gases, only inert gases – that's I-N-E-R-T. It means they don't change. Let's think of a few examples of each category. Iron is a metal. Zinc is a metal. Carbon is a non-metal. Hydrogen and oxygen are gases but they are not inert so they are non-metals. Inert gases include helium, with the symbol He. You find helium in balloons.

Lecturer D: We can classify all living things into five categories. The categories are called kingdoms. In the first kingdom are animals. In the second kingdom, we have plants. The third kingdom consists of fungi …The animal kingdom can be subdivided into many categories but I'm only going to talk about four: mammals, birds, fish and reptiles.

There are many examples of mammals, of course. We are mammals – humans. Bats are mammals. Whales are mammals, although some people think they are fish.

🎧 4.10

Presenter: **4.10. Exercise C2. Listen and tick the correct column.**

Voice: alone, although, flower, most, mountain, opponent, power, smoke

🎧 4.11

Presenter: **4.11. Lesson 4.4. Grammar for listening: Prepositions after the verb**

Exercise A1. Listen and number the verb + preposition phrases.

Voice:
1. Today we're going to look at types of literature.
2. Children must learn to rely on themselves.
3. OK. So, to sum up the problems …
4. I'm going to mention a few points and I'd like you to write down the most important one, in your opinion.
5. First of all we're going to hear about racing sports.
6. Children should try to reach for a target.
7. I don't want to go into detail here.
8. The spacecraft took off at 10.32 a.m. precisely.
9. Remove the old printer cartridge and put in the new one.
10. Traditional festivals are dying out all over the world.

🎧 4.12

Presenter: **4.12. Exercise A2. Listen to some more verb + preposition phrases. These verbs are probably new to you. Can you hear the preposition in each case? Number the prepositions.**

Voice:
1. come about	3. box in	5. fly at	7. let on	9. climb down
2. act for	4. look into	6. put off	8. work out	10. set up

🎧 4.13

Presenter: **4.13. Exercise B. Listen to the start of some sentences. Choose the correct phrase to complete each sentence.**

Voice:
1. First, we're going to look at …
2. You can look up …
3. It is difficult to look after …
4. OK. Let's look back …
5. People look forward …
6. Researchers look for …

Presenter: **4.14. Lesson 4.5. Applying new listening skills: Classifying ball games**

Exercise B2. Listen. Which game is the speaker talking about?

Voice:
1. People say that the game began at a British school. The children were playing football. Suddenly, one of the boys picked up the ball and ran with it.
2. This is a team game with five players on each side. You try to put the ball into a net with your hands.
3. You can play singles or doubles. You use a special bat with strings.
4. This is one of the oldest games in the world. People started kicking balls in China over 2,000 years ago.
5. Many people do not understand this game. It can last five days. You must try to stop the ball hitting three pieces of wood. You can only use your bat.
6. You need two teams of three players each for this game. You can only use your hands to touch the ball.
7. This is a target sport. You try to hit the ball into a hole with a long stick called a club.
8. This game is very popular in the USA and Japan. The batters try to hit the ball a long way with a long bat called … a bat!

🎧 4.15 DVD 9.C

Lecturer:
Today, I'm going to talk about ball games. As you know, there are many different ball games but it is possible to classify them into three groups. The first group contains games played mainly with the hands. The second group consists of games played mainly with the feet. Thirdly, there are bat sports – sports played with some kind of bat, stick or racket. So, I'm going to classify sports into three groups and give examples of sports in each category or group. Finally, I'm going to look at the importance of classifying ball games for Physical Education.

OK. So first, classification. As I said, ball games can be put into three groups. Let's look at the first group: hand sports. There are two sub-categories of hand sports. Firstly, there are sports where you can only use the hand. Basketball goes into this category. Secondly, there are sports where you can use the hand or another part of your body, usually your foot. Rugby fits into this category.

Now let's turn to the second group: sports played with the feet. Actually, there is only one major sport in this category. It's called *football*, of course. Players can use their heads but only one player can use hands in this sport – the goalkeeper. It is against the rules for any other player to touch the ball with their hands.

Finally, there are bat sports – sports played with a bat. In bat sports, you are only allowed to use the bat to hit the ball. It is against the rules to use your hands or your feet, for example. Of course, the bat has different names in different sports. For example, in tennis, the bat is called a *racket*. The word comes from Arabic, *rahat al yad*, meaning the palm or inside of the hand. So perhaps, at one time, players could use their hands in tennis, but not now. In golf, the bat is called a *club*. In ice-hockey, it is called a *stick*.

🎧 4.16 DVD 9.D

Presenter: **4.16. Lesson 4.7. Real-time speaking: Ball games for PE**

Lecturer:
OK. So we have heard about three categories of ball games – hand sports, foot sports and bat sports. Why is it important to classify ball games? Because at school, we must teach children to play at least one game in each category. This helps to build up their physical strength but also their physical ability.

Let's go into this point in detail. Young children often seem clumsy. They bang into things and knock over things. They can't balance on things well. Many children cannot work out the bounce of a ball. Why? Because children don't have co-ordination. They cannot move different parts of their body in the correct way, to throw a ball, for example, or to kick one. Ball games help to develop co-ordination.

Let's look at three groups again. How does each group of sports help co-ordination? Firstly, a hand sport develops the co-ordination between the hand and the eye. With the second group, a foot sport, of course, improves co-ordination between the foot and the eye. It also improves balance, because you have to balance on one foot to kick the ball with the other leg. Finally, bat sports. Bat sports help children to deal with a tool. They have to use the tool to hit the ball, instead of a part of their own body. Bat sports involve co-ordination again. But this time it is co-ordination with an extension of the body.

To sum up, then. Ball games are fun but we don't teach them at schools just because they are fun. We teach them to develop physical ability, especially co-ordination.

Before next time, think of ten more ball games and classify each one into one of the categories from today's lecture.

🎧 4.17 DVD 9.E

Lecturer:
Today, I'm going to talk about ball games for PE. There are many good ball games for children. Here are some of them. Firstly, there's football. Secondly, we have rugby. Next, tennis. Then we've got volleyball and, finally, there's hockey.

First of all, I'm going to talk about football because it is the most popular game in the world.

What type of game is football? Well, it's a team game, of course. It is played by two teams. Each team has 11 players.

🌐 4.18 [DVD] 9.F

Lecturer:	OK. So let's look at the value of football in PE. Firstly, it is good exercise. It is an enjoyable physical activity.
	Secondly, it helps with co-ordination. Children need to develop co-ordination and football helps with co-ordination between the eyes and other parts of the body.
	Thirdly, we have roles in a team. As we have seen, football is a team game, and team games teach children to co-operate with other people.
	Fourthly, football is a game for all shapes and sizes. Attackers are often short. Midfield players are often tall. Defenders and goalkeepers are often big.
	Finally, in competitive sports like football, children learn about winning and losing. Life is full of winning and losing, and children need to learn ways of dealing with both.

🌐 4.19

Presenter:	**4.19. Everyday English. Talking about games**
	Exercise B2. Listen and check. Practise the conversations.

Presenter:	Conversation 1.
Voice A:	What are you watching?
Voice B:	It's Brazil versus Germany.
Voice A:	Who's winning?
Voice B:	We are. We just scored.

Presenter:	Conversation 2.
Voice A:	What's wrong?
Voice B:	I was hopeless.
Voice A:	You weren't. You played very well.
Voice B:	But we still lost.

Presenter:	Conversation 3.
Voice A:	Same time next week?
Voice B:	Sure. Great game.
Voice A:	Yes, that was a brilliant shot just now.
Voice B:	I think it was just luck, really.

Presenter:	Conversation 4.
Voice A:	Was that in or out?
Voice B:	It landed on the line.
Voice A:	I wasn't sure. My point, then.
Voice B:	Yes, well played!

Presenter:	Conversation 5.
Voice A:	How did you get on?
Voice B:	Great! We won!
Voice A:	What was the score?
Voice B:	Three–one.

Presenter:	Conversation 6.
Voice A:	Do you know how to play this game?
Voice B:	Not really.
Voice A:	Do you want to learn?
Voice B:	OK. How do we start?

🌐 4.20

Presenter:	**4.20. Exercise C1. Listen and check your ideas.**
Voice A:	Don't forget there's a match on the 30th.
Voice B:	Sorry, did you say the 30th?
Voice A:	Yes, that's right.
Voice B:	Fine. I'll be there.
Voice A:	I'll meet you outside the sports centre at seven, OK?
Voice B:	Sorry, did you say seven or seven thirty?
Voice A:	Seven. Is that OK?
Voice B:	Yes, great. Seven o'clock outside the sports centre.

🔊 **4.21**

Presenter: **4.21. Lesson 4.9. Grammar for speaking:** *Must* **and** *should*

Exercise A2. Listen and check your answers. Notice the pronunciation of *must* **and** *mustn't* **in each sentence.**

Voice:
a. There must be an area around the goal which is called the penalty area.
b. The goalkeeper mustn't touch the ball with his or her hands outside the goal area.
c. The goalkeeper must wear clothes of a different colour from the opponents' clothes.
d. The interval between the two halves mustn't last more than 15 minutes.
e. The ball must cross the whole of the goal line to score.
f. When the ball goes out of play at the sides of the pitch, a player must throw the ball in.
g. A player mustn't push another player with his or her hands.
h. The referee must allow extra time for injuries and substitutions.

🔊 **4.22**

Presenter: **4.22. Exercise C2. Listen and check your answers. Notice the pronunciation of** *should* **and** *shouldn't.*

Voice:
You shouldn't use too many coloured backgrounds.
You shouldn't use a lot of effects, e.g., flashing words.
You shouldn't write full sentences on the slide.
You shouldn't read out the slide word for word.
You shouldn't stand in front of the screen.
You shouldn't talk to the slide.
You should talk to the audience.
You shouldn't speak quickly.
You should pause between sentences.
You should wait a few moments between slides.

🔊 **4.23**

Presenter: **4.23. Portfolio: Team games**

Presenter: Exercise B1. Group A: Polo.

Lecturer:
It is called the King of Games … and the Game of Kings. In fact, the following words appear on a tablet of stone in Iran. They come from the days of Ancient Persia: 'Let other people play at other things – the King of Games is still the Game of Kings.' Researchers believe that the game appeared in the area of modern-day Iran. Persian tribes played the game, perhaps to give some exercise to their horses. The first recorded polo match occurred in 600 BCE between the Turkomans and the Persians. The Turkomans won.

At first, the game was called *chogan* by the Persians. This later became *pulu* which then became *polo*. From Persia, the game spread to India. In the 19th century, two British soldiers, Captain Robert Stewart and Major General Joe Sherer saw a polo match in Manipur in Eastern India. In 1859, they held the first meeting of the first polo club, the Silchar Polo Club, and in 1863 they formed the famous Calcutta Polo Club. The club is still active today. From India, the game spread around the world. In fact, the current world champion is from South America. Argentina have held the title since 1949. Prince Charles of the UK is a famous player of the game.

Players wear special trousers called *jodhpurs* – J-O-D-H-P-U-R-S – and a helmet. Each player has a horse and a stick with two heads on one end. There are two goals – they are just sticks in the ground. There is no net.

There are four people on each team. Each plays on horseback. Players try to hit the ball with the stick towards the other team's goal. Each game has four or six parts, called *chukkas* – C-H-U-K-K-A. Each chukka lasts seven minutes. The objective of the game is simple. You must score more goals than the other team.

🔊 **4.24**

Presenter: **4.24. Exercise B1. Group B: Baseball.**

Lecturer:
The game first appears in a book by an American, John Newberry, published in 1744. Perhaps it developed from English sports such as rounders and cricket. The name of the game is baseball. It probably comes from the special equipment. Players must hit a ball and then run around four bases, or points on the ground.

A man called Alexander Cartwright wrote the rules of the modern game in 1845. He also designed the special field, which is in the shape of a diamond.

Professional baseball began in the United States in 1865 and the National League was founded there in 1876. In 1947, the first African-American became a professional player. Baseball is now a fully integrated sport.

All the players wear special trousers and helmets. One player is the pitcher – P-I-T-C-H-E-R. He or she tries to throw a ball past the batter. The pitcher has a glove on one hand. The batter has a bat – a long thin stick, made of wood. The batter tries to hit the ball with the bat. If the batter hits the ball, he or she tries to run around four bases. The other team try to run him or her out. They get the ball and throw it to one of the basemen. If the batter runs around the four bases, he or she scores a run. The objective of the game is simple. Your team must score more runs than the other team.

🔊 **4.25**

Presenter: 4.25. Exercise B1. Group C: Netball.

Lecturer: This game developed from a very old game. In around 1000 BCE, there was a game called *Pok-ta-pok* – P-O-K, T-A, P-O-K. The Indians of modern-day Mexico played the game. However, the game did not spread around the world.

In 1892, a man called Dr James Naismith took some points from the old game and invented basketball. But some people thought the game was too violent for women. So they developed a female version. At first, they called it 'women's basketball'. But then women started to play basketball, so, to avoid confusion, people changed the name of women's basketball to *netball*.

The new game became very popular in girls' schools in Britain and then in other parts of the world. For example, it is now very popular in Australia and New Zealand. It is now played by boys as well as girls, men as well as women.

Teams play on a special court with a high post at each end. There is a net on each post, just like basketball. Each player wears a bib, which is a piece of cloth with a hole for the head. Each bib has two letters on it. These letters give the name of the player's position. Each position has parts of the court that the player must not go into. For example, GS means goal shooter. The goal shooter can only go into the area closest to the other team's goal.

There are seven people on each team. Players pass the ball with their hands to each other and try to score in the other team's net. Players must only hold onto the ball for three seconds. They can only move one foot while holding the ball. They cannot bounce the ball more than once. The objective of the game is simple. You must score more goals than the other team.

🔊 **5.1**

Presenter: **5.1. Theme 5: Nutrition and health**
Lesson 5.1. Vocabulary for listening: Why do we eat?

Exercise A2. Listen and write the names of foods in the correct category.

Voice: apple, banana, beans, beef, carrot, chicken, lamb, mango, orange, peas, pork, salmon, shark, tomato, tuna

🔊 **5.2**

Presenter: **5.2. Exercise B. Listen and choose the best way to complete each sentence.**

Presenter: **Part 1.**

Voice:
1. Why do we eat? We eat because …
2. Well, that answer is true, in a way. But why …
3. We feel hungry because …
4. Energy is the ability …
5. Every part of the body needs energy …
6. We get energy …
7. However, we have to be careful. If we don't use all the energy from food, …

Presenter: **Part 2.**

Voice:
1. How does the body keep the energy? It stores it …
2. It is easy to use *new* energy from food. It is much harder to use …
3. So, what's the answer? We must eat the right …
4. … and we must take exercise to use …
5. The food we normally eat is called …
6. Of course, we must eat the right …
7. If we eat the right *amount* of the right *kind* of food, we will have …

🔊 **5.3** DVD **10.A**

Presenter: **5.3. Lesson 5.2. Listening review (1): Nutrients**

Lecturer: This week I'm going to talk about nutrients. So, this week, I'm going to define the word *nutrient*. Then, I'm going to classify the different nutrients. After that, I'll give you some examples of foods which contain each type of nutrient. Next week, we'll go on to look at food groups. We'll also talk about quantity. How much food do you need from each group?

🔊 **5.4** DVD **10.B**

Lecturer: OK. So what is a nutrient? It is something which the body needs to operate properly. Food contains nutrients, which are, basically, energy and chemicals. Energy has many meanings – for example, electricity. But in the human body, energy is the ability to do work. Chemicals are things like calcium and magnesium. These chemicals help the parts of the body to operate correctly. The body needs different amounts of each nutrient. If you have too much of a particular type, you can get fat. If you have too little of a particular type, you can get ill.

Presenter: **5.5. Lesson 5.3. Listening review (2): Vitamins**

Lecturer: OK. First, what are the different nutrients? There are five main types. Firstly, there are carbohydrates. Secondly, there is protein. Thirdly, we have vitamins. Fourthly, there are fats. Meat and fish contain fats. Finally, there are minerals. Food also contains fibre, which is important for digestion. But that is not a nutrient so I'm not going to talk about that today.

OK, so we've seen the five different types. But what is the value of each type? Let's take carbohydrates. This is the main energy nutrient. Most people get most of their energy from carbohydrates. Secondly, we have protein. The body needs protein for growth. It also needs it to repair damaged parts. Next, vitamins. As I'm sure you know, there are several different vitamins – A, B, C, etc. Each one helps with a particular part of the body. But in general, vitamins help with growth and repair, like protein. Fourthly, we have fats. Most people think of fats as a bad thing but some fats are necessary. They help to form chemicals called hormones, which carry messages around the body. Finally, there are minerals. We only need tiny amounts of these nutrients but again they are essential for growth and repair – almost every nutrient has a role in that – and they also help to release energy from other nutrients.

Right, so, we have classified the main nutrients and seen their function in the body. Let's turn now to the key question. Where do we find the main nutrients? Firstly, carbohydrates. These nutrients are found in food like bread, pasta and rice. There is protein in meat and fish. There is also protein in cheese. What about vitamins? Fruit, like apples and oranges, contains Vitamin C. Eggs have got Vitamin D in them and there's Vitamin E in nuts. Next, fats. Meat and fish contain fats. There are also fats in products like milk and cheese. Finally, there are minerals. We find minerals in many foods, but particularly in milk, meat and eggs.

OK. So … we have looked at nutrients and foods that contain them. Next week, food groups and how much food you need from each group. Before next week, could you look up food groups on the Internet and make some notes of different ideas about them. OK. So I want you to do some research on food groups on the Internet and make some notes about them.

🎧 5.6

Presenter: **5.6. Exercise A. Listen and number the expressions in order.**

Voice:
1. First, I'm going to talk about sociology.
2. Next, social distance. In other words, how close you should stand to people.
3. In the past, we called people like Plato and Ibn Khaldun philosophers.
4. These days, we call them sociologists.
5. A long time ago, in the 4th century BCE, the Greek philosopher Aristotle wrote the first book about the mind.
6. In 1970, Elizabeth Loftus obtained a PhD in Psychology. At that time, she was interested in learning.
7. How to be a good employee? I've told you some of the things that you must do.
8. You can see why this country is popular for holidays.
9. First there are speeches. After that, the girls get presents.
10. OK. So, there are several methods of flying.
11. So we have heard about the main inventions in the field of flying.
12. In my opinion, the Space Shuttle was the most important invention.
13. News is all around us. Is that a good or bad thing? First, let's look at some advantages.
14. OK. Those are some of the advantages. What about the disadvantages?
15. As you know, there are many different ball games.
16. To sum up, then. Ball games are fun, and they develop physical ability.

🎧 5.7

Presenter: **5.7. Exercise B. Listen to some more information about nutrition. Match the words and the definitions.**

Lecturer: I want to talk to you today about some very important molecules. A molecule is a compound of different elements. Water is a molecule. It is made of two parts of hydrogen for every one part of oxygen. Water is an important molecule for the body. It is the solvent for most chemical reactions. In other words, it is the liquid which chemicals are dissolved in. Dissolving is changing from solid to liquid. So water is very important, but there are some other very important molecules. They are called vitamins. You know that the body needs vitamins, but why? Because vitamins work with enzymes, which help the human body carry out chemical reactions. For example, the enzyme praline hydroloxase is in Vitamin C. It is very important because it makes collagen, which is essential for healing wounds in the skin.

🎧 5.8

Presenter: **5.8. Exercise C. Listen. Complete the notes with the important words from each sentence.**

Lecturer: Vitamin C may be the most important vitamin. As we have seen, Vitamin C helps to heal wounds. But it also helps the body to fight infections. It may even help in fighting cancer. Vitamin C occurs in green vegetables and in fruits like oranges and lemons. On average, you should take 60 milligrams per day.

5.9

Presenter: **5.9. Exercise D. Listen. Write the correct year in each space.**

Lecturer: Vitamin C helps fight the disease scurvy – that's S-C-U-R-V-Y. People have known about the disease for thousands of years. It led to many deaths in Ancient Egypt in 3000 BCE and later, in 500 BCE in Ancient Greece and 100 BCE in Ancient Rome. But nobody knew the cause. In 1536, native American Indians gave a French explorer a medicine contained in tree leaves, and his men recovered. But the knowledge did not return to Europe. In 1742, a British naval officer, James Lind, asked for fruits like lemons to be included in the food for all long voyages. But his idea was rejected. Then in 1768, another British naval officer, James Cook, gave lime juice to his sailors on a long voyage, and nobody died from scurvy. People began to realize there was a connection between fresh fruit and scurvy. However, it was another 150 years before the real cause of scurvy was established. In 1932, Charles King, an American researcher, proved the connection between Vitamin C and scurvy.

5.10

Presenter: **5.10. Lesson 5.4. Grammar review (1): Predicting; past and present, positive and negative, singular and plural**

Exercise A. Listen and find the information that comes next.

Voice:
1. A festival is [PAUSE] a special event in one country or several countries.
2. *Celebrate* means [PAUSE] 'remember a happy event'.
3. I made a hypothesis then [PAUSE] I did an experiment.
4. There's a mountain range [PAUSE] in the north of the country.
5. There aren't [PAUSE] any lakes.
6. There is a river in the south. [PAUSE] It is very long.
7. The first flight took place on [PAUSE] the 14th of December 1926.
8. She was born in [PAUSE] 1949.
9. The area consists of [PAUSE] forests and lakes.
10. First, I'm going to talk [PAUSE] about the history of the mass media.

5.11

Presenter: **5.11. Exercise B. Listen. Tick the correct column for each sentence.**

Voice:
1. Vitamins are essential parts of human diet.
2. Lack of vitamins makes a person ill.
3. For example, lack of Vitamin D causes a disease called rickets.
4. There are many different vitamins.
5. The name *vitamin* appeared in 1912.
6. Vitamin A was discovered between 1912 and 1914.
7. Researchers found other vitamins in the next ten years.
8. There are 13 vitamins that prevent disease.
9. Vitamin C prevents scurvy.
10. It occurs naturally in fruits like limes and lemons.
11. 1n 1742, James Lind realized the importance of these fruits.
12. But very few people used his discovery at the time.

5.12

Presenter: **5.12. Exercise C. Listen. Tick the sentence you hear.**

Voice:
1. The human body needs vitamins.
2. The human body can't make vitamins.
3. It gets them from fruit and vegetables.
4. Cooking can destroy vitamins.
5. Boiled vegetables don't have a lot of vitamins.
6. You should eat raw fruit.
7. Washing fruit doesn't remove vitamins.
8. Washing fruit removes most germs.

Presenter:	**5.13. Exercise D. Listen. Is the subject of each sentence singular or plural?**
Voice:	1. Fat's a solvent, like water.
	2. Fats are in meat, and also in milk.
	3. The vitamin's essential for strong bones.
	4. The meeting's at 2.00 p.m.
	5. The researchers are still working on the problem.
	6. The festival's very old.
	7. The manager's a very nice person.
	8. The banks open at 9.
	9. There's a river in the north.
	10. There are mountains in the east.

🔊 5.14

Presenter:	**5.14. Lesson 5.5. Listening review (3): The food pyramid**
	Exercise A1. Listen to each sound. It is the stressed syllable of a word connected with food. Can you identify the word?
Voice:	a. pro c. high e. vit g. pair i. ness
	b. new d. die f. min h. dam j. lees

🔊 5.15

Presenter:	**5.15. Exercise A2. Listen and check your ideas.**
Voice:	a. protein c. carbohydrate e. vitamin g. repair i. necessary
	b. nutrients d. diet f. minerals h. damage j. release

🔊 5.16 [DVD] 10.D

Lecturer:	Last week I talked about nutrients in food. I explained that there are five main nutrients. The main nutrients, if you remember, are carbohydrates, protein, vitamins, fats and minerals. This week I'm going to talk about food groups. Then I'm going to talk about healthy eating, that is putting these groups together in a healthy way. Finally, I'm going to ask you to think about your own diet.

🔊 5.17 [DVD] 10.E

Lecturer:	So, first. What are food groups? Well, you can probably work it out from the name. A food group is, simply, a group of foods. There are six main food groups. Some have the same name as the nutrients which they contain, but some are different.
	The six main food groups are as follows:
	Number one: fats. Number two: carbohydrates – they're both nutrients of course – then three: vegetables, four: fruit, five: dairy products and six: meat and fish.
	One food group may need some explanation. What are dairy products? They are mainly milk and the products from milk – in other words, butter and cheese. English speakers usually include eggs in dairy products, too.

🔊 5.18 [DVD] 10.F

Lecturer:	OK. So what is the connection between the six food groups and healthy eating? Scientists say that a healthy diet consists of the correct balance between the foods in the different groups. But what is the correct balance? There is quite a lot of argument about this. I'm going to give you one idea. It comes from American scientists.
	In the USA, food scientists have made a pyramid of the food groups. This pyramid shows the balance between the different groups. Fats are at the top of the pyramid. According to the American scientists, we should only have one portion of fats each day. At the next level of the pyramid, we have dairy products on one side, and meat and fish on the other. The American scientists recommend three portions of dairy products and two portions of meat or fish each day. At the third level, there are vegetables on one side and fruit on the other. Apparently we should have four portions of fruit and three portions of vegetables. Finally, at the bottom of the pyramid there are the carbohydrates. The scientists say we should eat ten portions of carbohydrates.

🔊 5.19 [DVD] 10.G

Lecturer:	Finally, today. What about *your* diet? Is it balanced? Think about a normal day. Do you have ten portions of carbohydrates – that's pieces of bread, pasta, rice, potatoes – not chips, of course, because they have fat on them. Do you have four portions of vegetables? Make a list of the foods you eat on an average day. Put the foods into the six main food groups. Work out a diet pyramid for you. Is it balanced? Or is it top heavy? Or does it stick out in the middle? We'll look at some of your food groups next week …

Presenter: **5.20. Lesson 5.6. Vocabulary for speaking: Portions.**
Exercise B. Listen and complete the text. Use words from the list on the right. Make any necessary changes.

Lecturer: We are often told to eat three portions of meat, or five portions of vegetables, etc. But what is a portion? Here is a guide to portion size for a number of common foods.
- a slice of bread
- a handful of pasta or rice
- a small bowl of cereal
- two small potatoes
- one large egg
- three thin slices of meat
- one piece of fish
- half a can of beans or peas
- a handful of nuts
- a glass of milk
- a small pot of yoghurt
- a small piece of cheese
- one apple, orange, etc.
- a small glass of fruit juice
- two handfuls of berries
- a teaspoon of fat
- a small piece of butter
- no spoonfuls of sugar! (It is in fruit, vegetables, etc.)

🔊 5.21

Presenter: **5.21. Lesson 5.7. Speaking review (1): Researching daily diet**

Exercise B1. Listen and look at the tables and figures.

Student: According to nutritionists, everyone should eat a balanced diet. We can see a balanced diet in Figure 1. I wanted to find out if I have a balanced diet, so I did some research.

Firstly, let me tell you about the research. I recorded my food intake for a typical day. You can see the results in Table 1. For breakfast, I had two slices of toast with butter and a cup of coffee with one spoonful of sugar. For lunch, I ate a burger and lots of chips with peas, then I had a carton of yoghurt. I also drank a glass of orange juice. For dinner, I had pasta with tomato sauce. I also had a chocolate bar in the afternoon. You can see it here in Table 1.

Now, I'm going to explain my analysis. I put each item into the correct food group. I estimated the portions at each meal and put the results into a table. Here are the results in Table 2. I converted the raw data into percentages. Then I drew this pie chart – Figure 2.

We can compare my intake with the balanced diet pie chart ... I had almost the correct amount of carbohydrates. I also ate almost the correct amount of vegetables, and meat and fish. However, I did not eat enough fruit and I had far too much in the category fats and sweets.

I am going to change my diet. I am going to eat more fruit and I am going to try not to eat chocolate bars! I don't think I will increase my intake of dairy products because I don't like milk or cheese.

🔊 5.22

Presenter: **5.22. Everyday English. Getting something to eat**

Exercise B2. Listen and check your ideas.

Presenter: Conversation 1.

Voice A: Are you ready to order?
Voice B: Yes. I'll have the chicken with noodles.
Voice A: Anything to drink?
Voice B: Just tap water, please.

Presenter: Conversation 2.

Voice A: What would you like to have?
Voice B: The curry, please.
Voice A: Rice or chips?
Voice B: Um, rice please.

Presenter:	Conversation 3.
Voice A:	That's £7.38 all together, please.
Voice B:	Could I have a bag?
Voice A:	Certainly. Here you are.
Voice B:	Thanks.

Presenter:	Conversation 4.
Voice A:	What can I get you?
Voice B:	Two coffees, please.
Voice A:	With milk?
Voice B:	Yes, please.

Presenter:	Conversation 5.
Voice A:	What do you want?
Voice B:	A cheese sandwich, I think.
Voice A:	OK. Put the money in here. Press G-1-2.
Voice B:	Thanks. I think I've got the right coins.

Presenter:	Conversation 6.
Voice A:	Good evening. Pizza Rapida.
Voice B:	Oh, hi. Can I order a pizza for delivery, please?
Voice A:	It will be about 45 minutes. Is that OK?
Voice B:	That will be fine.

a little (*n*)	5.6
a lot (*n*)	5.6
accept (*v*)	2.16
according to (*prep*)	1.16, 2.6
achievable (*adj*)	4.1
achieve (*v*)	4.1
achievement (*n*)	4.1
actual (*adj*)	5.16
actually (*adv*)	1.6
ad (*n*)	3.6
adult (*n*)	1.1
advance (*v*)	4.11
advert (*n*)	3.6
advertisement (*n*)	3.1, 3.6
advertising (*n*)	3.1
aerobics (*n*)	4.1
affect (*v*)	3.11
against (*prep*)	4.16
ago (*adv*)	2.1
aircraft (*n*)	2.1, 2.16
allow (*v*)	4.1
ancestor (*n*)	1.1
anniversary (*n*)	1.11
anthropologist (*n*)	1.1, 1.16
anthropology (*n*)	1.16
apparently (*adv*)	2.6
appeal (*n* and *v*)	3.11
appear (*v*)	3.1
appendix (*n*)	3.16
around (*prep*) [= approximately]	1.16
as a matter of fact	3.1
astronaut (*n*)	2.1
astronomer (*n*)	2.11
at all	2.11
attach (*v*)	2.16
attack (*v*)	2.11
attacker (*n*)	4.6
attend (*v*)	1.1
attitudes (*n pl*) [= how you see things]	3.11
attract (*v*)	1.11, 3.11
audience (*n*)	3.1, 3.6
avoid (*v*)	3.6

badminton (*n*)	4.6
balance (*n*)	5.1
balance (*v*)	4.1
balloon (*n*)	1.16
bar (*n*) [= piece]	5.11
bar (*n*) [= serving counter]	5.11
basically (*adv*)	5.1
basket (*n*)	4.6
bat (*n*)	4.1
battle (*n*)	1.16
belief (*n*)	3.11
bias (*n*)	3.1
biased (*adj*)	3.6
birth (*n*)	1.1, 1.6
birthday (*n*)	1.6
biscuit (*n*)	5.6
blood pressure (*n*)	5.11
board (*n*)	4.11
body rate (*n*)	5.11
bonfire (*n*)	1.6
bowl (*n*)	5.6
brake (*n*)	2.6
break (*v*)	2.6
breaking news (*n*)	3.1
brief (*adj*)	2.16
broadcast (*n* and *v*)	3.1
build up (*v*)	4.1
burger (*n*)	5.6
button (*n*)	2.6, 4.16

cake (*n*)	5.6
can (*n*)	5.6
candle (*n*)	1.6
canned (*adj*)	5.11
capture (*v*)	4.11
carbohydrate (*n*)	5.1
carbon (C) (*n*)	2.11
card (*n*)	1.6
carry on (*v*)	5.11
carton (*n*)	5.6
castle (*n*)	2.11
category (*n*)	3.16
cause (*n* and *v*)	4.16
celebrate (*v*)	1.1
celebration (*n*)	1.1
celebrity (*n*)	3.11
centre (*n*)	1.11
cereal (*n*)	5.6
ceremony (*n*)	1.1
channel (*n*)	3.1
character (*n*) [= in video game]	4.16
character (*n*) [= letter]	3.1
checkmate (*n*)	4.11

chemical (*n*)	5.1		decline (*n*)	3.11
chest (*n*)	4.6		decorate (*v*)	1.11
chew (*v*)	5.11		defender (*n*)	4.6
childhood (*n*)	1.1		definitely (*adv*)	3.6
chip (*n*)	5.6		deliver (*v*)	5.16
chocolate (*n*)	5.11		demographic (*adj*)	3.11
class (*n*) [= group]	4.1		demonstrate (*v*)	2.16
classification (*n*)	4.1		design (*n* and *v*)	2.16, 3.6
classify (*v*)	4.1		develop (*v*)	4.1
click on (*v*)	2.6		diabetes (*n*)	5.16
club (*n*) [= stick]	4.1		dice (*n*)	4.11
coin (*n*)	2.6		die out (*v*)	1.1, 1.16
collection (*n*) [= group]	3.11		diet (*n*)	5.1
colourful (*adj*)	1.6		disabled (*adj*)	3.6
common (*adj*)	3.16		discover (*v*)	2.11
community (*n*)	3.6		discuss (*v*)	4.1
compete (*v*)	1.11		disk (*n*) [= playing piece]	4.11
competition (*n*)	1.11		display (*n*)	1.11
competitive (*adj*)	4.1, 4.6		distribute (*v*)	3.1
concentration (*n*)	4.16		distribution (*n*)	3.1
condition (*n*) [medical]	5.16		divide (*v*)	4.6
conditions (*n*)	1.6		documentary (*n*)	3.6
conduct (*n* and *v*)	3.16		dress (*n* and *v*)	1.6
congratulations (*n*)	1.1, 1.6		dress up (*v*)	1.11
connect (*v*)	1.11		dried (*adj*)	5.11
consume (*v*)	5.16		drive (*v*)	2.16
control (*n* and *v*)	2.6, 2.16		duration (*n*)	4.6
convert (*v*)	3.16		during (*adv*)	1.6
cooperate (*v*)	4.1		during (*prep*)	1.16
co-ordination (*n*)	4.1, 4.6	**E**	each (*adv* and *pron*)	1.6
cope (*v*)	3.11		earlier (*adj*)	1.16
copy (*n* and *v*)	4.16		earlier (*adv*)	1.11
cosmetics (*n*)	3.6		educational (*adj*)	4.16
costume (*n*)	1.11		effect (*n*)	3.11
course (*n*)	4.6		effectively (*adv*)	3.16
court (*n*)	4.6		elderly (*adj* and *n*)	3.11
cover (*n*)	2.6, 3.11		electricity (*n*)	2.1
crash (*n* and *v*)	2.16		electronic (*adj*)	4.16
critic (*n*)	3.6		encourage (*v*)	4.16
critical thinking (*n*)	4.11		enemy (*n*)	2.11
crowd (*n*)	3.1		energy (*n*)	5.1
cultural (*adj*)	1.16		engage in (*v*)	4.11
culture (*n*)	1.6		engine (*n*)	2.1
D dairy product (*n*)	5.1		engineer (*n*)	2.16
damaged (*adj*)	5.1		engineering (*n*)	2.16
dancing (*n*)	1.6		entertainment (*n*)	3.16
deal with (*v*)	4.1		equipment (*n*)	4.6
death (*n*)	1.1		estimate (*n* and *v*)	4.11

ethnic (adj)	3.6	
even (adv)	5.16	
event (n)	1.1, 1.11	
evil (adj)	1.6	
examine (v)	5.16	
exercise (n and v)	4.16	
exercise (n) [= physical]	5.1	
exhibition (n)	1.11, 3.6	
explanation (n)	3.1	
explode (v)	2.11	
exploration (n)	2.11	
explorer (n)	5.1	
e-zine (n)	3.11	

F

failure (n)	1.11
far (adv)	2.11
fast (n and v) [= not eat]	1.16
fast food (n)	5.16
fat (adj and n)	5.1
fatty (adj)	5.11
feature (n and v)	3.11
feature (n)	3.6
female (adj)	2.6
festival (n)	1.1
fewer (adj)	5.6
field (n) [= area]	2.1
figure (n) [= model]	1.11
fill up on (v)	5.11
findings (n)	3.16
finger (n)	4.16
fire (n)	1.6
fire (v)	2.11
firework (n)	1.11
flag (n)	1.11, 4.6
flight (n)	2.16
flour (n)	5.16
fly (v)	2.16
focus (n and v)	4.16
formula (n)	3.16
fridge (n)	5.11
frozen (adj)	5.11
further (adv)	2.11
(the) furthest (adv)	2.11

G

(the) general public (n)	3.1
generalize (v)	3.6
generation (n)	1.1
glass (n)	5.6
glider (n)	2.16
goal (n)	4.6

goalkeeper (n)	4.6
God (n)	1.1
(the) gods (n)	1.1
guest (n)	1.1
guide (n)	1.6
gunpowder (n)	2.11

H

habit (n)	3.16
handful (n)	5.6
handwriting (n)	4.16
happen (v)	1.16
hard (adj) [= not soft]	2.6
head (n)	4.6
health (n)	5.1
healthy (adj)	5.1
heart attack (n)	5.11
heart disease (n)	5.16
helicopter (n)	2.1
historic (adj)	2.16
historical (adj)	1.11
hold (v) [= happen]	1.16
hole (n) [= in golf]	4.6
holy (adj)	1.16
home (n) [= target in game]	4.11
hopeless (adj)	4.6
hot-air balloon (n)	2.16
huge (adj)	1.6
human (adj and n)	2.1
humiliate (v)	4.16
hungry (adj)	5.1
hunter-gatherer (n)	5.16

I

ice hockey (n)	4.6
ill (adj)	5.1
image (n)	3.6
image (n) [= picture]	3.11
impression (n)	3.6
in (adj) [tennis]	4.6
in fact	3.1
in favour [of]	4.16
in many cases	3.1
in my opinion	2.1
in the air	2.1
incidentally	3.1
industrial (adj)	2.6
influence (n)	1.1, 3.1
ingredient (n)	5.16
inhabit (v)	2.11
insert (v)	2.6
instead of (prep)	5.16

intake (n)	5.6	
(the) Internet (n)	2.6	
invent (v)	2.1	
invention (n)	2.1	
inventor (n)	2.1	
issue (n)	3.6	

J

jet (adj and n)	2.16
jet (n)	2.1
jockey (n)	1.11
journey (n)	2.11
juice (n)	5.6
jumbo jet (n)	2.1
junk food (n)	5.11

K

keep (v) [= continue]	4.6
kick (v)	4.1
kill (v)	2.11
kite (n)	2.16
knock over (v)	4.1

L

land (v)	2.11, 2.16, 4.11
land on (v)	4.11
largely (adv)	1.16
last (v)	1.6, 1.11
later (adv)	2.1
launch (v)	2.11
lead to (v)	4.16
lean (adj)	5.16
leisure (n)	4.16
lemonade (n)	5.16
Lent (n)	1.16
less (adj)	5.6
let (v)	4.16
lifestyle (n)	3.11
light (v)	1.1
lit (v) [= past participle]	1.11
literacy (n)	3.1
live (adj)	3.1
local (adj)	1.6
look like (v)	1.11
lose (v) [= not have]	2.16
lose control (v)	2.16
loser (n)	4.1
lots (n)	5.6
low-fat (adj)	5.11
luck (n)	1.6, 1.16
lucky (adj)	1.6

M

machine (n)	2.6
magazine (n)	3.6
main (adj)	2.1
mainly (adj)	3.16
mainly (adv)	2.11
majority (n)	3.16
male (adj)	2.6
man/men (n) [= piece/s]	4.11
mark (v) [= show a change]	2.11
market sector (n)	3.11
marriage (n)	1.1
(the) mass media (n)	3.1, 3.11
material (n)	2.6
may (v)	3.11
meal (n)	1.6
measure (n)	4.6
medicine (n)	5.1
medium (n)	3.16
medium (n) [= way of communicating]	3.1
mental skills	4.16
mention (v)	4.11
message (n) [= what you want to say]	3.1
method (n)	2.1
midfield (n)	4.6
mineral (n)	5.1
minority (n)	3.6, 3.16
mix (v)	2.11
(the) Moon (n)	2.11
mosque (n)	1.16
mostly (adv)	3.6
motorcar (n)	2.6
motor skills	4.16
motorcycle (n)	2.1
move (n and v)	4.11

N

natural (adj)	2.11
natural death (n)	5.16
navy (n)	2.16
nearly (adv)	1.6
net (n)	4.6
(the) news (n pl)	3.1
normally (adv)	5.1
nowadays (adv)	1.1
nut (n)	5.6
nutrient (n)	5.1
nutritionist (n)	5.16

O

obesity (n)	5.16
objective (n)	4.11
occasion (n)	1.1
official (adj and n)	1.1
on average	3.16

on land	2.1	
on sea	2.1	
on the one hand	1.16	
opponent (n)	4.1, 4.6	
oppose (v)	4.16	
orbit (n and v)	2.11	
origin (n)	1.1	
original (adj)	1.6	
originally (adv)	1.6	
other (adj and pron)	2.1	
otherwise (adv)	3.6	
out of school	4.16	
oxygen (O) (n)	2.11	

P

parachute (n)	2.11	
parade (n and v)	1.11	
pardon?	2.6	
participant (n)	3.16	
particularly (adv)	5.16	
partner (n)	4.6	
party (n)	1.1	
pass down (v)	1.1	
pasta (n)	5.6	
pastime (n)	4.11	
pawn (n)	4.11	
PE (n)	4.1	
peanut (n)	5.11	
peculiar (adj)	1.11	
per cent (n)	3.16	
percentage (n)	3.16	
persuade (v)	3.6	
persuasion (n)	3.11	
petrol (n)	2.1	
physical education (n)	4.1	
pie chart (n)	3.16	
piece (n)	4.11, 5.6	
pilot (n)	2.16	
pitch (n)	4.6	
plan (n and v)	4.11	
planet (n)	2.11	
play (n)	4.11	
player (n)	4.11	
point (n)	4.6	
popular (adj)	1.11	
population (n)	1.11	
portion (n)	5.1	
portray (v)	3.6	
position (n)	4.6	
post (n)	4.6	

poster (n)	1.11	
potato (n)	5.16	
powder (n)	1.6	
power (n and v)	2.1	
power source	2.1	
powered (adj)	2.16	
powerful (adj)	3.11	
practical (adj)	2.6	
pray (v)	1.16	
prayer (n)	1.16	
present (n)	1.1	
preservation (n)	5.11	
preserve (v)	5.11	
press (v)	2.6	
primitive (adj)	1.1	
principle (n)	3.11	
printing (adj and n)	3.1	
printing (adj)	2.16	
privacy (n)	3.1	
problem-solving (n)	4.11	
procedure (n)	1.1	
procession (n)	1.6	
product (n)	2.6, 3.1	
promote (v) [= support]	3.11	
propeller (n)	2.1, 2.16	
protein (n)	5.1	
publisher (n)	3.11	
purpose (n)	3.6	
push (v)	2.6	
put on (v)	5.11	
pyramid (n)	5.1	

Q

questionnaire (n)	3.16	
queue (n)	5.6	

R

race (n and v)	1.6, 1.11	
racket (n) (or racquet)	4.1, 4.6	
raw (adj)	5.16	
raw data (n)	3.16	
reach (v) [= get to a target]	3.1	
react (v)	4.1	
reaction (n)	3.6	
reader (n)	3.11	
reality (n)	3.6	
realize (v)	2.16	
receipt (n)	5.6	
receiver (n)	4.6	
recent (adj)	4.16	
recipe (n)	5.11	
recommend (v)	5.1	

record (n)	2.6	
record (v)	3.16	
recover (v)	1.11	
reduce (v)	5.11	
reflect (v)	1.6	
reject (v)	2.16	
relationship (n) [= percentage, etc.]	3.16	
relative (n)	1.6, 1.16	
religion (n)	1.16	
religious (adj)	1.1	
repair (v)	2.16	
replace (v)	2.6	
report (v)	3.6	
reporter (n)	3.1	
represent (v)	1.6	
research (n and v)	3.16	
response (n)	3.16	
restrict (v)	4.16	
result (n)	3.16	
review (n)	3.6	
ribbon (n)	1.11	
ride (v)	2.1	
rider (n)	2.6	
riding (n)	4.1	
ring (n)	1.6	
rink (n)	4.6	
ritual (n)	1.1, 1.16	
rocket (n)	2.1	
role (n)	4.6	
row (v)	2.16	
rowing (n)	4.1	
rugby (n)	4.6	
ruins (n)	4.11	
rule (n)	4.6	
run out of (v)	2.6	

S

safe (adj)	2.6
safety (n)	2.6, 2.16
sail (n and v)	2.1
salad (n)	5.16
salt (n)	5.11
sample (n)	3.16
satellite (n)	2.11
saturated (adj)	5.11
sauce (n)	5.6
scene (n)	3.1
score (n and v)	4.6
screen (n)	2.6, 4.16
sector (n)	3.11

seed (n)	5.16
self-esteem (n)	4.16
self-image (n)	3.11
service (n)	3.1
set (n)	1.1
set (v) [= fix]	2.6
sexist (adj)	3.6
shape (n)	4.6
shocking (adj)	3.6
show (v)	3.6
shuttle (n)	2.1
significant (adj)	5.16
simple (adj)	4.16
situated (adj)	1.11
size (n)	4.6
slice (n)	5.6
slow down (v)	5.11
snack (n and v)	5.16
snack (n)	5.6
social science (n)	1.16
social skills	4.16
society (n) [= club]	1.11
(the) Solar System (n)	2.11
solution (n)	5.11
something else	3.16
song (n)	1.6
sort (n)	3.6
source (n)	2.1
space (n) [= universe]	2.1
spacecraft (n)	2.1
special (adj)	1.1
specialist (n)	3.11
spectator (n)	1.11
speed (n)	2.6
speed up (v)	5.11
spirit (n)	1.6
spoonful (n)	5.6
sporty (adj)	4.1
spread (v) [= move outwards]	4.11
square (n)	4.11
star (n)	2.11
starve (v)	5.11
statue (n)	1.6
steam (n)	2.1
stereotype (n)	3.6
stereotypical (adj)	3.6
store (v)	5.1, 5.11
stroke (n) [= medical]	5.11

stuff (n)	3.6	
submarine (n)	2.16	
substance (n)	2.6	
suffer from (v)	5.16	
sugary (adj)	5.16	
sulphur (S) (n)	2.11	
(the) Sun (n)	2.11	
sunrise (n)	1.6, 1.16	
sunset (n)	1.16	
support (n and v)	4.16	
surprise (n)	1.6	
survey (n)	3.11, 3.16	
swallow (v)	5.11	
sweets (n)	5.6	
swimming (n)	4.1	
switch on (v)	2.6	
symbol (n)	1.6	

T

take off (v)	2.16
take part (v) [in]	1.11
take place (v)	1.1, 1.11
take-away (n)	5.6
tally chart (n)	3.16
target (adj)	3.6
target (n and v)	3.11
team (n)	4.1
teaspoon (n)	5.6
technology (n)	2.6
teen (adj)	3.11
terrorist (n)	3.1
test (v) [= try out]	2.16
Thanksgiving (n)	1.16
therefore (adv)	3.1
through (prep)	1.6
throughout (prep)	1.16
ticket (n)	1.11
title (n) [= name]	3.11
tool (n)	4.1
touch (v)	4.1
tourism (n)	1.11
tourist (n)	1.1, 1.11
track (n)	2.1
tradition (n)	1.16
traditional (adj)	1.1
trampolining (n)	4.1
transmission (n)	3.1
transmit (v)	3.1
transport (n)	2.1
transportation (n)	2.1

trap (v)	4.11
travel (n and v)	2.1
tray (n)	5.6
trend (n)	5.16
turn (n)	4.11
typical (adj)	5.6

U

underwater (adj)	2.16
unhealthy (adj)	5.1, 5.11
universe (n)	2.11
unsuccessful (adj)	1.11
usage (n)	3.16

V

value (n)	3.11
values (n pl)	3.11
variety (n)	5.11
vegetable (n)	5.1
vegetarian (n)	5.16
vehicle (n)	2.6, 2.16
version (n)	4.11
versus (prep)	4.6
victorious (adj)	1.16
violent (adj)	4.16
visitor (n)	1.11
vitamin (n)	5.1
vote (n and v)	1.1
voyage (n)	5.1

W

war (n)	1.16
weapon (n)	2.11
wheat (n)	5.16
wheel (n)	2.1
while (adv) [= at the same time as]	3.16
win [a contract] (v)	2.16
wing (n)	2.16
winner (n)	4.1
work (v) [= operate]	2.6
wound (v) [= injure]	2.11
wreath (n)	1.6

Y

yoghurt (n)	5.6